Quentin Tarantino

Quentin Tarantino

Life at the Extremes

AARON BARLOW

Modern Filmmakers
Vincent LoBrutto, Series Editor

 PRAEGER

AN IMPRINT OF ABC-CLIO, LLC
Santa Barbara, California • Denver, Colorado • Oxford, England

Library of Congress Cataloging-in-Publication Data

Barlow, Aaron, 1951–
    Quentin Tarantino : life at the extremes / Aaron Barlow.
        p. cm. — (Modern filmmakers)
    Includes bibliographical references and index.
    ISBN 978-0-313-38004-4 (alk. paper) — ISBN 978-0-313-38005-1 (ebook)
    1. Tarantino, Quentin—Criticism and interpretation. I. Title.
    PN1998.3.T358B38 2010
    791.4302'33092—dc22   2009051236

ISBN: 978-0-313-38004-4
EISBN: 978-0-313-38005-1

14   13   12   11   10   1   2   3   4   5

This book is also available on the World Wide Web as an eBook.
Visit www.abc-clio.com for details.

Praeger
An Imprint of ABC-CLIO, LLC

ABC-CLIO, LLC
130 Cremona Drive, P.O. Box 1911
Santa Barbara, California 93116-1911

This book is printed on acid-free paper ∞

Manufactured in the United States of America

For Jan, Always

Contents

Series Foreword

The Modern Filmmakers series focuses on a diverse group of motion picture directors who collectively demonstrate how the filmmaking process has become *the* definitive art and craft of the twentieth century. As we advance into the twenty-first century we begin to examine the impact these artists have had on this influential medium.

What is a modern filmmaker? The phrase connotes a motion picture maker who is *au courant*—they make movies currently. The choices in this series are also varied to reflect the enormous potential of the cinema. Some of the directors make action movies, some entertain, some are on the cutting edge, others are political, some make us think, some are fantasists. The motion picture directors in this collection will range from highly commercial, mega-budget blockbuster directors, to those who toil in the independent low-budget field.

Gus Van Sant, Tim Burton, Charlie Kaufman, and Terry Gilliam are here, and so are Clint Eastwood and Steven Spielberg—all for many and for various reasons, but primarily because their directing skills have transitioned from the twentieth century to the first decade of the twenty-first century. Eastwood and Spielberg worked during the 1960s and 1970s and have grown and matured as the medium transitioned from mechanical to digital. The younger directors here may not have experienced all of those cinematic epochs themselves, but nonetheless they remained concerned with the limits of filmmaking; Charlie Kaufman disintegrates personal and narrative boundaries in the course of his scripts, for example, while Tim Burton probes the limits of technology to find the most successful way of bringing his intensely visual fantasies and nightmares to life.

The Modern Filmmakers series will celebrate modernity and postmodernism through each creator's vision, style of storytelling, and character presentation. The directors' personal beliefs and worldviews will be revealed through in-depth examinations of the art they have created, but brief biographies will also be provided where they appear especially relevant. These books are intended to open up new ways of thinking about some of our favorite and most important artists and entertainers.

Vincent LoBrutto
Series Editor
Modern Filmmakers

Preface

Each chapter in this book deserves at least a book of its own. Some of them do have books already, but the topics constantly grow and change, demanding more—and will, even after Quentin Tarantino stops making movies. Other chapters await their first in-depth studies. In each case, understanding changes, as do movies, and so do the cultures they entwine. Nothing can ever be said about a filmmaker like Tarantino with finality, certainly not about his films; everything bears repeating, for it is in the repetition that one sees the new, as Tarantino's movies constantly show. Changing contexts change meanings. So, like any study of film, this book is a work in progress—perhaps more so than others, for it concerns a director whose own work constantly reinvents itself, constantly changing with the world around it.

Tarantino defined American filmmaking of the 1990s and remains one of the country's most influential directors, and not simply through his directorial output (the subject of this book). As a writer, as a producer, and even as an actor, Tarantino continues to put his stamp on the entire film industry. His personality, as outsized as his jaw, has dominated Hollywood from the release of his first movie in 1992. He has changed the way we look at film and filmmakers, widening perceptions of "art" and challenging viewers to make themselves part of the films they watch, much as he had done for himself while growing up.

To Tarantino, film is the voice of his culture and its discussions, the raw material of the language he speaks and lives. His films make his point: without movies, not only could we not have contemporary culture as we experience it, but we would have much weaker tools for negotiating and understanding whatever culture had developed instead. Movies, at least as much as literature has done, provide us a way of looking at ourselves while looking away; they give us tools for talking about ourselves.

They also provide a means for challenging ourselves, especially when they begin to consider those aspects of life and culture that we'd rather not face—including our fascination with violence. There's a ghoulish side to each of us, though most of us manage to suppress it. We are drawn to stories that center on acts of violence, though each with differing levels of acceptance of intimacy with the acts themselves. Tarantino's movies provide a litmus test, a measure of where we draw the lines between what we'll face directly and what we'll turn away from.

Whatever his future may hold, Tarantino's place in the history of the American film industry is secure. He has created a body of work that is, in many ways, an ongoing conversation with his audience, one that will continue for quite some time. He challenges us to consider anew the way movies and the world interact—and to view with new eyes the world films exist within. As a result, engaged viewers return to his movies again and again, mining them for nuggets that can be melted into the gold that makes our greater cultural debates sparkle. And they will do so for the foreseeable future, for Tarantino has also changed the way *other* filmmakers approach their craft.

Any book about Tarantino, then, must also be about the dynamics of film and culture, and itself becomes part of Tarantino's on-going conversation with and about the world. Recognizing that, this book would still be in process, growing daily—had I my way in a perfect world. I can see dozens of lines of inquiry that have been examined here only in passing or that have not yet been looked into more than cursorily. In addition, I know quite well that there are people much more expert than I who could easily take what I have done and refute it or sharpen it, furthering our understanding of both Tarantino and the movies either way. I hope they will, and I will gladly bow to them as they prove me wrong or show where I could have gone but wasn't able to. One way or another, I know that this book will not be an end, but an addition to a discussion that will go on for a long, long time.

Here, I concentrate on Tarantino as a director, focusing on only one (though the major one) of his contributions to the Hollywood film industry and the culture of our time. I deliberately avoid examination of the screenplays he wrote that were directed by others, his contributions to television and collaboratively directed films (excepting *Grindhouse*), his acting (on stage and on screen), and his producing. All of these deserve attention, but none of them defines his vision and his art as clearly as do his films. Furthermore, not only have a long line of books on Tarantino already appeared, but many more will follow. There is no need to try to be comprehensive here; the ongoing conversation will take care of that.

For assistance in completing this book, I thank my wife, Jan Stern, whose patience, when I growled that I just need a few more minutes at the computer, lasted for months. Others who have helped make this possible include Jean Austin; Bambi Everson (whose father William helped create the field of films studies); Frank Coleman; my editor Daniel Harmon; my officemates at New York City College of Technology ("City Tech") Caroline Hellman and Johanna Rodgers, who had to put up with my grumbling and my piles of books; Laura Kodet, who kindly pointed out some of my many small errors; Vincent LoBrutto, series editor for Praeger's "Modern Filmmakers," of which this book is a part, who provided dozen upon dozen of useful suggestions for improving this book; and Peter Romanov, who kindly supplied me with a copy of his master's thesis on music and Tarantino. Finally, I must express my appreciation to the City University of New York, of which City Tech is a part, for providing the support and the release time that has made timely production of this book possible.

Tarantino in the World of Ideas

What matters to Quentin Tarantino? To many who write about him, "What matters, to Mr. Tarantino, is the filmmaking."[1] They see him as a talented creator of "worlds" who is stuck in his movies and in the older films that have influenced him, finding within them, not in the world outside or in the lives people actually lead, the end-all of the existence he wishes to present. They dismiss him, this way, in a fashion they would never use against a novelist such as, say, Thomas Pynchon, whose 1973 novel *Gravity's Rainbow* has about as much relation to World War II as Tarantino's *Inglourious Basterds* and whose 1966 *The Crying of Lot 49* explores the creation of worlds much as does *Death Proof*.

Try to imagine anyone writing, "What matters to Mr. Pynchon is the novelizing." The most likely response would be a quizzical, "So?" In the cases of both the filmmaker and the novelist, creation of artwork is the job they've taken on, so of course the act of creation of that artwork matters to them. Saying so should be no slight, but there's a tinge of dismissal in it sometimes. Both Pynchon and Tarantino bring the nuts and bolts of their craft to the forefront of the experience of the art, both revel in popular culture, and both play with history for the purposes of their storytelling. Yet that faint air of disdain in the comments about Tarantino is never present in consideration of Pynchon, who has literary tradition and respect for the novelist's art behind him.

Perhaps because of the long tradition of the novel, we are more accepting of self-reflexivity, something both Pynchon and Tarantino indulge in, in fiction than in film. Perhaps our familiarity with the way language grows through its own metaphors makes it easier for us to watch—and embrace—the process in ways we can't yet do when it comes to film, in which sound and sight augment (and sometimes replace) words. Maybe we are still so fascinated by the mechanics of the movies that we can't imagine that those who create art through them might not simply see the films as their tools.

Whatever the reasons, we hold movies to a standard different from fiction. When Robert Coover and John Barth and Don DeLillo* write novels about writing novels, they are esteemed. No one implies that they degrade their craft by "only" writing about writing. We always assume, with novelists who show their craft as they write, that much more is going on beyond simply showing off one's skills and knowledge. With Tarantino, though his work is related to fiction as much as to film, we are not so sure. When we call *him* "postmodern," then, it is sometimes with something of a smirk to hide our confusion, our suspicion that we are missing something.

Tarantino has said, "I'm looking to my movies as my passport to the world."[2] This "passport" takes him into the world quite literally (it was film that got him out of the United States for the first time), but it also provides figurative entry into the great discussions that broker our visions of the reality we live in and, for our own perceptions, help construct it. Tarantino's assertion, furthermore, is that of an enthusiast, not of someone of jaded or ironic sensibility. Grounded in tradition and exhibiting a forthright affection for his art and his audience, Tarantino has little in common with any "postmodern" sensibility, with those who might try to remove their art from the world and from culture. If anything, his goal is the opposite. As D. K. Holm writes, "Tarantino's references project out from the screen only to turn around and point back to it, aiming at the immediate narrative and thematic and artistic intention behind the reference."[3] In other words, everything—world, culture, film, and anything else one can think of—interrelates for him.

Not that the appellation "postmodern" has much utility in most instances anyway, having become "a catchword for anything that's irregular or 'unreal.'"[4] It sometimes seems things have gotten to the point at which, when we cannot find the center of a work, its anchor, we decide the work lacks any tethering at all, so we give up on it and dismiss it, calling it "postmodern." For, in a postmodern sensibility, according to Jerome Charyn, "we no longer have any historical context; we ourselves have become packaged, like culture itself. We're the walking wounded, the reader of signs that never stop replicating in a culture of hype and hucksterism. We have come to view ourselves as products, as being more dead than alive."[5] This, however, is definitely not Tarantino's view of the world. He is all about context, all about packaging but not about being packaged, all about creating signs and hype out of signs and hype, all about being the huckster totally in

---

*Robert Coover (1932–), a master of metafiction, is the author of *The Public Burning*; John Barth (1930–), perhaps best known for his collection of short stories *Lost in the Funhouse* and the novel *Chimera*, is a master of self-reflexive fiction; and Don DeLillo (1936–) wrote, among much else, the novel *White Noise*, which explores the position of the scholar and writer and creator in American consumer society.

control, all about creating products as proof that he is alive—and all about the world.

Yes. At his core, Tarantino is all about life and adventure and about the joy of living, even in a crazy world. This is why he makes movies and why he takes chances in his movies. It is what may make him *seem* postmodern. However, like Odysseus, Tarantino has made sure he is tied firmly to the mast, that the seductions of the world, the Sirens, can't draw him away, can't draw him completely into movies about movies, into a "postmodern" universe of nothing more than artifice signifying artifice. Again like Odysseus, he has other goals, places he wants to go, things he wants to accomplish in the world, and not just in film.

Perhaps because of ideas such as those of Jean Baudrillard, who posits (possibly appalled, possibly with irony) that the relations between reality and art are becoming reversed today[6]—giving precedence to film itself, for example, instead of what had seemed its depictions—it has become easy to fall into the further assumption that all movies, and not just those of Tarantino, are only about movies, that the world has fallen out of the motion picture. Certainly, our contemporary discussions of reality are often based, in their terminology and imagery at least, on movies, as are our vocabularies and our conceptions of our reality. Sure, we can and often do tell ourselves, "It's only a movie," but each film does temper the way we look at the world once we are back outside. Films fall solidly into the world and stay there.

Even so, as Catherine Constable notes, the perception for some once moved in another direction, reaching a Baudrillard-like point at which "the real itself becomes film-like."[7] There's truth there: despite the apparent circularity implied by such a statement, one cannot ignore the quite real impact of film on society. Unfortunately, by focusing too much on film and not also on society, the pleasing postmodern conceit of a reality constructed through film (or perception of it constructed through film) sidestepped consideration of the real role that film (and all mass media) plays in American, Japanese, Indian, and European societies—and, more and more, in all societies. It's not that films don't temper our vision of reality—they do—but that films are only a means to an end; they are never the ultimate definers, the truth, the reality, in themselves. For all its grandiosity, Baudrillard's vision in which, as Constable puts it, "the construction of the real as film is said to mark the destruction of reality"[8] did not encompass the full extent of the "real" position of film in contemporary society, for it belittled and underestimated the real, the ultimate subject matter of film. Movies (and other electronic media), of course, haven't destroyed the real—they cannot—but have, instead, irrevocably altered the way we think, talk about, and react to our shared experiences of the real. Movies don't mask the world; even when they try to hide it, they expose it—even if only through the point of view of the artist.

Baudrillard's mask, as opposed to the mask presented by the science-fiction writer Philip K. Dick* (whose thoughts on the subject of simulacra and the mask generally do complement Baudrillard), covers nothing. Dick, like today's filmmakers, realized that the mask can be worn explicitly to hide a reality—but, by so doing, it reflects something about that reality (one never wears a pretty mask to hide a pretty face or an ugly mask to hide an ugly one). Film, as Baudrillard's mask instead, hides a *lack* of acceptance of a reality beyond that aspect of it tempered by the work of art (in this case, film). Dick would likely reject this view, as would Tarantino. M. Keith Booker describes "Baudrillard's vision of postmodern society as increasingly dominated by technologically generated forms of culture and experience, leading to the death of conventional reality and the growth of 'hyperreality,' in which all is simulation and all experience is mediated through images—particularly 'simulacra,' images that exist only in their own right, representing nothing in reality."[9] All of this, however, remains mere perception, not substance. The substance is the world behind the mask. Without it, the mask is no more than a balloon with no air, formless and limp.

Refusal to include the fullness of the reality behind the mask demeans the work of a filmmaker, of an artist such as Tarantino, who is perhaps the first director to speak "film" natively and fluently in his discussions of the world. He negotiates reality through film—something quite a bit more intriguing, and certainly more positive, than what we find through Baudrillard's rather apocalyptic vision. Tarantino integrates the mask and the wearer, film and reality, in a way even Dick never managed. Favoring the former over the latter will always diminish understanding of his work and has done so, as persistence of the "movies about movies" motif demonstrates. Contrary to public perception, Tarantino never simply makes movies about movies and never has. What he does, instead, is *speak* "movies," speaking movies via film to help him explore the reality he experiences.

---

*Philip K. Dick (1928–1982) didn't gain broad attention until close to the time of his death in the aftermath of a stroke. Since then, his books have been the inspiration for a number of films, including *Blade Runner* (Ridley Scott, 1982), which was in production when he died and based loosely on Dick's 1968 novel *Do Androids Dream of Electric Sheep?*; *Confessions d'un barjo* (Jérôme Boivin, 1992) from his early 1960s novel (not published until 1975) *Confessions of a Crap Artist*; and, from his 1977 novel *A Scanner Darkly*, Richard Linklater's 2006 film of the same name. Like Tarantino, Dick grounded his work in a genre but refused to be confined by it—his 1981 novel *VALIS*, for example, combining science fiction, autobiography, and a parts of a religious "exegesis" that Dick worked on over the last decade of his life. His 1978 talk, "How to Build a Universe That Doesn't Fall Apart Two Days Later," contains the confession that he *did* want his universes to fall apart, an attitude that Tarantino, perhaps, is coming to share.

Scholar of postmodernism (among many other accomplishments) Fredric Jameson has managed to capture one important and quite interesting aspect of film as it relates to Tarantino, connecting a number of filmmakers to a changing cultural conversation and orientation in his essay "Postmodernism and the Consumer Society." Unfortunately, in doing so, he, too, diminished and limited consideration of movies by artists such as Tarantino, making them out to be much less than they are in order to address his own agenda, to make his own separate points about society. A Marxist scholar, he wanted to press everything into service of the dialectic of cultural history and change he has constructed.

Even though Tarantino is *not* postmodern in sensibility, he is now absolutely associated with "postmodernism" in the public mind because it is an easy catch-all phrase for that which is new and that which we don't completely understand: a Google search on the two words "Tarantino" and "postmodernism" will turn up close to 200,000 hits. Therefore, it is worth taking a look at Jameson's view of the postmodern film, even if it is somewhat outdated, especially given that one of Jameson's sweeping statements is that everything influenced by Jean-Luc Godard is postmodern—and Tarantino certainly has been as influenced by Godard as by any other director (as by anybody at all, for that matter). Among many possible examples of this influence, Tarantino's use of title cards (or "intertitles") for his film chapters is certainly a deliberate homage to Godard, who has inserted similar cards as one of his ways of drawing attention to the artifice of film; the drowning out or bleeping of Beatrix Kiddo's name in parts of *Kill Bill* is another, a bow to Godard's *Made in U.S.A.* (1966).

Jameson posited postmodernism as a reaction against what he saw as the cultural snobbery of modernism, a snobbery that created a divide between an elite-accepted high culture and low popular culture. For that conceit to work, however, an anger against the snobbery has to exist—an anger that Tarantino, along with most of his generation, doesn't exhibit. Instead, like many of his contemporaries, Tarantino is a cultural omnivore, rejecting categorization, ingesting all he finds with equal fervor and delight—or seeing each as simply a first course for whatever larger meal he wishes to create and dig into. This is likewise true of his use of film genres, almost all of which he relishes (excepting, perhaps, only porn) and many of which he utilizes, though only as starting points for his films, most gleefully then crossing genre (and other) boundaries and categories at will. He certainly does not efface genres or other delimiters; he simply uses them without constraint and as he might see fit, ignoring *their* constraints when it suits the needs of the points he is trying to make.

Jameson, like many scholars of his generation, accepted that the divide created (or, in the eyes of the modernists, identified) between high and low culture through modernism is, in fact, real—and has had a continuing impact. That divide, it is true, has long been an accepted part of most views of Western culture. Writing in 1953, Dwight McDonald commented that "Mass Culture [his phrase for "popular" or "low" culture] is to some extent a continuation of the old Folk Art which until the Industrial Revolution was the culture of the common people, but here, too, the differences are more striking than the similarities. Folk Art grew from below. It was a spontaneous, autochthonous expression of the people, shaped by themselves, pretty much without the benefit of High Culture, to suit their own needs."[10] The assumptions McDonald makes and Jameson doesn't contradict are ones that an artist such as Tarantino not only doesn't share, but (more importantly) ignores. The hierarchy of cultural values, the idea of distinct high and low arts with intrinsic difference in value, doesn't exist in his universe—reflecting an attitude that is perhaps the most important difference between the modernists and their children.

MacDonald goes on to make the somewhat contradictory claim that "Mass Culture is imposed from above. It is fabricated by technicians hired by businessmen; its audiences are passive consumers, their participation limited to the choice between buying and not buying."[11] Here again, the real distinction between the modern and the postmodern (taken most broadly and literally) is highlighted by an older statement of another hierarchy or distinction, not one of cultural value but of commercial interaction, and of a basic misunderstanding of that interaction: consumers in Western capitalist systems have never been passive, nor have they been provided with simplistic, stark choice of one or nothing.

If an artist such as Tarantino were to have any reaction to claims such as those of MacDonald, it would probably simply be a piqued interest in what MacDonald sees as kitsch, the output of commercial culture. In making his argument, MacDonald cites Clement Greenberg's even older article "Avant-Garde and Kitsch," in which Greenberg distinguishes between the two types of artifacts in his title, extolling the avant-garde not as experimental, but as the leaders, the artists trying "to find a path along which it would be possible to keep culture *moving* in the midst of ideological confusion and violence."[12] He sees them as removing themselves from the public completely and concentrating solely on art for its own sake and on "pure poetry," providing an artistic base when all else seems fluid. Though working in complete disregard to pop-cultural currents, the avant-garde ultimately, Greenberg implies, provide the path to the future, justifying their art and their seclusion. Their understanding of culture is as something to aspire to, though not something that the general populace might own.

Kitsch, by contrast—in Greenberg's view—belongs nowhere but among the people and far away from real culture. It is a product of commerce, not art, and probably shouldn't even be mentioned in discussions of art, for it is fake, "ersatz culture, kitsch, destined for those who, insensible to the values of genuine culture, [who] are hungry nevertheless for the diversion that only culture of some sort can provide."[13] Greenberg goes on: "Kitsch is mechanical and operates by formulas. Kitsch is vicarious experience and faked sensations. Kitsch changes according to style, but remains always the same. Kitsch is the epitome of all that is spurious in the life of our times. Kitsch pretends to demand nothing of its customers except their money—not even their time."[14] The reaction, today, to such a description might actually be an unironic, "Cool, let's have some." Tarantino most certainly feels that way.

Kitsch, by this definition, is the very starting point for twenty-first century art by the likes of Tarantino. It is real art, of a sort that Greenberg or even MacDonald did not even imagine would come to be. It ultimately integrates kitsch and the avant-garde, completing a process of melding that started, self-consciously, in the 1950s but that is now something of an assumed, seamless, and forgotten (on the surface) base for contemporary artistic creation.

Noël Carroll further describes, and more favorably, Greenberg's distinction between kitsch and avant-garde, the one that Tarantino ignores: "Avant-garde art is abstract, whereas mass art ostensibly favors representation. Avant-garde art is reflexive, whereas mass art is generally imitative. Avant-garde art is introverted—it is about itself (it is about its medium). Kitsch is extroverted; it is about the world."[15] Tarantino, for all those tired claims that he makes movies only about movies, is extroverted in just this way, and without apology, but then again, there is also an introverted, almost avant-garde aspect to his work, a confirmation of his lack of regard for distinction. He is imitative, but reflexive through it, and original in the way he uses his source material. His work is representational, but there is always an element of abstraction included. Lacking any sort of overt ideological base, Tarantino and those he influences see both the avant-garde and kitsch not simply as pieces for collage or pastiche but as sources for their own art and as metaphors in the new language they are in the process of creating for discussing and negotiating their world, as pieces to be carefully selected, trimmed, and sealed together into a sort of linguistic decoupage.

At its heart, their work is *both* reflexive and imitative, about the medium and about the world. Their reaction to modernism isn't to reject high art in favor of low, but to reject the value of any such hierarchical or oppositional distinction—to reject, in many respects, hierarchies and dichotomies altogether, certainly to deny them as absolutes. Their work certainly isn't simply a cobbling together of pieces but a new way of incorporating the old, a new decoupage.

In talking about film music specifically, composer Michel Chion uses "decoupage" instead of pastiche, pointing out that the composition of this sort, of decoupage, creates a whole, not a collection, something certainly true of Tarantino's work. Claudia Gorbman, Chion's translator, describes the use of "decoupage" as emphasizing "the conceptual planning of a scene's shooting and editing, whereas its counterpart, *montage,* in French stresses the postproduction process of editing."[16] This removes any overt sense of external commentary from the planning and the choices themselves, satiric or otherwise, making the items included within the process simply pieces useful for constructing the new work with all that implies.

Ultimately, by bypassing the models people have constructed and the discussions of theory, by either simply ignoring them or by incorporating both sides of the various dichotomies assumed, Tarantino ends up reflecting *and* creating a new type of "mass art," one without boundaries, taking a step beyond older attitudes and yet embracing them. Until recently, as Carroll argues, mass art has been ignored through the bias of those devoted to high art, "demoting mass art of the rank of either kitsch or pseudo art."[17] The theorists, in his view, started from a bias toward the avant-garde, so they were never able to consider mass art dispassionately. They saw the weaknesses, therefore, and ignored the strengths of anything but that which they've already deemed as real "art." "They observed, with some cause: that mass art is formulaic; that, in certain pertinent respects, the response to mass art was what they considered to be passive; that mass art is generally designed to induce certain predetermined effects; that mass artworks are not unique; and so on."[18] They proved the old maxim that just about anything can be made to look bad if one tries hard enough. Tarantino, by ignoring objections to mass art, takes a giant step toward making them irrelevant.

Though postmodern theorists generally rejected the observations such as those Carroll describes, observations stemming primarily from modernist perspectives, just as the modernists did, they still carried forward assumptions and attitudes—and judgments—that contemporary purveyors of mass art (such as Tarantino) ignore. In fact, in holding onto what they see as the abandonment of the avant-garde by what they call "postmodernist" artists (including Tarantino), the theorists often continued the very avant-garde/kitsch duality that many of those so-called postmodern artists are ignoring today. In other words, the "real" postmodernism cannot be defined through a preference for kitsch any more than by any overt abandonment of modernism—for the real postmodernists don't react against much of anything; they embrace whatever they find useful, rejecting only labels—including "postmodernism."

Instead of "postmodern," many of these artists (again, including Tarantino) are better described simply as "mass artists," people working within the traditions of mass art that have arisen over the past century or so who are aware of those traditions (and others) and who mine them—for reasons inherent in the very definition of "mass art." Carroll argues that a work becomes "mass artwork" if it is (1) not singular, (2) both produced and distributed through mass technology, and (3) "is intentionally designed to . . . promise accessibility with minimum effort, virtually on first contact, for the largest number of untutored (or relatively untutored) audiences."[19] Tarantino's art, like much contemporary art, meets all three of these requirements and quite precisely.

Carroll sidesteps questions of whether certain works of mass art should be called "art" at all by arguing that they are descended from categories that have long been accepted as "art." Movies, of course, come from drama, etc. The first condition, then, is primarily that the work not be singular, such as an unrecorded or broadcast-live performance of a play or a concert. The technologies of the second condition have changed, of course, over the years, starting with Gutenberg and the printing press, but all share the purpose of disseminating the work of mass art as broadly as possible. Carroll defines the "delivery system as a technology with the capacity to deliver the same performance or the same object to more than one reception site simultaneously."[20] It is the reliance on technology that distinguishes mass art from popular art, a broader category that encompasses mass art.

Of his third condition, Carroll writes, "Here, the parenthetical qualification concerning 'relatively untutored audiences' is meant to accommodate the fact that, to a certain extent, audiences may be tutored by the repetition and formulas of mass art itself."[21] Furthermore, "Mass art gravitates not only toward certain formal features for the sake of accessibility; mass art may also gravitate toward the exploration of certain generic affects . . . because they are commonly recognized."[22] He goes on to say that genres such as action/adventure are mass-art naturals, "since it is easier for the average movie-goer to comprehend how a kick-boxer fights . . . than it is to comprehend the intricate and crafty financial manœuverings of leveraged corporate take-overs."[23]

As an artist deliberately working in the mass arts, Tarantino is particularly attuned to the third of Carroll's conditions. Like the writer Stephen King, Tarantino understands where he needs to start in the construction of a mass-art artifact—but that such a starting point is never a limitation or constraint. Both artists know that an audience "learns" as it experiences the work of art (one of the basic points of narrative construction) and that they can pull audiences along *within* the work just as they have been doing externally (the "tutoring" Carroll refers to). Tarantino may start with genres and with what his audience already "knows" as viewers of films, but he can then move his audience (one *he* knows extremely well) toward discovery of a new way of accessing his work, "tutoring" the audience toward understanding a new way of accessing the art.

In *The Classical Hollywood Cinema*, David Bordwell titles the first chapter of the section he wrote, "An Excessively Obvious Cinema,"[24] a title fitting well with Carroll's broader conception of mass art (not surprising, the two of them have worked together). In it, Bordwell reiterates the fact that successful film viewing requires audience participation in the illusion along with the "even more . . . required for that imaginative involvement solicited by narrative. No story tells all. . . . It is clear that the protocols which control this activity derive from the system of norms operating in the classical

[Hollywood] style."[25] A master of this "system of norms," Tarantino is able to take it apart and put it together again within the films he creates, building new systems, though ones still excessively obvious (to steal Bordwell's term) to movie audiences, at least at the start of each movie.

Jameson, for understanding of Tarantino, simply didn't go far enough in his thinking about the impact of modernism or the implications of a developing mass art, but was satisfied to discover an imagined whole through a narrow ideological lens, one of rather limited focal range. He did, however, make a significant point about influence and reference, the point that artists such as Tarantino don't bother to "'quote' such 'texts' as a Joyce might have done, or a Mahler; they incorporate them."[26] The reason for this, however, is that film, for Tarantino, becomes a part of language itself, not a Jameson pastiche, not parody, nor simple self-referentiality. It becomes another of the basic pieces of language, to be used without the need of quotation marks to represent borrowings—for the pieces have dropped into the language, their referentiality negligible. "Lions, and tigers, and bears" today draws the inevitable chorus, "Oh, my!"—degree of knowledge of the source movie, *The Wizard of Oz* (Victor Fleming, 1939), notwithstanding. What happens is not, as Christine Gledhill claims, that "postmodern practices treat the past as a superstore for picking and mixing,"[27] but that film reference has retreated into the common parlance, available for the picking and mixing regardless of origin or even knowledge of origin. Like "thug," descended from a Hindu word but having lost, in American usage, any connection with South Asia, phrases and images from movies have entered into the language, losing their referentiality to the past or to anything else, meaning now resting within them and not simply through them. They are manipulated freely for purposes even completely unconnected with the source movies, let alone with what *those* were depicting. And accuracy doesn't even matter: the title line to Woody Allen's *Play It Again, Sam* (1972) is never spoken in the source movie *Casablanca* (Michael Curtiz, 1942). Ilsa Lund (Ingrid Bergman) says, "Play it once, Sam, for old time's sake," then "Play it, Sam," and Rick Blaine (Humphrey Bogart) says, "You played it for her and you can play it for me," and then "Play it!" But so what? The aspect of parody or pastiche that Jameson describes has been subsumed as film references (and usages) become part of a greater conversation—recognition of which is the critical step toward understanding films in society and toward understanding of the use of films in films by the likes of Tarantino that Jameson did not seem willing to take.

Given the weave of cultural references that make a whole of what can *seem* almost random pastiche, it is not surprising that contemporary film (in what many see as its "postmodern" manifestation) begins to *appear* to lose its classical Hollywood narrative and continuity traditions. Some such movies become, in Alissa Quart's term, "hyperlink films" that toggle "back and forth between . . . ending and beginning."[28] Booker expands on this concept, saying these are films "in which multiple narratives intertwine in a single film, allowing (and requiring) viewers to jump about in time within a story and from one story to another much in the way they jump about among websites on the Internet,"[29] though he quickly notes that the analogy may not really be appropriate: "After all, the latter [surfing the Web] gives users much more control over where they go, even if they are likely to encounter unexpected information along the way."[30] Rather than allowing viewer control akin to Internet possibilities, the interweaving of stories and timelines that Tarantino excels in is instead an exhibition of authorial control over narrative pace and structure. This type of clever wink to authority goes back at least to Laurence Sterne in the eighteenth century. Such nonlinear construction was used sparingly in classical Hollywood and is relatively rare today, but Tarantino demonstrates once again (for he was not the first to do so) that nonlinear (and subjective) narratives *can* fit within a classical structure. In this, he does not innovate, but borrows from the novel and expands on the accepted and usual flashback, as *The Killing* (Stanley Kubrick, 1956), a great influence on *Reservoir Dogs,* does, and as do *Citizen Kane* (Orson Welles, 1941) and *Stage Fright* (Alfred Hitchcock, 1950), to name but two other films using some unusual variation of the standard flashback. Directors such as Martin Scorsese, Oliver Stone, and, more recently, Todd Haynes have done (and do) much the same thing.

J. David Slocum writes that the "postmodern gaze ranges over stylistics and narrative, the status of cultural myths, the role of ideology, and the relations between institutional practices and individuals."[31] This broad vision of postmodernism, following Jean-Francois Lyotard[32] and much more inclusive than Jameson's, sees a purpose-driven aesthetic of rejection of the grand visions of modernism and, in fact, of any system restrictive in definition. Following this line of thought, Slocum goes on to characterize contemporary cinema as producing movies of no historical depth as a result of replacement reference to mediated visions of the past. Referencing past movies instead of studies of the past itself becomes (to Slocum) a sign of collapsing aesthetic and cultural hierarchies, postmodern "rejection" of the past as past, not artifact. But Hollywood has never been in the business of recreating or explicating history, and it should not be criticized or valorized for failing to do what it never set out to do. In Slocum's sense (which ignores the way these "mediated visions" drop into language in the first place), Hollywood has always been postmodern anyway: what matters isn't the grand sweep of things, but immediate performance. If something works, try it again; if not, try something else. Hollywood has always been purveyor of attitudes and theories by default, not by design, working in reaction to what plays. It shapes because the particular shaping sells, not from any ideological stance of its own or for, say, educational purposes. And it takes the pieces for the shaping from whatever has worked in the past, assuming that what has been popular will be popular.

To understand how movies operate in this regard, it can be useful to look at how music is used in film, a usage that has resembled "pastiche" from its earliest days. In the silent era, "The construction of music to fit the perceived demeanor of specific films resulted in a compound of classical pieces and popular tunes."[33] This completely extra-diegetic use of music, naturally enough, still influenced how music was incorporated once sound and sight were able to be more closely and immutably linked, allowing synchronization of speech and sight starting in the late 1920s. However, the studios quickly found it more economical to have music composed and performed in-house rather than reaching outside for popular tunes, as had been the case in the silent era, when it "had been the fashion to weave a pastiche of existing musical pieces into the musical flow of a film's accompaniment."[34] Still, the basic nature of this aspect of the medium has changed little, and even today, "Film music is usually fragmentary and relies on a logic that is not an organic part of the music but a negotiation between the logic of the film and the logic of the music."[35] If this line of reasoning is expanded to all aspects of film, what seems to some as "postmodern" then might more simply be seen as a function of the nature and history of movies, of an art form that constantly borrows and even cannibalizes to create anew.

On a basic level, then, in terms of film, what some call "postmodernism" is an aspect of a developing language based on filmic metaphor and reference that serves no sequential cultural purpose of the sort often assigned to it by theorists of postmodernism, no dynamic of history or change, no dialectic. In fact, this aspect of the medium has been a part of film since its beginning, simply growing in power as the raw material for these new additions to the language of movies increases. It even becomes difficult, then, to call someone who speaks this language fluently, one such as Tarantino, "postmodern" in order to distinguish him from directors of the past, for he is simply using the language he has learned since childhood, a language developed by the older directors, the very ones a commenter might be hoping to distinguish him from. If, for example, Tarantino's movies are postmodern, Stanley Donen's *Charade* (1963) must be, too, for it involves just the sort of "pastiche" one sees in *Jackie Brown*, say. Not to forget his *Two for the Road* (1967), which plays with temporal sequence much as Tarantino's films do a generation later. For Tarantino, there is no apparent self-conscious desire to break with the past or to call particular attention to any innovative aspect of his art. However, there certainly is, within Tarantino's work, a reflexivity, a great deal of textual play, and a refusal to place "artistry" in the background for the duration of the filmic experience. Tarantino, in the words of D. K. Holm, "takes as his birthright the option to quote from his elders, either as an act of fealty or as an attempt to improve, provide a variation on, or examine more closely certain cinematic ideas. Tarantino came of age just as sampling became prevalent in rap and hip-hop music and from the artistic side of his brain . . . Tarantino appears to take the view that anything in the culture is up for grabs."[36] But these are only some of the aspects of his filmmaking art, and they lack any centrality. What he wants to do is make movies, exactly as his classical Hollywood predecessors did—exactly as his New Hollywood peers do. Exactly as a novelist, Pynchon, for example, wants to write books.

Significant to understanding why Tarantino (and New Hollywood in general) should never have been labeled simply "postmodern" is the framing of Hollywood, both classical and New, as an entertainment business. The art of Hollywood film is part of the entertainment and part of the business and does not exist for its own sake or for experiment, propaganda, or anything else. Furthermore, there is no room in Hollywood business models for attempts to break completely with the past; in fact, the opposite is encouraged. Even "high concept,"* one of the bases of New Hollywood filmmaking, stems from bringing the past forward through initial expression of the proposed movie's basic structure in terms of older films and established film personae.

Instead of recognizing the essential conservative nature of filmmaking in Hollywood, Jameson placed the filmmaker (and those like him) within a cultural "periodizing concept whose function is to correlate the emergence of new formal features in culture with the emergence of a new type of social life and a new economic order."[37] It is this, to Jameson, that makes what he saw Tarantino and his like doing pastiche and not (as he said) parody, imbuing pastiche with a cultural weight he denied to parody. "Both pastiche and parody involve the imitation or, better still, the mimicry of other styles and particularly of the mannerisms and stylistic twitches of other styles."[38] Parody, however, is little more, for Jameson, than mockery based on deviation from the normative linguistic values of society, whereas pastiche operates within a postmodern environment in which recognition of a societal center as a norming force has disappeared. Jameson sees a great fragmentation that leaves no basis for the parodying of any particular private idiom, for the loss of standard makes the act of parody meaningless to all but a tiny audience, rendering it ineffective within the broader society. At this point, Jameson argued, pastiche takes over, using the tools of parody but without the now-meaningless mockery: "Pastiche is blank parody, parody that has lost its sense of humor."[39]

It's not so simple, really. Though it may be true that the standards parodists once played off against are gone, it does not follow that humor also has

---

*"High concept" films are those that can be summarized in a single phrase that often relies on common knowledge of a movie, a star, or an event. The idea, parodied quite successfully in Robert Altman's *The Player* (1992), arose in the 1960s and is associated with Barry Diller and Michael Eisner, particularly through their *Movie of the Week* at ABC. It reached the heights of Hollywood in the mid-1970s with movies such as *Jaws* (Steven Spielberg, 1975) and *Star Wars* (George Lucas, 1977) and its depths, perhaps, with David Ellis and Lex Halaby's 2006 *Snakes on a Plane*.

disappeared or that pastiche has done anything less than find new standards for use in creating humor, be it parody or satire. The language of the parodist has grown, now including film and the private languages of splinter groups.

Jameson disparaged pastiche as a response to a situation in which no room remains for innovation, in which artists no longer have the option to do anything but imitate the past, "to speak through the masks and with the voices of the styles in the imaginary museum."[40] Pastiche becomes nothing more than a response to the failure of creativity that, to him, is a hallmark of the postmodern culture. In actual usage, of course, pastiche is much more than that. Pastiche, or decoupage, along with its composites are themselves becoming a new standard, a common language, if you will, with referents and standards as clear as those that Jameson sees as being lost—though the new ones are built from a myriad of "private languages" as well as from the films (and other artifacts) that have become cultural landmarks. The in-jokes resulting from fragmentation become among the many building blocks of a larger, though diffused, decentralized and new, basis for conversation. As Tarantino has said, "I just talk in movie terms."[41] And talking in "movie terms," we are beginning to learn, is not just talking about movies. It is a way, also, of talking about culture and about reality—and not simply about culture and reality as envisioned by one constructed through movies.

One non-Hollywood example of how pastiche unifies, how it helps make a new language readily accessible, how it sets its own new standard and making a cultural point with humor and what initially seems a reliance on the old, is the work of British/Nigerian artist Yinka Shonibare. Though he creates in various media, the signature of Shonibare's art in a liberal use of what is known as "Dutch wax" printed cotton cloth of a type ubiquitous in West Africa and of colors and designs associated with African culture—but manufactured in Europe. Shonibare uses the cloth to fabricate clothing of Victorian and Enlightenment style, often using it to dress headless dummies placed in poses themselves statements on imperialist European cultures and assumptions. Taking bits and pieces from different cultures and different times and places to build his art, Shonibare makes clear (and often very funny) commentary on status, cultural authenticity, and assumptions about history. His pastiche, then, is not pastiche as the postmodern theorists saw it, but building material for statements that have nothing to do with rejection (for example) of the possibility of a grand narrative. In fact, Shonibare is constantly in the process of creating his own grand narrative, though through an art that will always *seem* more postmodern, in form than modern.

Another example is the work of Tarantino's idol Godard, a giant of the cinema whose work, paradoxically, as Pauline Kael says, may

> seem inconsequential and slighter than it is: it is as if the artist himself were deprecating any larger intentions and just playing around in the medium. . . .

Because Godard's movies do not let us forget that we're watching a movie, it's easy to think he's just kidding. Yet his reminders serve an opposite purpose. They tell us that his aim is not simple realism, that the lives of his characters are continuously altered by their fantasies. If I may be deliberately fancy: he aims for the poetry of reality and the reality of poetry. . . .

It's always been relatively respectable and sometimes fashionable to respond to our own experience in terms drawn from the arts: to relate a circus scene to Picasso. . . . But until recently people were rather shamefaced or terribly arch about relating their reactions in terms of movies. . . .

Godard's sense of the present is dominated by his movie past. This is what makes his movies . . . seem so new: for they are movies made by a generation bred on movies.[42]

Kael goes on to say that the statement of Godard's films is, "You play at cops and robbers but the bullets can kill you."[43] Significantly, all that she said about Godard could be said today about Tarantino, and without a word changed. Her comments about analogies, about terms, certainly fit Tarantino. Long before most anyone else writing about movies in America, Kael understood how a director can use movies as language, not merely as subject. Her words clearly connect Tarantino back to Godard and lay the basis for understanding not only the art of these two directors but of contemporary film in general. Though she retired a year before *Reservoir Dogs* appeared and though she never loved Godard the way Tarantino certainly does, Kael's reviews had been important to Tarantino throughout his youth. He certainly paid attention, for example, when, in reviewing Brian De Palma's *Phantom of the Paradise* (1974), Kael lauded De Palma who, though he "can't tell a plain story, does something that a couple of generations of students and underground filmmakers have been trying to do and nobody else has ever brought off. He creates a new Guignol,* in a modern idiom, out of the movie Guignol of the past . . . De Palma's method is very theatrical, with each scene sharply divided from the next. De Palma loves the clichés for their shameless, rotten phoniness. The movies of the past haven't made him their innocent victim; rather, they have wised him up."[44]

Jameson, who mistook usage of pastiche for nostalgia, picked out *American Graffiti* (George Lucas, 1972), *Chinatown* (Roman Polanski, 1974), and *Il Conformista* (Bernardo Bertolucci, 1970) as films looking back through pastiche, creating a genre that, he said, would soon include movies such as *Star Wars, Episode IV: A New Hope* (George Lucas, 1977) and

---

*Originally created by Laurent Mourguet in the early nineteenth century as a puppet, Guignol is a wit from the lower classes whose verbal talent outshines all he encounters. The Guignol "type" influenced movies certainly from the advent of sound. Though they generally focused on the upper classes, screwball comedies, for example, owe a great deal to Guignol.

Raiders of the Lost Ark (Steven Spielberg, 1981), all of them providing a re-experiencing of something that the viewer has never experienced firsthand and often only knows through the movies or—in the later two cases—through recreating the childhood experience of B movies and serials. Jameson, however, did not take the step that Kael did and that these films themselves do. That is, the filmmakers all knew they were making movies for contemporary audiences and framed their visions of the past to address contemporary issues. Most of the people who grew to love *Star Wars* and *Raiders of the Lost Art* best were, after all, too young to have experienced the objects of homage (the pastiche aspect of the movies) firsthand, if they had seen them all. It didn't even matter if they hadn't, to either filmmakers or to their audiences. In fact, a certain part of the aesthetics of these seemingly nostalgic films was based on the exploitative and often over-the-top trailers for the older films and even on lobby cards, and not quite so much on the films themselves.

Jameson saw the utilization of film not as an extension of language and its metaphors but as a retreat to Plato's shadows on the wall of the cave. To him, as to Baudrillard, this is a supplantation of reality, not a means of supplementing human framing of reality. But we've always negotiated the experiential world through language and not merely through direct experience; today, that language has simply grown to include film and all it implies. And film even does more: in an era of fragmentation of language into a variety of jargons and dialects, film (and electronic media in general) becomes the one universal, a standard like that one Jameson saw as having, in the past, allowed for successful parody.

Relationships Jameson also spoke of, such as Jacque Lacan's sign and signifier/signified, extend to a referent, both for filmmakers such as Tarantino and for his viewers. The idea of a contained universe of sign and signifier alone makes little sense to them, for movies are part of their experiential world and an important part, for they become means for making sense of the world and for discussing it with others. The idea of a limited universe makes little sense, too, because the filmmaker's art is, for most, a primarily commercial art. The world of the work is constantly informed and shaped by the world of commercial demand and experience. In other words, context always has to be paramount to the filmmaker within the Hollywood commercial tradition. In discussion of Jacques Derrida's thoughts on genre,[45] Stephen Neale follows Derrida in observing "that all texts, all utterances, all instances of discourse are always encountered in some kind of context, and are therefore always confronted with expectations, with systems of comprehension."[46] That context, however, can (as postmodernist theorists asserted) become emptied of meaning, which is where discourse on postmodernism can still assist in understanding the place of film, and film violence in particular, within a contemporary framework. Slocum argues,[47] with limited justification, that even the most graphic violent image is drained of meaning and originality within a contemporary media context of repetition and replication. The question, then, becomes one of the impact and amplification of the image as it takes its place as a piece of language, simply a new word, one represented in a way distinct from the grapheme, not serving as a direct representation of reality but as a commonly understood touchstone.

Yet, the overriding importance of context, whatever its genesis, makes the study of film differ in important ways from the study of other arts, particularly from literature, in which the training of many film scholars still lies. Filmmakers, unlike these scholars, are not simply literary artists and students in another medium; rather they work within a distinct and different framework of possibility and constraint. The contrasts are particularly strong for Tarantino. Still, there are aspects of literary studies quite useful in approaching film—even if, on occasion, the use lies in drawing distinctions, not parallels.

Key to the differences, of course, is audience. Unlike literature, which grew from an oral tradition to a literate one requiring certain training and experience for even minimal participation in the enjoyment of the art, film required little besides eyes and a nickel when it first appeared. The commercial aspect, therefore, did not grow onto a tradition of art predating it by generations, but was part and parcel of the very development of the art. The tradition of film, then, is a tradition of commerce in ways that the tradition of literature is not. Commerce, of course, is concerned with the buyer, the audience, much more directly than the tradition of literature. Part of the genius of Tarantino is that he understands and embraces this in a fashion distinct from that of artists working in other traditions, allowing him to draw on things outside of the distinct rules and genres, if you will, defining film and literature.

It has become a commonplace to point out that Tarantino uses film genre as the starting point for all of his films, looking to the conventions of the past to construct his new work. So, at least a little background in the meaning of "genre" as used in discussions of film (as distinct from genre in literature) is useful to any discussion of Tarantino's movies. As Rick Altman points out, there is a real difference between literary and film genres: "Whereas literary genre was primarily a response to theoretical questions or to practical large-scale classification needs (such as library organization), early film genre terminology served as shorthand communication between film distributors and exhibitors."[48] This suited the growing studio system as it became formalized in the years after World War I. Though a constantly evolving set of subgenres soon arose, Hollywood settled into two major (or umbrella) genres, according to Altman, melodrama and comedy. All of Hollywood's other genres descend from these.

"Genres do not consist solely of films. They consist also of specific systems of expectation and hypothesis which spectators bring with them to the cinema and which interact with films themselves during the course of the viewing process,"[49] writes Neale. Hollywood's genres, built on interplay between filmmakers, distributors, exhibitors, and audiences, often are looked upon by "cultural commentators not as the law of Culture, but as the law of the market. It is therefore hardly surprising that genre was—and still is—principally associated with an industrial, commercial, and mechanically based art such as the cinema and with its most obviously industrial, commercial, and popular sectors such as Hollywood in particular."[50] Genre, in other words, is seen as predicated on something other than art, giving it (in some minds) a rather unseemly odor. In this view, it is associated with kitsch of the sort Greenberg describes, imposed for commercial reasons by people whose sole concern is profit.

For a director such as Tarantino, on the other hand, genre becomes something of a freeing factor. It gives a solid place to start, where audiences will understand what is going on, a firm launching pad for a shot that will take the director who knows where: "I love it when someone just starting out in the movies reinvents an entire genre from inside out. . . . I love playing with my viewer's expectations and, in the end, crossing him up."[51]

Though he long ago took on the role of participant in the creation of film, Tarantino has never lost his sense of himself as a member of the audience. In fact, by seeing himself as the audience for his own films, he increases the feeling of participation that his best audiences feel, making them part of the film experience just as he has been since childhood. All of those years as a clerk at Video Archives made Tarantino aware of just how active and enthusiastic a film audience can be and how the best viewing experience is one in which the audience and the filmmaker recognize that they meet each other halfway, cooperating to make a film work. As Bordwell writes, "just as we project motion on to a succession of frames, so we form hypotheses, make inferences, erect expectations, and draw conclusions about the film's characters and actions."[52] And we share these almost immediately, with others in the audience, in conversation afterward, and in the recommendations we make . . . affecting box office and, of course, the shape of movies to come.

Movies to come, one way or another, will have been affected by Quentin Tarantino. Whatever one calls him, he is of our time, an amalgamation of the past and a signpost to the future of American film.

History and a World of Influence

Given his high-profile media persona and the nature of the referentiality used as a tool in his movies, it is easy to fall into simplistic discussions of biography and/or influence when examining the directorial output of Quentin Tarantino. Both his biography and the signs he leaves of influence have, in fact, sparked minor industries: to date, there are at least five books on Tarantino in print with strong biographical elements[1]—this, for a man still in his 40s—as well as an informal on-going parlor game of "Tarantino Pursuits" centered on Web sites such as The Tarantino Archives (http://www.tarantino.info/) and God Among Directors (http://www.godamongdirectors.com/index.shtml). Tarantino doesn't help simplify matters, encouraging concentration on himself as a personality through appearances as an actor, as an interviewee, as a producer (in name or in fact), and even as the sponsor of his own film festival in Austin, Texas. In addition, as David Bordwell points out, Tarantino deliberately tantalizes his audiences by constantly signaling "his sources in order to tease pop connoisseurs into a new level of engagement,"[2] making it tempting to join in the Easter egg hunt in order to find the sometimes major but often sly and fleeting references to the movies that influenced Tarantino's development, references that have become part of his filmmaking language. Unfortunately, as enjoyable as this may be, concentration on either biography or influence, as important as they are in this particular case, can deflect us from analysis of the movies themselves—which, after all, should be the prime topic in any consideration of Tarantino as a director.

Yes, biography and influence certainly distract when the desire is to analyze the important, though still rather slender, *œuvre* of Tarantino. Still, he cannot be removed from the context of his biography or of his influences; both need to be included in discussion of his work. In this chapter, then, I will concentrate on the background of these two aspects of Tarantino's art, putting Tarantino within the context of the developing film industry of Hollywood, something his movies can hardly be understood without.

Quentin Jerome Tarantino was born in Knoxville, Tennessee, on March 27, 1963. Except for his earliest years, however, he only spent one extended period in Tennessee (and that just a matter of months when he was about ten years old), with most of his childhood being spent in California. The general outline of Tarantino's youth deviates little from that of tens of thousands of others: child of a young mother whose husband had disappeared; a step-father arrives but proves impermanent; a lack of interest in education becomes increasingly evident. The differences were a mother who proved unusually strong and able, carving out a career for herself and providing a pillar of personal stability for her son—and the movies.

At the time Tarantino was born, movie audience numbers were slipping, down to 1.06 billion from 1.29 billion movie views the year before.[3] The average ticket price of $0.85, however, would translate into $5.90 in 2008 dollars, still a bargain and well within reach of most Americans. The biggest box-office success that year was *Cleopatra* (Joseph Mankiewicz), a film that has gathered little sustaining interest except as an example of excess in filmmaking. If anything, 1963 was a year of doldrums for Hollywood. Television had established itself as the center of American entertainment, now even featuring fairly recent A-list Hollywood films through showcases such as "Saturday Night at the Movies" (which had debuted on NBC in 1961 with Jean Negulesco's 1953 *How to Marry a Millionaire* with Betty Grable, Marilyn Monroe, and Lauren Bacall). Faced with this change, movies didn't seem to know what to do with themselves.

Little else changed in the movies over the first few years of Tarantino's life. Hollywood's biggest draws during his infancy were movies such as *My Fair Lady* (George Cukor, 1964) and *The Sound of Music* (Robert Wise, 1965), both musicals coming at the end of that dwindling Hollywood tradition. The next year's top hit was *Hawaii* (George Roy Hill), like *Cleopatra* an attempt at an historical presentation of a sort of film producers felt could not be matched by television—a trend that, over time, came to be seen as another sign of the exhaustion of Hollywood.

Things seemed like they were going to start to get interesting, however, in 1967, when a number of unusual movies appeared, such as *Guess Who's Coming to Dinner* (Stanley Kramer), with its consideration of interracial relationships, and *The Dirty Dozen* (Robert Aldrich), in which criminals are forced to become war heroes. Both movies were among the year's top moneymakers. The situation of the industry was certainly looking up. At last, Hollywood had, in Robert Sklar's words,

> created several films that brought movies once again to the center of national attention. One was *Bonnie and Clyde*, directed by Arthur Penn; another was *The Graduate*, directed by Mike Nichols; a third was *Planet of the Apes*, directed by

Franklin J. Schaffner. The first was a gangster picture; the second a boy-meets-girl, boy-loses-girl, boy-gets-girl; the third, science fiction. All three, significantly, were made with an eye to drawing the largest possible mass audience, from all classes and age groups. Yet they were also particularly attuned to the political and social values emerging in the college generation of the 1960s.[4]

Bonnie and Clyde not only changed the national conversation on how violence is used in movies (Bosley Crowther of *The New York Times* decried the film's violence, leading Pauline Kael to come to its defense) but also introduced the massive American audience to some of the techniques that had been developing in France as part of the *nouvelle vague. The Graduate* addressed the questions of the evolving youth culture in a noncondescending way for one of the first times in film, and *Planet of the Apes* provided a commentary through science fiction on racial (and other) bias. These would all be films, though Tarantino probably didn't see them immediately (he may actually have seen *Bonnie and Clyde* during its first run), that formed part of the basis of the growing boy's conception of Hollywood—an image substantially different from that someone born even a short decade earlier would have developed, for they were movies that started to reflect, however lumberingly, the cultural changes of the greater American society around them.

Part of the reason for the changes of 1967, which also saw the U.S. release of Sergio Leone's Clint Eastwood trilogy,[5] focusing attention on the "Spaghetti Western," was the revision (the death, essentially) of Hollywood's Production Code in late 1966 following MGM's decision to release *Blowup* (Michelangelo Antonioni, 1966) without Code approval. In 1968, the Motion Picture Association of America (MPAA) established the Code and Rating Administration with its first rating system intended to arm viewers with at least minimal information about the sorts of things the films might contain and to keep young viewers from certain types of movies. Albert Auster and Leonard Quart write, "Gone were the twin beds and in to replace them came full-frontal nudity. Though this freedom was used by some filmmakers as an excuse for sexual titillation, and spawned a successful independent cottage industry of hard and soft-core pornography, it did permit a widening of the range of permissible film topics."[6] Also significant was the death of political blacklisting that had begun in the late 1940s. Though its impact lingered, its back had been broken in 1960, when Stanley Kubrick's *Spartacus* and Otto Preminger's *Exodus* were released, both with writing credit going to Dalton Trumbo, who had been blacklisted for a decade.

As Stephen Prince points out, *Bonnie and Clyde* would prove to be an extremely influential film, not only for its utilization of techniques and approaches of the French *nouvelle vague,* then hardly known in America, but because director Arthur "Penn was the first American filmmaker to utilize the cinematic techniques that quickly became the normative means of filming violent gun battles. Taking his cue from Japanese director Akira Kurosawa, who had used these techniques in *Seven Samurai* (1954) and other films, Penn employed multicamera filming (i.e., filming with more than one camera running simultaneously), slow motion, and montage editing (i.e., building a sequence out of many, very short, brief shots). To these techniques, which rendered gun violence with greater intensity than ever before, Penn added squibs. Probably more than any other effects tool, squibs changed the way screen violence looked."[7] In film, a squib is a small packet of blood-like liquid that can be exploded to simulate the bloody impact of a bullet.

Bright spots aside, things for the industry overall didn't get better after 1967, certainly not in the Hollywood studios. In fact, they continued to get worse. When the decade ended, MGM, once the greatest of all the studios, was in the hands of financier Kerkor Kerkorian, who soon sold off everything from the backlot to the distribution system to (quite famously) the ruby slippers from *The Wizard of Oz* (Victor Fleming, 1939), effectively sealing the decentralization of an industry that had become, it was true, top-heavy, overly concentrated, and inflexible.

By the time Tarantino was born, Hollywood's studio system, as it had been configured for at least 40 years, was in its death throes, if it was not already dead (the year of its death is often, if rather capriciously, set as 1960[8]). The group of bosses that had overseen the Hollywood of the Great Depression and its extension through and after World War II had been pushed aside—and their successors, as Sklar points out, were themselves in the process of being shoved aside as corporations (or speculators such as Kerkorian) with no prior connection to the film industry in Hollywood began to take control. According to Steven Jay Schneider:

> The final and perhaps most important factor in Hollywood's late 1960s transformation was the literal and figurative "bottom line." Simply stated, the late 1960s and early 1970s marked a period of severe economic distress for the American movie industry, due mainly to the crippling failure of big-budget blockbusters and the surging youth market. As Hollywood lost touch with the mainstream and catered to more dependable but increasingly rebellious younger moviegoers, revenues dwindled and the box-office charts were dominated by an eclectic mix of modestly performing films.[9]

The industry was backing itself into a situation in which, according to Sklar, "fewer and fewer pictures were made, and fewer still made money, but those that captured the box office earned enormous sums. It was as if the rules of baseball had been changed so that the only hit that mattered was a home run. The studios became interested only in the motion-picture equivalent of a home run."[10] This situation, though with various attempts to provide a countervailing force, has continued into the twenty-first century; it has been, in fact, the industry standard for all of Tarantino's life. And, in fact, one of these attempts to create an alternative would, in the early 1990s, provide Tarantino with his own entry into the film business. By then, as David Bordwell points out (using the same metaphor as Sklar), studios had begun to realize that they "also need to hit doubles and triples, successful movies brought to them by independent producers, shot on mid-range budgets."[11] Studios do still swing for the fences but are sometimes willing to bring in less powerful pinch hitters, such as filmmakers and producers from the independent sector. Tarantino was first seen as one of these, though after 1994 and the success of *Pulp Fiction,* he too was expected to produce blockbuster after blockbuster.

Part of the reason for all of this, again according to Sklar, was the movement back to an earlier model for the business, the one, in fact, that the studio system had replaced in the 1920s, one with control in the hands of distributors, not the production companies. For a distributor, a film that can be placed on hundreds (now thousands) of screens at once is more lucrative than any group of smaller movies filling the same screens and even drawing, as a group, as big an audience.

At the same time as the growth of concentrated distribution power, however, there were a number of small, usually urban (or college-town) theaters that were moving away from showings of Hollywood's new releases. Taking their cue from Henri Langlois, his *Cinémathèque Française,* and the *nouvelle vague* concentration on film tradition, these theaters had begun, in the 1950s, showing British, Italian, Japanese, and French films along with the older Hollywood films that were even then beginning to be recognized for their influence and the importance of their art. These theaters were, according to Sklar,

> generally small neighborhood theaters in university towns or large cities which could not have survived in their old role as inexpensive late-run outlets for Hollywood films but discovered that they could draw a steady audience for first-run foreign films at higher prices than they used to charge for double features. There may have been no more than four or five dozen such theaters in the country, but that was enough to encourage small independent distributors to bring in foreign films.[12]

Though the art houses never reached a point of becoming a significant financial factor in the American film business, they did, at least, show that not all theaters had to show movies for all people. Some filmmakers responded to this: "Films made for discriminating audiences, it was argued, would not make big money, but there was a potential audience large enough at least to recover the costs of production."[13]

Not only were these theaters pioneering a new business model, one that did not rely on the traditional distribution systems, but they tried to replace a concentration on newness with one on quality, betting that they could gain an audience by offering products substantially different from those of the first-run houses that were now moving away from American downtowns.

They also opened the door for what would become the "grindhouses" of the 1970s, theaters serving various niche audiences with everything from porn to slasher films. Tarantino, as a teenager, worked as an usher in one of these, a theater dedicated to porn (which may account for his aversion to pornography in his own work), and certainly darkened the doorways of many another, providing the base for his almost encyclopedic knowledge of grindhouse movies.

Few mourned the loss of the studios and the system they had operated under, a system of conformity and even self-censorship. Though "classical" Hollywood still influenced the way films were conceived and structured, it was becoming possible to envision alternatives anew, infusing an excitement into the industry that had been missing for quite some time. Diminished studio control of the industry allowed for a resurgence of niche filmmaking—including a new type of youth film, sparked by movies such as *Easy Rider* (Dennis Hopper, 1969) that had little resemblance to what Thomas Doherty calls "clean teenpics"[14] of the previous decade, along with what came to be known as "blaxploitation" movies.

The change in Hollywood, over less than a decade, was enormous and reflected much more than just a restructuring industry. Much of what was happening in Hollywood reflected societal upheaval, toned down at the beginning but leading to all hell breaking loose. Take, for example, the changes reflected through *Guess Who's Coming to Dinner* (Stanley Kramer, 1967): it was an Oscar-winning film stuffed with big-name stars;[15] and it created quite a stir with its self-congratulatory social-problem daring; and *Sweet Sweetback's Baadasssss Song* (Melvin Van Peebles, 1971), released just four years after *Guess Who's Coming to Dinner* and the most influential of the early blaxploitation films. In that short time, the lead black character goes from a respectable doctor designed to show that African Americans can achieve just like whites to a sex worker/criminal who couldn't care less. In light of the reality of an increasingly violent urban world, no longer could even the film industry ignore what had proven to be "the total blindness and irrelevance of . . . [*Guess Who's Coming to Dinner*'s] liberal, integrationist impulses . . . [in face of] to the rage and despair of the black community."[16] Van Peebles, who had to find independent backing for his film, saw what the studio moguls could not: pulling punches and softening the lighting was no longer going to work.

The first decade of Tarantino's life was certainly the decade when violence, shown graphically, became a dominant media focus. He wasn't even a year old when the Kennedy assassination set that stage; he was not quite five at the time of the Tet offensive in Vietnam, which brought home the pervasive images of military violence through constant film on television news. That same year of 1968, of course, brought fresh assassinations and more of the urban rioting that had already become a news media staple. Freed by the new ratings system to reflect changed attitudes toward violence in media, *Bonnie and Clyde* and *The Wild Bunch* (Sam Peckinpah, 1969) ushered in an acceptance of bloodiness on screen that laid the groundwork for acceptance of films such as *M*A*S*H* (Robert Altman, 1970) and *Catch-22* (Mike Nichols, 1970) and the visions of violence that grew increasingly common as the 1970s (and Tarantino's teens) progressed. The sanitized (i.e., bloodless) violence of previous decades, like the older, sanitized visions of race relations, all but disappeared.

One of the side-effects of the popularity of movies of this sort, particularly of *Bonnie and Clyde*, was the exposure of many American filmgoers to the "language" of that French movement best known through the movies of Jean-Luc Godard and François Truffaut. This was one of the new languages of film, one built on "free-intercutting of time and space, the use of slow and accelerated motion . . . little vignettes ending in visual and verbal puns à la Truffaut and the alternating of comic and violent moments apropos of Godard."[17] Even before he had reached his teens, Tarantino had been exposed to the film techniques that he would one day make his own.

There can be an advantage, as Malcolm Gladwell argues in *Outliers: the Story of Success*,[18] to when one is born. This was certainly the case with Tarantino, who followed hard on the heels of the baby boom generation that included his teenage mother. It was the baby boomers, raised on the cheap movie fare on television before the advent of broadcast of A-list movies in the early 1960s, who first developed a nostalgic passion for the B-movies and the cheaper of the genre films that did show up on their home sets. For Tarantino, television offered an even greater access to movies with the advent of cable and, in 1972, of Home Box Office. Hollywood, now facing stiff competition, had to please people like the Tarantinos, mother and son, and could only do so by utilizing the very past the boomers had discovered. To do this, moviemakers started taking the genres of cheap fare that had appeared on earlier television, for example, and updating them, as George Lucas did most memorably with *Star Wars* (1977). This must have been film heaven for young Quentin, for he was perfectly placed to soak in the movies and film milieu surrounding him. Through these and other films, Tarantino began to learn the strategies and methodologies of classical Hollywood *writ large* for a new and expanding cinema even before he had reached puberty.

A child herself when her son Quentin was born, Connie Zastoupil (as she became on remarriage), neé McHugh, became an adult as she was raising her son. "I guess Quint and I grew up together in more ways than most mothers and sons,"[19] she says. She loved movies, and she took her young son along, no matter what the subject matter might be. Movies they saw together that had a memorable impact on her son included *The Wild Bunch*, even though it was considered at that time to be the most violent movie ever made, *Carnal Knowledge* (Mike Nichols, 1971), and *Deliverance* (John Boorman, 1972).[20] She also read to him and with him, everything from comic books to classics, and encouraged him to read on his own, but it was at the movies that the two really bonded and where young Quentin discovered his life's passion.

As Tarantino was growing up, the national conversation about movies focused (and still does for the most part) only on a few of the movies that were made, something that surely disappointed a kid who loved *all* movies. On the other hand, with the art-house movement's slight popularity making the genre films, the foreign films, and many more available, there was the possibility for a young person to feel that he or she was finding the other, seemingly unknown movies on her own, on his own. Young film fans embraced movies like *King of Hearts* (Phillipe de Broca, 1966), which was often paired in revival houses with the equally popular, though also outside of the mainstream, *Harold and Maude* (Hal Ashby, 1971). Another example is John Waters's outrageous (for the time) *Pink Flamingos* (1972). The thrill of discovery was quite readily available, more than usually so, for it was now possible to find things in ways that were not simply repeats of what others nearby had done before: the young explorer of film could develop a sense of ownership propelling her or him into further exploration, leading, in Tarantino's case, into a situation in which he makes his films not by simply borrowing from the past but by using films that have become, in an extremely personal sense, his own. The possibilities would only increase throughout the 1970s as the VCR added an almost entirely new way of viewing movies at will—though it also sealed the fate of the grindhouses, which could not compete with the new home viewing possibilities.

For most of Tarantino's early childhood, the price of a movie ticket remained relatively cheap, and cheaper still for a child. Movie theaters were relatively accessible, not set off in distant malls with their multiplexes, but rather downtown, with comparatively fewer seats and only single screens. Yet, over his first decade, ticket prices did rise to an average of about $1.75 ($8.50 in 2008 dollars), making movie-going a great deal more expensive than it had been for a young addict a decade earlier—and children's tickets, as a regular feature, had begun to disappear. Partly as a result, and partly because industry offerings were not fully clicking with audiences, attendance had continued to go down. It bottomed at 864.6 million in 1973, though box office receipts had risen to $7.74 billion in 1972 from $6.585 billion a decade earlier (both in 2008 dollars) thanks to the ticket price rise and the boost given that year by the blockbuster *The Godfather* (Francis Ford Coppola), which grossed, in 2008 terms, some $680 million.

Yet, for all the chaos of the previous years, by the time Tarantino was ten, the movie business had started to exhibit a new strength artistically. In fact, the next few years would see a resurgence of Hollywood, both artistically and financially, at just the time Tarantino was coming to a point of real awareness of himself, of movies, of his culture, and of their combined possibilities. By 1975, the lure of the blockbuster was confirmed by *Jaws* (Steven Spielberg), which doubled the box office receipts of the 1974 top draw, *The Towering*

Inferno (John Guillermin and Irwin Allen) and even that of the next year's top, *Rocky* (John Avildsen), which succeeded thanks (in part) to a no-holds-barred advertising and publicity campaign and the presence of an up-and-coming superstar as actor and writer. There was real money, once more, in Hollywood: the $260 million *Jaws* took in would translate into well over $1 billion 2008 dollars, a stunning number for a movie, then or now.

But it was films such as *The Last Picture Show* (Peter Bogdanovich, 1971), *The Godfather,* and *Mean Streets* (Martin Scorsese, 1973) that had recently shown that a new generation of filmmakers could seriously build on the work of the more innovative of their working elders. These elders, directors such as Arthur Penn, Sam Peckinpah, and Robert Altman, had themselves recently taken the place of the last of the great directors of classical Hollywood. Change was happening, and fast. As a result, the next few years, up to the time Tarantino left school at the end of the decade, proved to be one of the great flowerings of Hollywood film, sparked by the young directors, something of a minor (at least) golden age.

Significant to the maturing aesthetic sensibilities of young Tarantino, this was also a time of B-movie flowering. Roger Corman's New World Pictures, founded at the beginning of the decade, soon began to take the central position in B-movie production from his old home, American International Pictures (though AIP did continue to be a strong presence, particularly in the growing blaxploitation genre) with a mix of chase pictures, slasher films, and other B genres. Tarantino, in the book accompanying *Grindhouse* (Robert Rodriguez and Quentin Tarantino, 2007), details his youthful dream of working for Corman, even calling his company: "I ended up just talking to his assistant. I told her my little story. . . . She actually stopped to give me a ten minute pep talk, to say that I had the right idea and that I should just keep going on. That I shouldn't wait for Roger Corman to make my dreams come true, but make them come true myself."[21] B-pictures from other companies, of course—including *Vanishing Point* (Richard Sarafian, 1971) and *Dirty Mary, Crazy Larry* (John Hough, 1974), both of which contributed to his own 2007 film *Death Proof*—also fascinated Tarantino. All movies, again, did.

Even though the B-pictures and the work of the younger directors flourished during the 1970s, they were a sideshow, each one appealing only to a small portion of the larger audience, none expecting to move into the big tent. There, where the money was, one had to appeal much more broadly—or so the filmmakers believed. Many of them, however, wanted to be in both places. As Nöel Carroll observes:

> At many late-seventies premieres, one frequently had the feeling of watching two films simultaneously. There was the genre film pure and simple, and there was also the art film in the genre film, which through its systems of allusions sent an esoteric meaning to film-literate exegetes. . . . It seems that popular

cinema wants to remain popular by developing a two-tiered system of communication which sends an action/drama/fantasy-packed message to one segment of the audience and an additional hermetic, camouflaged, and recondite one to another.[22]

These two major strands of Hollywood filmmaking of the 1970s (outside of the B-picture realm), the blockbuster and the more serious, socially conscious film, would eventually become indistinguishable. In the meantime, the American New Wave, consisting of directors such as Bogdanovich, Scorsese, Woody Allen, and John Boorman, was able to ensure that simple demand for profit would not overwhelm the industry. The demands for money and the lure of the blockbuster, however, made the "high concept" (reducible to a single phrase encompassing genre, plot, and situation) movie king, relegating almost all of the rest to an also-ran status that would last through the 1980s, a situation that would only be reversed with the rise of the "indy" at the end of the that decade, a rise that Tarantino himself, of course, would be a major part of. In the meantime, the focus on the blockbuster led to the death of smaller movements aimed at specific audiences even affecting the B-picture industry. As Novotny Lawrence writes:

> Hollywood turned its attention to a new phenomenon that began during the blaxploitation movement—the emergence of the blockbuster feature. Thus, the new cycle began as blockbusters, such as *The Godfather* (1972), *Jaws* (1975) and *Star Wars* (1977), which were produced across varying genres, became a staple in Hollywood. These films profited from both black and white audiences and effectively eliminated the need for Hollywood to continue producing films targeted specifically toward blacks.[23]

The blockbuster, in effect, destroyed (for a time, at least) the possibility of multiple American cinemas, one that had been growing over the previous decade. Combined with growing possibilities for at-home viewing and a dearth of product not available on VCR and not aimed for blockbuster success, this also spelled the death of the grindhouse theater.

When Tarantino was in junior high school, the introduction of the Betamax and then the VHS systems (along with the advent of HBO) revolutionized home viewing of movies and increased access to films (including porn, which, as with the Internet a generation later, was the economic engine behind the revolution) a thousand-fold (and also, with the DVD and Blue Ray of the next generation, revitalized the niche filmmaking it had helped to kill) and added new ways for viewers to interact with movies.[24] One of the older visions of the movie audience is that of the passive receptacle. The movies are breathed in, not out. For Tarantino, as for most young movie fans by the 1970s, this was certainly not the case. There was an interaction between audience and film that required willful participation on the part of the viewer, even though the code of behavior in movie theaters in most of America has long reinforced the idea of the passive audience, with audience sound and movement discouraged. Tarantino, restless in many ways, saw movies with a variety of audiences, including primarily African American ones, in which it was (and is) much more acceptable to yell back at the screen and to interact with others in the audience. He learned that watching a movie is best when it becomes a communal experience and has kept that clearly in mind in his own filmmaking and career.

Tarantino had become an aficionado of movie theaters themselves, placing him in an unusual position: not only was he young enough to take full advantage of the new and extensive home movie-viewing possibilities, but he had already established the habit of seeing films in theaters, of seeing them there as something of a special event. The older theaters, built when going to the movies *was* an event, were disappearing or were being cut into smaller, indistinguishable boxes so that multiple films could be shown at one venue. The newer movie houses, generally in the malls dominating the American retail experience, offered little of the allure of the older movie palaces. It was as if the mall were the attraction, not the movies.

Certainly, a lot was going on in Hollywood during the mid to late 1970s. Changes that had begun with the fall of the studio system were finally beginning to bear fruit in the production of a better class of product than had been seen in years. Though it did seem that the formal film schools had replaced apprenticeship within a studio as the means for learning one's craft, there were still plenty of examples of outsiders breaking in—especially in the areas of acting and screenwriting, two of the areas that interested Tarantino most. Small, private schools for acting were flourishing, and the demand for "how-to" books on screenwriting was growing.

Unfortunately, though there certainly was an upsurge of creative output from Hollywood during the last half of the 1970s, that other change, that of concentration on the "home run," the blockbuster generally based on "high-concept" structures, was also occurring, one that would lead to what can best be characterized as an industry malaise through the decade following. It resulted from what Sklar sees as a reversion to what the industry had been before Adolph Zukor's rise at Paramount around the time of World War I.[25] Prior to Zukor and the change he brought about, the three primary aspects of the film industry, production, distribution, and exhibition, were separately controlled—but the distributors effectively called the shots. The rise of the studio system occurred, in part, because of the consolidation, led by Zukor, of the three aspects within single umbrella organizations; its fall led to the reassertion of dominance by the distributors.

One problem with the new paradigm of the late twentieth century was that the tendency to look solely for the "home run" was exacerbated—with little room or interest left for simply getting on base (breaking even) or scoring a run (making a small profit). Naturally enough for people whose interest in the industry was in distribution, in screen numbers and audience size, the new powers in Hollywood wanted nothing less than the fireworks associated with a four-bagger.

Even so, the years from 1975 through 1979, the last of Tarantino's formal schooling, saw the release of a startling number of films now considered either classics or, for one reason or another, particularly significant to film history—or that were certainly memorable to a young movie fanatic. These include *Nashville* (Robert Altman, 1975), *Dog Day Afternoon* (Sidney Lumet, 1975), *One Flew Over the Cuckoo's Nest* (Milos Foreman, 1975), *Jaws, The Rocky Horror Picture Show* (Jim Sharman, 1975), *Taxi Driver* (Martin Scorsese, 1976), *Network* (Sidney Lumet, 1976), *Rocky* (John Avildsen, 1976), *The Deer Hunter* (Michael Cimino, 1976), *Star Wars, Eraserhead* (David Lynch, 1977), *Annie Hall* (Woody Allen, 1977), *Saturday Night Fever* (John Badham, 1977), *Close Encounters of the Third Kind* (Steven Spielberg, 1977), *Days of Heaven* (Terrence Malick, 1978), *Invasion of the Body Snatchers* (Philip Kaufman, 1978), *National Lampoon's Animal House* (John Landis, 1978), *Dawn of the Dead* (George Romero, 1978), *Superman: The Movie* (Richard Donner, 1978), *Apocalypse Now* (Francis Ford Coppola, 1979), *Being There* (Hal Ashby, 1979), *Alien* (Ridley Scott, 1979), *Monty Python's Life of Brian* (Terry Jones, 1979), *Manhattan* (Woody Allen, 1979), *The Warriors* (Walter Hill, 1979), and *Mad Max* (George Miller, 1979). Though nowhere near complete (certainly not in terms either of blockbuster status, influence, or aesthetic value), these are all probably among the movies that Tarantino saw in something close to first release while in his mid-teens. Certainly, even a glance at them can provide a glimpse into what must have been the then-developing film intelligence in his head. Add a few of the B-movies he also surely saw, such as *A Boy and His Dog* (L. Q. Jones, 1975), *Death Race 2000* (Paul Bartel, 1975), and *Eat My Dust* (Charles Griffith, 1976), and a clear picture of the movies shaping the aesthetic of this young man begins to appear.

One of the surprises in watching a Tarantino movie can be the lack of sex, explicit or otherwise. The 1970s, after all, were the years of the rise of explicit porn, exemplified by movies such as *Deep Throat* (Gerard Damiano, 1972), *Emmanuelle* (Just Jaeckin, 1974), and *Debbie Does Dallas* (Jim Clark, 1978). Suddenly, pornography wasn't limited to hard-to-find erotic scenes but presented itself in the open to the mainstream with full-length, plotted picture. When one learns that Tarantino spent many hours of his teens working in a porn house and negotiating its clientele, the surprise lessens. At 16, he was bouncing unruly customers and seeing, over and over again, the most unseemly aspect of the industry he had already decided to join. This is the one branch of his industry that he does not seem to revel in.

By the end of the decade, Tarantino had begun to study acting, working in a community theater and taking lessons. He quit school and began to move toward a life centered completely on the movies. "I was like the dumb kid who couldn't keep up with the class,"[26] recalls Tarantino. "I fucking hated school. I was left back, so I was like, sixteen in ninth grade. I wouldn't even make the effort to just keep up with it, to do the little bit of work that I needed to do to get by. I wanted to be an actor."[27] Never to become much of a speller, much less an academic, the somewhat disruptive Tarantino was kept from a school-suggested drug regimen by his mother before finally replacing formal education with one in which it was he, himself, who directed his restless energies.

Too young for the heyday of the art-house theater movement, Tarantino found the community of movie aficionados he craved through his acting lessons and, more importantly, through a place called Video Archives, a rental store for the newly popular VCR where, first as a customer and then as an employee, he moved from fan to expert and began to think seriously about writing and making movies of his own. "That's the only thing I ever was, a film buff," he says. "It's funny. I meet people who are twenty, twenty-five, whatever, and they don't know what they want to do with their lives. I've known since before I can remember. As a kid, I wanted to be an actor because, when you love movies, that's what you gravitate toward."[28] Certainly, by this time, his knowledge of movies was growing, becoming extensive enough for him to seriously imagine doing even more than acting. "Tarantino wasn't the typical fanboy. When a customer wanted to know about a film, he would act out entire scenes; he knew the décor and the dialogue by heart."[29] It was during this time, too, that he became immersed in the works of Jean-Luc Godard, an art-house favorite of the past decade and the director who would become one of the most important of all of the influences on Tarantino's own movie-making.

Places such as Video Arcades and Kim's Video in New York City, where young film buffs congregated, made possible a sensibility toward film and an understanding of the nature and history of movies not seen since the *nouvelle vague* in France, surpassing anything sparked by the art-house movement in America or even the film schools. It became the one place where the nonacademic cinephile could be sure to find kindred souls. Tarantino had found a home: "I loved exploitation movies. I loved in the 1970s when New World was cranking out their pure stuff. . . . And all the Roger Corman stuff, drive-in movies. At the same time, I loved crime and horror films. Also at the same time I discovered, it sounds like a cliché, I discovered Godard."[30] As a fan of Godard, the similarity between the video store and the cafes of Paris where enthusiasts had gathered after *Cinémathèque Française* showings must have been clear to Tarantino. In fact, the works of Godard, with their pointed references to earlier films, must have seemed both liberating and confirming to the young video buffs soaking in decades of film through the new VCRs. In any case, the influence Godard on Tarantino's films and on his attitudes toward filmmaking should never be underestimated. Tarantino named his production company "A Band Apart" in honor of Godard's 1964 film *Bande à Part.* The debt is deep and fundamental: it's not just in little borrowings or sly homage that Tarantino shows the impact of Godard, but in the very structure of his films, as well as in the camera work, the editing, and especially in the way he manipulates film as language. *Death Proof,* with its focus on the makers of movies, can be traced to Godard in more ways than one, continuing the discussion of the relation between filmmaking and the world that Godard put forward. In *Le Mépris* (1963), Godard uses Fritz Lang playing Fritz Lang; in *Death Proof,* it is stunt specialist Zoë Bell playing Zoë Bell. The poster of Bridgitte Bardot dominating an apartment shown at the start of the film is, according to production designer Caylah Eddleblute, probably from a photograph taken on the *Le Mépris* set,[31] setting up the continuity between the two films.

At the heart of the video-store culture was the list, immortalized in Nick Hornby's 1995 novel *High Fidelity* and by the movie version, directed by Stephen Frears in 2000. Although the venue was a record store and the topic was music instead of film, the passion for compiling life into references to popular art is the same—as it is, also, in comic stories, something Tarantino recognized when he switched the setting to a comic store for the start of his script for *True Romance* (Tony Scott, 1993). Benchmarks were created by recognition of relative importance of specific pieces of individual works and friendly one-upmanship spurred people into further development of their own knowledge. The list, itself never static, was a tool for organization, understanding, and competition, not itself a product or simply a showing of knowledge.

Though there was lots of energy for film in places like Video Arcades, energy that would coalesce into the "indy" movement of the early 1990s, the film industry, by the time Tarantino was able to seriously consider entering into it, had once again stalled, its engine flooded by the lead-foot industry driver, the executive intent only on the high RPMs of the blockbuster. Again, after that period of rejuvenation in the 1970s, the addiction to the "home run" had proven impossible to break, and the independent producers, with their doubles and triples (and even singles) had yet to have a significant impact on Hollywood—though that would be coming soon, marked by the success of *sex, lies, and videotape* (Steven Soderbergh, 1989) at just about the time Tarantino was beginning to really develop his skills as a screenwriter. Soderbergh's film marks the start of contemporary American independent film and laid the groundwork for Tarantino's success just three years later.

Yet, if nothing else, the 1980s provided a young film fanatic such as Tarantino a chance to look back rather than constantly looking around, to study the films of the past with a leisure (and a choice) that few people ever had before. He was able to consider even the 1970s as more than the blockbusters and the films that had found favor with the critics. He saw it as the decade of blaxploitation, Kung Fu, and other genre movies (save the sexploitation ones that he had gotten his fill of while working as an usher)—and was able, in the relatively creative quiescence of the time, to plan how he would build on what he knew best, creating his own movies without distraction.

While working at Video Archives, Tarantino continued to develop his skills through his acting lessons, movie watching, and an attempted movie, *My Best Friend's Birthday,* a film he worked on, off, and on, for almost four years. His break into the movies, however, came elsewhere, with two screenplays, *True Romance,* which Tony Scott eventually directed and which was released in 1993, and *Natural Born Killers,* directed by Oliver Stone and released in 1994. He was starting to get noticed as these screenplays made the rounds, and established filmmakers saw his potential, making it possible for him, finally, to direct his own screenplay.

Developed through a stint at the Sundance Institute Film Lab in 1991 and with the support of Harvey Keitel, Tarantino was soon able to find backing for a third script, *Reservoir Dogs,* this time with himself as director. Released in 1992, it quickly established him as a force in American cinema, a position cemented two years later with the release of *Pulp Fiction,* which earned a screenwriting Oscar for Tarantino and Roger Avery as well as a *Palme d'Or* at Cannes for Tarantino for directing. There was no more becoming for him; he had arrived.

Because of the influence of Godard the *nouvelle vague* of the 1960s, Italian directors such as Bernardo Bertolucci and Sergio Leoné, and barrier-busting (read "bloody") American films such as *Bonnie and Clyde* and *The Wild Bunch,* it can be tempting to call Tarantino an "anticlassical" director. This is especially true when one considers the additional influence of cult filmmakers such as Ted Mikels (whose 1973 movie *The Doll Squad* may be an ancestor of *Kill Bill*); B-movie filmmakers such as William Castle (whose 1964 *Strait-Jacket* contains the sort of twist Tarantino adores); blaxploitation movies such as *Coffy* (Jack Hill, 1973), *Sweet Sweetback's Baadasssss Song* (Melvin Van Peebles, 1971), and *Shaft* (Gordon Parks, 1971); and Hong Kong action movies such as *Come Drink with Me* (King Hu, 1966), *Vengeance* (Chang Cheh, 1970), and *Executioners from Shaolin* (Lau Kar-lueng, 1976). This would indicate, however, that his films turn their back on the traditions developed in Hollywood during the "classical" period starting about 1910 and continuing to about the time Tarantino was born. But Tarantino is not limited in his influences or his artistic stance. In fact, he makes films as much in the classical tradition as someone such as Steven Spielberg, the crudeness and apparent verité of his dialogue and the explosiveness of his violence (to be fair, he has not made anything with the graphic, violent impact of Spielberg's 1998 film *Saving Private Ryan*—one of the many films showing the influence of *The Wild Bunch*) notwithstanding.

In *The Anxiety of Influence,* one of the most important works of literary criticism of its time, Harold Bloom argues that the success of a poet depends, in large part, in grappling with, and besting, the poets most admired by the tyro. Success lies in moving beyond being derivative, and it is the anxiety that arises from recognition of the influence of the past that spurs poets to originality. Though there may be much to be said for Bloom's model, it doesn't hold for an artist such as Quentin Tarantino, one who goes about building his art *through* the derivative, taking what he has found elsewhere and incorporating it, often without disguise, into the newer work. In fact, Tarantino may be exhibiting a comfort with influence that itself could be said to be part of the classical Hollywood tradition. Tarantino would most certainly agree with the classical Hollywood studio executives who generally insisted on derivation over innovation, making even the best directors use the former to produce the later, just as Tarantino tries to do today.

In simple, generational terms, Tarantino follows naturally from the work of Martin Scorsese, who also found inspiration in the *nouvelle vague* and classic Hollywood (among other places). There's a difference in attitude, however, one that has had a major influence on Tarantino's approach to film-making, a difference perhaps best expressed through a story Scorsese has retold often, of John Cassavetes's comment after screening *Boxcar Bertha* (1972), Scorsese's exploitation film for Roger Corman at American International Pictures. Scorsese biographer Vincent LoBrutto calls it "career-saving counsel."[32] Essentially, Cassavetes told Scorsese that his ambitions should be higher. Twenty years later, and addressed to Tarantino, someone of Cassavetes's stature saying (essentially) "Kid, you're better than this" might have been career ending rather than saving. Rather than making something better than a B-picture, Tarantino had decided to make B-pictures better.

It may be Tarantino's open acknowledgement of influence—in fact, a utilization of it that comes close to pastiche (though a better word might be "decoupage")—that makes many see him as a postmodern or, at least, postclassical director. Certainly, his attitude arises from the film culture of his youth, characterized by Nöel Carroll, who writes that, from the time Tarantino had come of age;

> The queue at the box office is dominated by teenagers seeking a hearth away from home. These consumers know what they want and Hollywood has listened to them; after the experimentation of the early seventies, genres have once again become Hollywood's bread and butter. And the viability of genres is what makes allusionism a practical option. The film-historically conscious director can deftly manipulate the old forms, satisfying the adolescent clientele while also conveniently pitching allusions to the inveterate film Gnostics in the front rows.[33]

Like Shakespeare playing to the pit and to the boxes, a director of Tarantino's sort searches for—and finds—ways of pleasing both audiences. The desire, for Tarantino, is not, as in Bloom's assumption for the poet and his or her audience, for originality but for reference for a place within the traditions he loves as well as motion beyond them. As Carroll observes, "Allusions to Hitchcock, Hawks, Ford, and Fuller became a means by which directors following these masters could pretend to the same preoccupations and to the same intensity as the originals."[34] Having himself grown up loving to seek and find references, Tarantino early on recognized that providing references for his audiences to find would thrill his own audiences—as well as allowing him to "pretend" to the themes of his elders while developing his own out of theirs. This dovetailed well with the introduction of the World Wide Web in the early 1990s, allowing networking of information to a degree never before imagined. As Bordwell notes, soon after their release, "Websites, both authorized and amateur, cataloged the dozens of films cited in *Kill Bill*'s two 'volumes.'"[35]

One of the first films finding success in America that openly catered to the love of the sort of cinematic voyeurism that Tarantino would manipulate in his own movies was *C'era una volta il West* (Sergio Leone, 1968). In fact there is much in Leone's film that illustrates the attitudes that Tarantino would bring to his own decades later. The use of actors Woody Strode and Jack Elam in the opening scene of the movie, for example, not only is a nod to the influence of earlier Westerns but to the filmmaking of an earlier time as a whole, to the "recycling" of actors because of certain characteristics and even of their presence within a "family" of actors appearing in many of one director's films (Woody Strode was part of John Ford's "family" for a time), both important parts of Tarantino's filmmaking. Then there was the use of a star, Henry Fonda, against type—much as John Travolta was used in *Pulp Fiction*.

As in Tarantino's films, the references to earlier movies in *C'era una volta il West* are really too numerous to count. The homages to *Johnny Guitar* (Nicholas Ray, 1954), to *Shane* (George Stevens, 1953), and to *High Noon* (Fred Zinnemann, 1952) are only the most obvious of dozens of references and allusions. None of these, however, not even the eyes of a child killer that prove to be the eyes of Henry Fonda, provides a necessary piece for enjoyment—even understanding—of the film. This is not simply because the movie works on multiple levels, but because the levels do not work separately. Instead, each amplifies another, all working together and circularly to construct what is, finally, a seamless whole and not simply a collage, a pastiche, or even decoupage.

Such a design, of course, has never been exclusive to film. Readers of Vladimir Nabokov's *Lolita,* for example, can follow the novel without familiarity with the sly and often arcane references Nabokov uses to texture his narrative. Among the writers who use the same technique (it could be argued that there are few who don't) are two of Nabokov's students, Richard Fariña, whose career was cut short when he died in a motorcycle accident soon after his one novel, *Been Down So Long It Looks Like Up to Me* (filled, like Tarantino's movies, with popular culture references), was published, and

Thomas Pynchon, perhaps the contemporary master of the technique in fiction—as Tarantino is, in film. In *Gravity's Rainbow*, Pynchon writes that "Red, the Negro shoeshine boy, waits by his dusty leather seat. The Negroes all over wasted Roxbury wait."[36] It doesn't matter, to understand the passage or even the scene it appears in, that "Red" is Malcolm Little, the future Malcolm X, nor that "wasted Roxbury" was a massive Boston inner-city slum. Few readers, even without this information, will miss the implications of the passage—and even if one were to miss them, the story as a whole would not be interrupted. In transferring this to film, in the way he structures his stories and uses "chapters" to define their parts, Tarantino shows the consistent influence of the novelist's art. As Jeff Dawson puts it, "Tarantino has long coveted for filmmakers the freedom of expression that novelists have, with the liberty to not only play about with chronology but to allow characters to float in and out of different stories."[37] And so, he constantly pushes his own art toward acceptance of the freedoms so willingly granted to those who work solely on paper.

Like many directors before him, but perhaps more explicitly, Tarantino sees himself as a novelist in a cinematic age, working with the range of tools available to him, not simply with the pen encompassing all, as it did before the advent of electronic media. By embracing an expanded tool set, Tarantino also takes on an expanded language, one encompassing all of the books, records, TV shows, and movies (and more) that he has experienced within its vocabulary.

Often described as the essence of "cool," Tarantino takes Marshall McLuhan's "hot" medium of the movies, cools it down, and places it squarely in the hands of the audience, transforming it into "cool" in McLuhan's sense, not simply in terms of popular perception. He does this because he understands movies best from the point of view of the moviegoer, and constantly draws on his own background as an audience, taking what he has experienced in the theater (and elsewhere) and forming it to create a new experience containing the old and allowing for the next viewer/listener to do the same, in turn.

Mayhem and Farce, the World and the Movies

In 2005, there were nearly 40,000 automobile accidents in the United States involving at least one fatality.[1] For 2008, the Federal Bureau of Investigation reported close to 1,400,000 incidents of violent crime, or about 4.5 for every 1,000 people.[2] Included were over 16,000 murders. Add to these numbers death and injury from fire, natural disaster, and other sources, and a picture of common violence emerges. Yet most of us would rather pretend none of this exists, living our lives on the assumption that we, somehow, will be the ones to make it through unscathed and that our children will grow up unaffected—a not unwarranted assumption, given the odds, but still *only* an assumption.

Though we avoid consideration of violence in our own lives (even to the point of denying it exists, as is common in domestic violence situations), we remain drawn to it as voyeurs. Few feet don't ease up on the gas pedal when passing an accident. Few others stride on without hesitation when a crowd gathers around a knifing victim. The sound of gunshots makes us duck, but we peek—not to see if it is safe to come out, but to view the commotion. Violence, though we pretend it won't affect us, still fascinates us.

Without Tyburn-like public hangings to mesmerize us, for many of us, movies and other visual media have taken the place of live voyeurism of violence. No longer do we have to run to watch a fire; instead we can simply switch on the TV. In a quite real fashion, the mechanicals of media do protect us, separating us from violence, making us *feel* safe, at least, and excusing our watching. This doesn't apply only to the end viewers: on 9/11, as I walked away from the New York City College of Technology campus on the Brooklyn side of the East River, I saw camera after camera pointed from the tops of buildings toward the sparkling, tragic smoke across the water behind me. At first I was angered by the idea of these people who, I thought, were clearly recording for the future rather than living in the moment of our common disaster. I couldn't imagine trying to think beyond the moment, but seeing them forced me to, and I resented it. Later, I realized that they were only keeping themselves safe by keeping their cameras between themselves and massive death, mediating violence by camera, protecting themselves much as cameraman John Cassellis (Robert Forster) thinks he is doing at the start of *Medium Cool* (Haskell Wexler, 1969)—or (on the audience side) as Chance (Peter Sellers) does when he tries to click away threatening young men with a remote control in *Being There* (Hal Ashby, 1979). The medium, in these situations, isn't the message; it's the barrier and the cocoon.

Even though I finally understood why they had been created, years passed before I was able to look at 9/11 images. For me, they removed the personal from the violent. And violence, ultimately, is nothing if not personal—which may be part of the point. Which may be why we turn to media so quickly in violent situations: we want to *remove* it from the personal, something media do seem to allow and even encourage.

But violence, again, is always personal. To know so, I need look no further than to my own life. I have been lucky: most of the violence I've experienced having been around me and not to me—or having been threatened, not executed. Yet mayhem has certainly been part of my life. In the past two years, four people have died by violence in three incidents within three blocks of my house. I stumbled into a border war in Africa a quarter of a century ago, and I survived a variety of attempted *coups d'état*—not to mention auto accidents, the unfortunate swing of an axe, a head bloodied by fists, and even an ill-advised attempt to stop a purse-snatcher. At one point—it was during that border war—I was led at gunpoint into the brush, and I believed I was being taken to be shot, out of sight. Though I understand the desire to use media as a barrier against violence (as well as a window upon it), I've never felt protected from violence or aside from it or exempt from it by past experience, as Gnossos Pappadopoulis believes he is, in Richard Fariña's novel *Been Down So Long It Looks Like Up to Me*. As many Americans also seem to believe today—or did, before 9/11.

On the other hand, I've never loved violence, either. To me, it's simply part of my environment, a sad one, but real. For that reason, perhaps, I've less trouble with violence in entertainment than have many people: I can laugh at Punch and Judy without worrying that it is going to promote more real violence. I found *Straw Dogs* (Sam Peckinpah, 1971) annoying not for the violence but for what I saw as a crass effort to manipulate my emotions, the same reaction I had, a few years later, to *Jaws* (Steven Spielberg, 1975), one of the only movies I have ever walked out on—not because of the violence, but because I felt cheated by what I saw as cheap and too obvious attempts to manage my reactions through the soundtrack. In fairness, the very thing that bothered me about the movie is part of what makes it work, of what makes it one of the most successful movies of all time. Film audiences, in general, *want* to be manipulated.

My vision of screen violence in particular was perhaps first crystallized by the death of a college classmate killed by a car as she walked from a movie theater. It wasn't the movie that killed her, but a driver who was probably drunk. I learned from the incident, learned that, to put it a little facetiously, movies don't kill people, people kill people. On the other hand, as William Rothman notes, it does remain true that, "As Freud also recognized . . . a clear boundary between real and symbolic violence is difficult or impossible to draw. 'Real' violence can have symbolic meaning, and 'symbolic' violence can have real consequences."[3] Also, people do tell stories of having been put into trances by movies, the screen vision becoming so real that they don't remember leaving the theater or even how they got home.

Perhaps the dividing line that I imagined between what happened in that theater and on the road outside is murkier than I would like to think. The more I consider it, the less completely comfortable I am with the idea that "the world on film differs from the real world by being exempt from real violence."[4] The link between the two is real, and is us, the viewers. The attitudes that we develop in the theater are sometimes brought into the real world—and vice versa. The question is: what is the extent of these attitudes, and the impact?

Unfortunately, "the guiding focus of most of the century's social and institutional attention to film violence has been on censorship itself or effects on viewers, or institutional modes of regulation, specific social concerns, or marginalized groups—all worthwhile projects, but rarely allowing for a more synthetic understanding of film violence. . . . Cinematic, cultural, and historical contexts have been neglected in favor of assertions regarding individual films and the repetitive production of scandals that rehearse a narrow range of viewpoints."[5] Questions relating to the place of violence within our culture and entertainment in general, questions certainly in need of consideration, often take second place to what almost amounts to voyeuristic accusations of specific responsibility on the part of movies in particular, but also television and music, one of the things Michael Moore explores in his *Bowling for Columbine* (2002).

In his examination of film violence, J. David Slocum argues that, if

> violence is a function of relations of power, of violations, victimizations, oppression, and harm, or of legitimate social and political change, a greater variety of presentations—relations between genders, say, or races, or economic classes, or throughout everyday life—can be construed as violent. . . . [T]he emphasis of research on "film violence" tends to isolate and decontextualize cinema, or the popular culture of which it is part, as discrete and distanced from individual lives or larger social practices.[6]

If the line between filmic violence and real violence is ambiguous, that between the conceptualization of violence (in film and elsewhere) and individual experience is even more problematic. Violence is never simply an act but is also an attitude—and a threat. When Walter Sobchak (John Goodman) says to Smokey (Jimmie Dale Gilmore) in *The Big Lebowski* (Joel and Ethan Coen, 1998), "You're entering a world of pain," and then repeats himself, it's not the fact of the gun he holds or even what it could do physically that's at stake, but a very personal conception of the world. When Sobchak and Lebowski (Jeff Bridges) leave the bowling alley where the incident occurred, they talk about it:

> **Lebowski**: Walter, you can't do that. These guys're like me, they're pacifists. Smokey was a conscientious objector.
>
> **Sobchak**: You know Dude, I myself dabbled with pacifism at one point. Not in Nam, of course—
>
> **Lebowski**: And you know Smokey has emotional problems!
>
> **Sobchak**: You mean—beyond pacifism?
>
> **Lebowski**: He's fragile, man! He's very fragile!

Having a gun pointed at you can change your attitude toward life—even if it is never fired. Threatened violence of this sort is *close* to the ultimate intrusion, and it reduces any confidence in the future. Though the impact is nothing like that of being shot, it can still be life changing. In other words, and once again, violence is always personal. And it remains so even when seen on the screen. Screen violence cannot be fully considered, as Slocum implies, outside of that context.

In fact, it was the changing context of violence in the 1960s that has altered our view of the impact of violence in movies. Early on, it wasn't the violence in movies itself that concerned people, but the moral impact viewing it could have, or so some believed, on the audience. So, as Stephen Prince writes, "crime films were bad because criminals provided poor role models. . . . By contrast, the violence that occurred in war films or Westerns was often recuperated by the genre. It did not seem as subversive as the violence in crime or horror pictures."[7] Violence in the name of right was OK. Clearly, it was the consequence of violence that raised concern, not the act itself.

Raised in a Quaker environment in which violence is considered no option at all, I have wondered since my teen years about the attraction that violence in the movies (and on television and even in books) holds for me. At one point I wondered if there weren't a part of me that actually wanted to *be* violent, if the movies were some sort of wish fulfillment. But, no: though I can kill a chicken and prepare it for the table, there's no joy in it for me—and I've no serious fantasies about revenge or physically destroying anyone. As I have been in the presence of violence and have been the victim of physical attack, I certainly don't use movie violence as a way of imagining how I would react to violence, for I have learned that one reacts differently to each situation.

Prince writes that the "key development of the sixties was the emergence of 'violence' as a discrete category disentangled from issues of behavior—from the considerations of criminality or genre that had subsumed it in previous decades."[8] Prior to the late 1960s, as I have mentioned, violence had often been excused as a vehicle for something else, generally for a moral point of some sort. From that time on, it began to be something else. Not only did it begin to be seen as a thing in itself, untied from any point the movie might be trying to make, but it began to seem to become the point of a few movies in and of itself.

The graphic nature of new film violence was made possible by technological advances, but also by the violence seen in other media, violence (like almost all of the "real" violence of the experiential world) that seemed to make no sense at all, completely at odds with the screen violence of the previous three decades, in which that moral point of some sort was most always present. Leo Charney sees this as the start of a "seemingly escalating decontextualization of those moments [of violence], their apparently increasing tendency in contemporary action movies to stand on their own, as if for their own sake, no longer the handmaidens of an orthodox cause-and-effect story."[9] Some might see this as simply the advantage of the moment in a continual struggle between spectacle and storytelling in cinema: "violence and kinetic sensation have become the fall guys for a perceived decline in coherent storytelling that implicitly defines 'films' as conventional classical narratives."[10] On the other hand, as Marsha Kinder argues, violence can be used by a filmmaker "to structure not merely an individual sequence but the stylistic and narrative design of the entire film—that is, to use representations of violence as a series of rhythmic eruptions that orchestrate the spectator's emotional response."[11] Violence sometimes serves as spectacle, sometimes for narrative. And it is here, in this duality, where one encounters the problem of how best to consider violence in film.

Two of the movies I remember most vividly from my early years are *The Counterfeit Traitor* (George Seaton, 1962) and *The Dirty Dozen* (Robert Aldrich, 1967), both World War II movies, though the former tells heartbreaking tales of sacrifice amidst horror, whereas the latter is "an uncommonly cynical World War II action picture about hardened criminals."[12] Like almost everyone I knew growing up, my father was a veteran of that war but, again like my friends' fathers, he rarely ever talked about it—except in the presence of other vets, and then only in rather veiled terms. It's not surprising that my generation was drawn to movies about our parents' experiences: often, it was the only way we had of finding out anything about that time that had so shaped our lives even before we were born. But it wasn't their history that I took from these movies.

Whereas *The Counterfeit Traitor* shocked me, and seeing it has, over the years, proven to be a defining experience in my moral and political development, *The Dirty Dozen* was a lot more fun to watch, though it is little more than a romp. Though it was shocking, too—I had never imagined there could be a film making me sympathetic with such a rotten bunch or that I could cheer the destruction of unarmed people, including civilians, trapped in an underground bunker—it showed me almost nothing about the realities of power relationships, individual responsibility, or the consequences of choice. In other words, it gave me nothing to think about, exactly the opposite of the earlier movie.

While watching *The Counterfeit Traitor,* I could almost feel the pervasive violence of Nazi Germany—or believed I could. The movie portrays an atmosphere of intimidation, of paranoia, and of the willful embrasure of a violent hierarchy as self-protection. The horror for the viewer is that good and evil are mixed together in the movie in a way much more frightening than that seen in the rather simplistic *Schindler's List* (Steven Spielberg, 1993), say, in which the two are carefully delineated. In *The Counterfeit Traitor,* one spy for the Allies, for example, sees a school bombed and children killed as an accidental result of information she may have provided. Her remorse leads her into a confessional where a Gestapo agent (who has been trailing her) replaces the priest. This, not surprisingly, leads to her arrest and subsequent death.

After examining the "making and marketing" of *The Great Train Robbery* (Edwin Porter, 1903), Peter Kramer identifies "the divergent discourses of effectively and respectability . . . [providing] a model for mainstream narrative in American cinema as a whole . . . the generation of 'excitement,' by whatever means necessary, has been the primary objective, running parallel to, yet being hidden behind and occasionally at odds with, complex narrational procedures and their associated aesthetic and moral qualities."[13] Most movies do utilize both spectacle and narrative; the question has always been one of balance, with *The Counterfeit Traitor* and *The Dirty Dozen* falling on different sides.

Watching *The Counterfeit Traitor* and *The Dirty Dozen* led me to believe that there's screen violence and then there's graphic screen violence—and that the two are completely different things. One, I thought, is a tool for story and the other uses story to justify spectacle. They are, I argued to myself, as different as melodrama and comedy, as mayhem and farce . . . yet I have since realized that we continually must and do combine them into one, judging one by the standards of the other, and vice versa. We have no real way of extracting one from the other in our conversations any more than in our movies, sometimes rendering us inarticulate when it comes to explaining our feelings and fears regarding the relationship between our lives and what we want to see on the screen.

Sissela Bok, in her book *Mayhem,* pins the fault for the confusion directly on the screen itself: "The screen renders experience both less and more real in its own right. It both mediates violence and makes it seem more immediate, exposing viewers to levels and forms of violence they might never otherwise encounter. It helps cross boundaries between real and reenacted, between art and entertainment, between being near the violence and being at a distance."[14] And that is certainly so. *The Counterfeit Traitor* brought the reality of Nazi Germany (accurately or not) home to me in a way that nothing else ever has, outside of a visit to Auschwitz-Birkenau decades later. *The Dirty Dozen,* however, did nothing of the kind, though, as I said, I enjoyed watching it very much. Perhaps, then, Bok must be talking here about only one of the two kinds of film violence, the one that is not just for fun. The problem is, the two cannot be effectively divorced.

Bok goes on to write that, "A killing in a movie is watched by real people on whom it may have real effects."[15] Yes, but when is a killing on screen a killing? There's an Eastern bloc comedy Western called *Limonádový Joe aneb Konská opera* (Oldrich Lipský, 1964) in which the dead come back to life at the end. Are the deaths that have been earlier depicted actually "killings"? The trouble is that Bok is making an extremely important point, but it reaches into an ill-defined world of screen action that makes even the most careful discussion problematic and likely too broad, for it must ultimately bring comedy and spectacle into the arena of "real" violence. The two sides, again, cannot be permanently separated.

The questions for movies get even more complicated: is a killing off screen a movie killing? It's not watched, after all. The death of Marvin (Phil LaMarr) in *Pulp Fiction* happens off screen—but the blood shoots all over the screen image. Does that count? There's lots of death associated with *Reservoir Dogs,* but little of the violent action is actually seen. Do those deaths count? These questions verge on the facetious, but they have a point: there are plenty of movies dealing with questions of violence that are never criticized for their violence, because it is sanitized, because it is elided, or because it is kept in the background. Do these deaths and acts have less of an impact than graphic on-screen violence?

To Bok, and I think, mistakenly, there's a distinct difference between on-screen violence and other violence referred to or otherwise relating to the narrative. She sees the graphic depiction as something of an authorization to violence, a glamorization of it, and a deadening of reaction from overexposure creating pitilessness. To her, these three things in combination "enable spectators to experience heightened pleasure from violence."[16] The visual aspect of movie violence, the spectacle, then, is what bothers her most, not the inclusion of violence in the narrative, though the other does certainly enter into her concern.

Rothman asks, "What is it about the medium that is so frightening that it led film's earliest critics to believe—and so many continue to believe—that movies are 'capable of evil, having the power for it'?"[17] Maybe it is, simply, that the violent image has more power than violence portrayed in other ways, with the power growing the more graphic the violence becomes, adding new sorts of temporal elements to violence carried by film (witness contemporary slow-motion depictions and repetition of the violent act through cameras set to different angles, both common techniques today and used to great effect by Tarantino in *Death Proof*), making filmic violence more disturbing than, say, that of painting or photography. With a still image, we can look away quickly knowing the picture will not change. A moving image constantly tempts us back. Perhaps, because motion makes them closer to "reality," "films do not simply present us with images of violence (or of the effects of violence). They also represent violent actions,"[18] making them not about violence, but violence themselves.

Perhaps the greatest problem with violent depictions in movies is enjoyment, that is, as Prince argues:

> To a large extent, the cinema cannot present violence in other than a pleasure-inducing capacity, and . . . serious social consequences follow from this. The medium inevitably *aestheticizes* violence. The arousal and expression in cinema of 'negative' emotions—fear, anxiety, pain—typically occur as part of a please-inducing aesthetic experience. Admittedly, there is much about this phenomenon—why viewers seek emotional experiences in art that they would avoid in a nonfictional context—which is little understood. But it seems likely that representations of violence on screen that are unrelentingly horrifying, nauseating, or disgusting will fail to attract viewers, in comparison with films that provide aesthetic pleasures, even when the work in question . . . aims to be shocking and upsetting.[19]

Perhaps because our interactions with movies have become so strong emotionally in so many ways, our relation to screen violence has become affective as well. After all, movies work visually, aurally, and temporally, creating wholes with immediate emotional impact greater than just about any other art form. Rothman comments, "Because it is not real violence, it would not be possible for film violence to harm us were it not for the massive ways we involve movies in our lives. . . . We have an appetite for film violence, an appetite that film violence feeds, and perhaps also creates."[20] As far as I know, no one has made a similar claim about violence in still photography, for example, though Cindy Sherman and others have changed that somewhat. So, for the claim to be true, there has to be a qualitative difference between violence on film and violence shown elsewhere—and that difference must be the temporal unfolding of film action.

If the temporal element is significant, then examination of the use of violence in drama, though it has of necessity a less graphic aspect, could be useful, or as Bok does for her study, one could examine contests such as those of the Roman gladiators. Also possible would be inquiry into those sports with a heightened and common violent aspect, such as boxing. In boxing, at least as in film, as viewers, Rothman writes:

> we might well also find ourselves thinking, at this moment, that if it is so thrilling merely to be imagining that we are throwing this punch and feeling its impact, it must be infinitely more pleasurable to be living what we are only

imagining. If it has the power to motivate us to think such a thought . . . then film violence is capable to stimulating, or even creating, an appetite for violence, a blood lust, that, we imagine, we can more fully gratify by performing or suffering real acts of violence than by merely viewing violence (or the effects of violence) on film.[21]

This, I suspect, is the heart of the problem people often have with depictions of violence on screen—or in the arena or on the racetrack: because it looks real, it can too easily cross that line and *become* real. What's worse, we are liking it more the closer it gets, part of what is explored in movies such as *Fight Club* (David Fincher, 1999), in which it gets very close, indeed.

Another aspect of the movies that makes people uncomfortable in relation to depictions of violence is the huge popularity of film, especially when laced with violence. This must, they say, have impact on the general population. Bok writes, relating to children's viewing but stating specifically that no age escapes vulnerability, that "as with all consumption, viewing intake can be harmful in two ways. It may either simply displace activities needed for adequate for [sic] growth and sustenance, or else be actively toxic, at times addictive. It is in this context that questions concerning media violence enter in."[22] This widespread view presupposes, as Bok admits, that movie watching is a passive activity of consumption that, furthermore, takes "away opportunities for sports and play and creative activities and the give-and-take of reciprocal engagement with others."[23] This concern is hierarchical: movies just aren't as good, Bok implies, as these other activities—and there cannot be room for all.

Though the idea of movie viewing as passive consumption is quite old, it really doesn't fit the real, observed relations among movie makers, the films themselves, and the audience. Herbert Gans noticed more than 50 years ago "that there is active, although indirect interaction between the audience and the creators, and that both affect the makeup of the final product."[24] Gans refers specifically to the consideration of audience choice in filmmaking, but the implication comes clear the more one looks at the dynamics of the film industry: viewers play an active role, even if only in the choices they make for viewing. This, perhaps, is even more worrisome to Bok: viewers *participate* in the movies they see.

In fact, they are active in film in many ways, as the life of Tarantino attests. Movies never pacified him, but electrified him, as they have done, now, for generations of Americans. The very fact (one that Tarantino draws upon for creation of his movies) of the changes in language brought about by film makes clear that the interactions between the audience and even the screen are a great deal more complex than the idea of a passive, receptive audience allows. The proof of this has come with the advent of the World Wide Web, which now provides outlets for audiences, for these very people to participate, people who had once been seen as little more than passive receptacles waiting for media masters to fill them. Will Brooker and Deborah Jermyn observed the audience of a contemporary British TV show, finding that audience members didn't simply watch, but "went online to debate its flaws, emailed its characters, watched clips that were never shown on TV and wandered off onto other sites."[25] In prior decades, such activity was generally confined to discussions among family and friends—but it happened even then. From the beginning of motion pictures, audiences have reacted immediately to what they see on the screen, sometimes in fright, sometimes in anger, sometimes in debate. Sometimes, it is feared, in violence.

From the beginning of motion pictures, also, there have been those wishing to protect those same audiences from themselves as well as from the predators among them, believing they were too naïve or were too vulnerable to make their own determinations about what they see. At the start, "the belief among film's earliest critics that movies caused harm to society was inseparable from their puritanical sense than movie viewing was in itself immoral."[26] A slight taint stemming from that belief remains even today.

The puritanical view of movies wasn't the only that presented film as, if not inherently immoral, intrinsically violent. Rothman writes that:

> [Sergei] Eisenstein believed that every frame of every film had, as it were, the blood of the world on it, due to the violence of the camera's original act of tearing pieces of the world from their "natural" places. The idea that the camera is an instrument of violence was taken up, at least implicitly, by André Bazin (if the film image is a "death mask" of the world, must not the camera be implicated in killing the world?), for whom Eisenstein's ideas were otherwise anathema, and, in turn, by Stanley Cavell (in its transformation into the world on film, the world undergoes a metamorphosis, or transfiguration, so profound as to be akin to death and rebirth).[27]

The association of movies and violence, in this view, is so basic that, here again, the two cannot be split asunder: even the most benign-appearing movie would still be introducing violence, confirming those old puritanical suspicions.

Though questions of violence in film have been around from the first, it was only in the 1960s that that the current specific concern over movie violence began to arise, thanks to the death of the old Production Code and the institution of the Motion Picture Association of America's rating system—which made room, for the first time in Hollywood, for films such as *Bonnie and Clyde* (Arthur Penn, 1967) and *The Wild Bunch* (Sam Peckinpah, 1969), movies that created a new attitude toward graphic depiction of violence, an attitude that Tarantino shares, though he is generally nowhere near as graphic in his violence as many contemporary directors. The rating system also changed how violence was viewed conceptually. According to Prince, before "that time, 'violence' did not exist as a 'thing in itself,' perceived as an irreducible feature of cinema irrespective of considerations such as genre or the dramatic content of a given scene. There are, for example, no sections of Hollywood's Production Code that deal with what we now call 'violence.'"[28] Here again, the debate moves from the impact to the depiction of the act.

Since the beginning of cinema, there have been people who simply find violence on the screen disturbing and uncomfortable and not for any specific ethical or moral reasons. These people have had an impact, too, on movies and on cultural opinions about their violence. Pauline Kael once wrote that people "*should* feel uncomfortable, but this isn't an argument *against* the movie. Only a few years ago, a good director would have suggested the violence obliquely, with reaction shots . . . and death might have been symbolized by a light going out, or stylized, with blood and wounds kept to a minimum. In many ways, this method is more effective; we feel the violence more because so much is left to our imaginations. But the whole point of *Bonnie and Clyde* is to rub our noses in it, to make us pay our dues for laughing. The dirty reality of death—not suggestions but blood and holes—is necessary."[29] On the other hand, as Geoff King suggests, "Violent events often provide the disruption of equilibrium so basic to the establishment of the classical-style narrative trajectory, a shift out of 'routine' or 'ordinary' life into the heightened register of the world we usually experience vicariously on screen. Violent events, confrontations, or climaxes are handy ways of rendering conflict into a form that is clearly manifest, visible, and audible. Some would argue that violence is a 'lazy' narrative device for this reason, an easy alternative to the exploration of more complexly shaded areas of experience."[30] Necessary challenge or cheap technique, violence remains one of the most important tools of the filmmaker, which is one of the reasons Tarantino won't even consider discussing how violence should be used in film. Even the discussion itself, by its very nature, would limit his tools.

That decade of tremendous social shift, the 1960s, has informed American cultural debate in quite a number of arenas, including film. Slocum writes that, "For policymakers, critics, and the public today, the contests over the meaning of 'film violence' redound upon their views of the decade [the sixties], its place in history, and the legacy of the politics that are seen to have defined it."[31] Certainly, the filmmakers of the time did not see what they were doing as isolated from public attitudes or from the need for cultural change. Slocum claims, for example, that "Peckinpah's stated aim was to undermine viewers' conventional, distanced, and finally safe vantage points for watching movie violence."[32] Furthermore, by "heightening the artifice of violence in his films, he [Peckinpah] claimed to hope to convey the horrors of the era to viewers inured to society's real violence—as he might put it, to wake viewers up to what violence was really all about."[33] Violence to cure violence—something of a homeopathic approach—today simply seems more of an excuse to explore the impact of violence, when one looks back on

Peckinpah's films. Within the discussions of the early twenty-first century, Slocum claims:

> the invocation of "film violence" continues to tend strongly toward a critical and public discourse premised on the issue of behavioral "effects" of viewing (putatively) violent movies. In so orienting discourse, the trope of "film violence" effectively delimits the scope and focus of attention to cinematic brutality and bloodletting. It also enables the ready attachment of moral judgments—of Hollywood film being "good" or "bad" for its violence—to these supposedly more objective or scientific evaluations. Such readings of film violence as a matter of effects have become naturalized through repetition and the legitimation accorded by the funding, policy debates, and even industry pronouncements, though upon closer inspection they can also be seen to rely directly on formulations that were consolidated in the historically specific conditions of the 1960s.[34]

This makes it extremely difficult to look at the films outside of one's preexisting belief in the impact of media violence on perpetrators of physical violence.

Some, however, do find ways to sidestep the debate. Tarantino faces it head on but rejects it, brushing it off as irrelevant to what he is doing: "Does violence put ideas in people's minds? It probably does. . . . I'm not going to be handcuffed by what some crazy fuck might do who sees my movie. . . . The minute you put handcuffs on artists because of stuff like that, it's not an art form anymore."[35] Slocum continues:

> The nub of many claims of postmodern violence is their reflexive critique of institutional, media, and social relations, and the supposition that the bases of individual identity and social life have been irremediably changed since the 1960s. To expand a discussion of "film violence," postmodern critics thus posit different assumptions concerning cinema, society, psychology, and violence— or, at least, a greater willingness to interrogate traditional assumptions. Rather than assuming a coherent contemporary society and cultural order comparable to that which existed during the period of classical cinema, critics critique the foundations of the received social contract and mythical compact, and emphasize the fragmentary quality of social experience.[36]

Thus, blaming the movie for a cultural situation fraught with violence becomes somewhat akin to blaming the messenger.

So far, I have concentrated here on the one type of screen violence, spectacle, that depicting graphic gore for purposes having nothing to do with comedy or relaxed enjoyment, though I have mentioned that I see the two types as inextricably linked, as Tarantino also seems to believe. In this first type of screen violence, the violence is imagined by some to reach from the screen and into audience lives. Then there's that other type of screen violence, that encompassing comedy, but extending far beyond it and that can even embrace spectacle. Bok recognizes that, at least, an argument can be made for the distinct existence, if not the value, of this sort of violence: "Picturing or describing a violent scene, first of all, can shed light on it in such a way that it provides, at the very least, harmless amusement, possibly insight and joy. As both Plato and Aristotle pointed out, we do delight in representations of objects and emotions that would evoke altogether different responses in real life, but most of us side with Aristotle in refusing to regard this as corrupting or maiming in its own right. We laugh at the pratfalls and pies thrown at people's faces in slapstick movies as we would not in real life."[37] The word, the stage, and the screen keep the fiction before us. But this, I think, is a slippery slope that leads us away from the obvious tautology that violence, not matter how it is framed, is still violence.

Even at his most graphic, Tarantino also keeps the screen explicitly and concretely between the violence and the audience, as he does in *Death Proof* (2007), where he uses "signs" of an overused print (scratches, splices, etc.) to retain focus on the fact of the screen and the separation it represents, perhaps making his most gruesome scene of violence a little more palatable. In other instances in his films, the violence is off screen or so over-the-top that it can hardly be considered as anything more than farce. Only in *Jackie Brown,* in which the violence is secondary to the romance, and *Reservoir Dogs,* in which the effect of violence is part of what the movie studies, are the uses of violence by Tarantino much more than farce, though they always do serve his narrative purposes.

According to Jessica Davis in her book *Farce,* the guiding rule of the genre

> is to tread a fine line between offence and entertainment. . . . Farce favors direct, visual, and physical jokes over rich, lyric dialogue . . . and it declares an open season for aggression, animal high spirits, self-indulgence and rudeness in general. In contrast to satire and "black humor" (which can of course be equally licentious and violent), the style of humor in farce is essentially conservative: it has little reforming zeal—or even much despair—for the ways of the world.[38]

Violence is an essential part of farce, of course, and even serves the purpose of keeping viewers from identifying too closely with the characters and situations of the drama. Davis says about the dungeon episode of *Pulp Fiction* that the "farcical incongruities and comic inversions of the situation reinforce the viewer's detachment from their [Marcellus Wallace (Ving Rhames) and Butch Coolidge (Bruce Willis)] plight, as does awareness of the fact that neither of the victims should have the slightest objection to the other being bumped off (which was their mutual purpose in the first place), as long as he himself escapes."[39]

Farce provides a means of distancing from the (deserved) fates of the victims, allowing the audience to laugh even at the most explicit and gory examples of violence: "The targets of aggression and violence are presented as largely responsible for inviting their own fate. . . . They receive their punishment on behalf of a much wider set of offenses than those they present personally. And always they lack self-consciousness, being totally unaware of their own limitations. Over their fluid humanity is plastered the restrictive plating of self-absorption, so that communication with them only takes place on their own terms and warnings go unheeded."[40] At the same time, at least some of the characters need to be well enough presented to elicit audience identification and sympathy. For farce to work, at no point in the movie should anyone in the film (or controlling the camera or editing) join in with the laughter. A sense of gravity on screen should allow the audience to decide when to laugh, something that bothers many who want to find fault with violence in cinema, for all of the overt signals are signals of seriousness.

Davis further states that farce "must keep the audience in constant play between anticipation of predictable action-and-reaction on the part of the characters on stage, and delightful surprise at some unexpected development revealing a more complete symmetry of events."[41] Tarantino is a master of this. Think, for example, of that death of Marvin in *Pulp Fiction,* which comes just as the audience has been lulled into thinking it is in for another example of the sort of offhand dialogue between Jules Winnfield (Samuel Jackson) and Vincent Vega (John Travolta) that centered their earlier (and introductory) driving scene. True, that bit of offhand dialogue also anticipated violence, but this one leads to it directly, and while they are still in the car. Though it may be hard to characterize the death of Marvin as "delightful," it does set up the marvelous "The Bonnie Situation" chapter and allows for the introduction of Winston Wolfe (Harvey Keitel), a delight all by himself.

The scene in *Pulp Fiction* that Davis focuses her discussion on, the "meeting" on the street of Coolidge and Wallace and its aftermath, has all of the elements of farcical misunderstandings and chance meetings, with the audience able to see the situation from both points of view due to the unorthodox structure of the narrative, seeing neither completely as the villain though each aggressively goes after the other. The audience's privileged knowledge of the motivation on both sides, and relatively positive feelings for both, allows for laughter when they find the two characters bound and gagged next to each other—and for acceptance and understanding of Coolidge's action when he escapes and Wallace doesn't. Davis describes this sort of situation: "two independent, on-stage perspectives or narratives intersect, so that the resulting (single) event is interpreted in different ways by different parties to it, while the audience (which occupies a position of privilege) is able to see both sides and to enjoy the hilarity of detached superiority."[42]

Davis divides farce into four categories.[43] Each is used by Tarantino, often in a number of ways and differently in each film. The first she calls

Humiliation or Deception Farces. Though it is not primarily farce, the end of *Jackie Brown* leaves Ordell Robbie (Samuel Jackson) to his fate without regret—and without the possibility of his retaliating against anyone—and no one watching the movie feels much remorse either for the deaths of Beaumont Livingston (Chris Tucker), Melanie Ralston (Bridget Fonda), or Louis Gara (Robert De Niro), even though all three roles are played by "name" actors we would expect to have sympathy for. Except for the daughter of character Vernita Green (Vivica Fox), no one in *Kill Bill* survives the fury of "The Bride" (Uma Thurman) in any condition to do future damage. Davis characterizes this sort of farce as unidirectional in the humor and points out that the victims have to be built up to a point at which they appear (in audience minds) to deserve what they get. The death of Mr. Blonde (Michael Madsen), which brings forth laughter of shock tinged with delight, in *Reservoir Dogs* fits in here as well, as does much of what happens to the characters of *Pulp Fiction*. The entire build-up in *Death Proof* is meant to lead to audience satisfaction in the brutal beating of Kurt Russell's "Stunt-man Mike," making the whole movie an exercise (among other things) in this type of humiliation farce.

The second is *Reversal Farces. Death Proof* fits in here too. In the first half, "Stuntman Mike" is the grisly joker in the deck. *Pulp Fiction* contains a number of reversals, from the death of John Travolta's character on the toilet to the successful exit of "Pumpkin" (Tim Roth) and "Honey Bunny" (Amanda Plummer)—and more. In *Jackie Brown,* it's the *possibility* of reversal that drives the suspense. *Inglourious Basterds* is built on reversal from the very start and uses it to the very end. Third comes *Equilibrium or Quarrel Farces.* Here, no one gets the best of things; the struggle just keeps on going. When "The Bride" indicates to the daughter of Vernita Green in *Kill Bill* that the struggle could be taken to the next generation, she is hinting toward this. Also, it is this pattern that Jackie Brown (Pam Grier) and Max Cherry (Robert Forster) are both trying to break in *Jackie Brown.* Tarantino doesn't use this type of farce in his movies except as a repelling force, as in *Inglourious Basterds,* in which the audience thinks, toward the end, that Colonel Lande (Christoph Waltz) is going to get away with his traitorous actions.

Finally, Davis describes *Snowball Farces. Reservoir Dogs, Pulp Fiction,* and *Kill Bill* all contain elements of this type of farce, which is based on mistakes and misunderstandings that get out of hand. Here again, Tarantino often goes against the expectation for the farce, not taking it to the extreme that might be expected, as he does a number of times in *Pulp Fiction* and also in *Inglourious Basterds,* in which things seem to start to snowball, but get side-tracked, as happens with the Lt. Archie Hicox mission, nearly aborted by his death and transformed into something altogether different. An example from *Pulp Fiction* is the "date" between Vincent Vega and Mia Wallace (Uma Thurman), which seems heading for snowball effect but ends up without consequence, with only the promise that its consequences never be spoken of. The same is true for the scenes following the death of Marvin, in which it seems things are going to spiral out of control until Mr. Wolfe arrives and restores order. In other places, Tarantino takes it as far as he can, as in the "House of Blue Leaves" scene in *Kill Bill,* in which the number of attackers just grows and grows. Generally, in this type of farce, after things have gotten crazy, they also get back to normal in something of a circular effect—again, a pattern (of sorts) in *Kill Bill.*

No matter how well structured or executed, farce has always been seen in something of a negative light, just as Tarantino is seen today and for exactly the same reason. In addition, these questions of farce are structural and avoid the real concerns of staged violence.

Violence in entertainment, when not understood as somehow edifying, is often cast as "gratuitous." Yet in classical farce, as in Tarantino's contemporary version, there is nothing at all gratuitous about anything that occurs. In both cases, there is an element of challenge to the audience: can you laugh at what shocks you? Can you admit to the primal connection between fear, pain, and laughter? In both cases, can you admit that you enjoy what you don't necessarily like to see happen? In both cases, also, there is a severe moral point, though it is often hidden so well that only the extremely attentive can find it, and there is also a basic belief in a moral structure to the world: "With all its rules and formalities, farce is good at fluidly producing order out of apparent chaos and at paradoxically liberating laughter by its tight control of events."[44]

Davis finds five tendencies in contemporary farce: that it becomes intertwined with romantic comedy, a container for angst and black humor, a vehicle for in-jokes, a means for desensitization toward violence, and a self-reflective commentary on theatre.[45] Tarantino follows each of these as well, at least to a short distance, perhaps making it more appropriate to call him "*farceur*" than "postmodern." *Jackie Brown* is a romantic comedy containing farce; angst and farce are certainly present in *Reservoir Dogs;* and black humor is the center of *Inglourious Basterds* and, to a lesser degree, *Pulp Fiction.* The in-jokes of all of Tarantino's films, like the in-jokes of stage farce, provide a connection between the characters and the audience that Tarantino wants to reinforce as frequently as possible; the blood of *Pulp Fiction, Kill Bill, Death Proof,* and *Inglourious Basterds* certainly desensitizes audiences toward gore; and *Pulp Fiction, Death Proof,* and *Inglourious Basterds* all carry heavy-handed commentary on the film industry they grow out of. In this, Tarantino's movies certainly also fall within the developing tradition of New Hollywood. As King argues:

> A close combination of comedy and aestheticization is characteristic of many of the most celebrated/notorious examples of New Hollywood violence in recent years. . . . Moments of violence in these films are often coded as 'witty' and stylized, and more detached from potentially 'real' implications than might otherwise be the

case. . . .The overall effect is one of great intensity and cinematic impact but also an encouragement of awareness that this is an operatically confected, *staged*, exaggerated attraction, a veritable production-number of violence.[46]

Though many may reject this as a part of the comfort zone they are willing to establish for viewing, violence is—and will remain—a tool for filmmakers, now and in the future.

Concerns over depictions of violence in movies cannot be adequately satisfied as long as some acts of violence are acceptable and others are not—which is why Tarantino refuses to be drawn into the slightly nonsensical debate over when violence becomes too violent. Attempts at classifying violence end up as attempts to create aesthetic standards upon ethical and morals bases—and these, of course, change as culture changes. No clear and fast lines can be drawn.

Some attempt to reduce questions of violence in media to questions of spectacle, ignoring narrative completely as an aspect of media that merely clouds the issue. That is, they ask the question of what, when *seen* in art, oversteps the bounds of taste and sense. Once, blood represented the line, and there is still a large part of the movie-going population that wishes that this line were respected. But this, too, becomes a question of aesthetics. Why is blood worse than, say, torture represented without blood?

Others try to see representations of violence simply in terms of impact, making moral judgment on the narrative. What might violence seen lead a viewer to do or think? Is a barrier removed when violence is visualized, especially in a relatively accurate fashion? If so, where does it end? What about extreme, over-the-top violence, such as that found in Peter Jackson's *Braindead* (1992)? How is a viewer, particularly a naïve viewer, to know what is violence and what is stylized spoof?

In all discussions, the primary goal seems to be to find limits, to determine what depictions of violence should be seen as acceptable and what are not, for few seem willing to argue that *all* violence in art should be proscribed. This is the essential problem of all discussions of media violence, for the line always finds itself based on either aesthetic judgments or moral ones, neither providing the clarity desired. The very discussion, then, can never lead to satisfactory results.

When an artist is tagged as "violent" it apparently becomes impossible to reverse that view, for almost all narrative art, and nearly all film (all, if one accepts Eisenstein's contention that all movies can be considered violent by their very nature), contains an element of violence and can be shown to exceed at least one person's standard. At this point, if Tarantino remade *Mr. Hobbs Takes a Vacation* (Henry Koster, 1962) faithfully to the original, there would still be many who would refuse to see it, certain of its violence.

Perhaps the only way to resolve the debate over violence satisfactorily is to turn it on its head, to say that it is not the depictions of violence that should worry us but the ways in which we react to a violent world. Both film and the world contain violence. Could it be that the debate is more about the world than about film? Because we cannot contain it completely in the world, is the only way that we (or some of us, at least) can feel safe is by limiting it in art? Could it be that the debate over movie violence is nothing more than an extension of our attempts to control a world that, more often than not, seems of the verge of careening out of control?

If films influence the world, they also reflect it, creating a circularity of impact that gives rise to an intricate gyre allowing us to explore ourselves and our relationships to our world with detail that few, before film, could manage and in a dynamic made possible only through the interactions of the motions of the art and of our lives. Exploring violence in film, in this view, is little more than a means of exploring violence in us. We may not like the violence in certain types of films or presented in certain fashion, but the focus of criticism shouldn't be on the film, but on us. Why don't we like it? What do we do to change it? We certainly don't have to watch it in movies and should be able to turn away at will. But understanding what there is, in us, that makes us react as we do when we watch movies provides more to our current and future lives than does any attempt to use our reactions to impose limitations on the creations of others, violent or otherwise.

Reservoir Dogs: Stuck in the Middle with Nietzsche

No matter how much Quentin Tarantino seems to be focusing solely on movies as he makes movies, it is really the illusion that films create that seems to interest him most—and the reality behind movies that allows the illusion. Friedrich Nietzsche, writing almost a century before Tarantino was born, captured his attitude: "The beautiful illusion of the dream worlds, in the creation of which every man is a consummate artist, is the precondition of all visual art. . . . But even when this dream reality is presented to us with the greatest intensity, we still have a glimmering awareness that it is an *illusion*."[1] Nietzsche goes on to equate reaction to art and reaction to dreams to what the philosopher does in reaction to existence, claiming that it is the combination of the three that prepares one for life. Illusion doesn't exist without life; life may be impossible for humans without illusion. This, one of the points made through *Reservoir Dogs,* has been part of the discussion of drama and other narrative arts for thousands of years. Movies can't be simply about movies any more than illusion can be about illusion. Both are tied to life, and reflect it, just as life reflects illusion.

Seventeen years may not seem a long time in the larger stream of things, but *Reservoir Dogs* has been a focus of film students and film scholars for what now amounts to nearly a generation. In that narrow sense, it's old and picked over. We've fallen into assumptions about it, and about Tarantino, perhaps even making the film stale and uninteresting to some jaded eyes. "Everything's already been said," one might complain as even another study of the movie, of the things Tarantino "imitates" or incorporates, of the violent impact of his work, appears. And that may be. After all, I certainly am not the first to see in *Reservoir Dogs* reflections of Nietzsche's discussion of Greek tragedy in *The Birth of Tragedy*.[2] Nor am I the first to see classical tragedy in a gangster film— Robert Warshow did that in *Partisan Review* way back in 1948. In his essay,

Warshow also describes the city and the gangster and their relationship to each other—and to the worlds of the audience, relationships that are also at the heart of *Reservoir Dogs,* giving rise, finally, to some of the meanings that can be extracted from it. Speaking of gangster films generally but in an essay in which he refers specifically to *Scarface* (Howard Hawks and Richard Rosson, 1932) and *Little Caesar* (Mervyn LeRoy, 1931), Warshow writes:

> The gangster is the man of the city, with the city's language and knowledge, with its queer and dishonest skills and its terrible daring, carrying his life in his hands like a placard, like a club. For everyone else, there is at least the theoretical possibility of another world—in that happier American culture which the gangster denies, the city does not really exist; it is only a more crowded and more brightly lit country—but for the gangster there is only the city; he must inhabit it in order to personify it: not the real city, but that dangerous and sad city of the imagination which is so much more important, which is the modern world. And the gangster—though there are real gangsters—is also, and primarily, a creature of the imagination. The real city, one might say, produces only criminals; the imaginary city produces the gangster: he is what we want to be and what we are afraid we may become.[3]

The very themes and their presentations in *Reservoir Dogs* were forecast more than 40 years before it was made—through an examination of even older movies. Some things about the movie go back even in other ways: "Despite its postmodern glaze, the film is morally conservative in a way that earlier, classically made heist dramas [as opposed to most gangster films] . . . are not: none of the thieves lives to profit from his crime."[4]

All is old. We don't want to forget what James Agee reports Mack Sennett as having claimed: "Anyone who tells you he has discovered something new is a fool or a liar or both."[5] The new, the rare to the point of nonexistence, can't be the focus of our interest exclusively, or we will find ourselves rather bored, having very little to discuss. So, not finding the new certainly isn't reason for shutting up; we can contribute to the conversation just as much as, in the larger sense, a filmmaker such as Tarantino does, by taking the old and making it new, *revitalizing* a genre, a career, or a film—all of which Tarantino has done through his movies. All of which we can do each time any of us talks about cinema.

Even David Bordwell, following his sometime collaborator Kristin Thompson, makes use of the concept of revitalization to change the focus of discussion on films made over the past four decades. He moves from "post-classical," signifying a break, to "hyperclassical," a term of embracing the old—in effect, making it new.[6] That, of course, is exactly what Tarantino does in *Reservoir Dogs* in respect to the styles of classical Hollywood and even of the genre of classical tragedy—not to mention his possible use of Ringo Lam's 1987 film *City on Fire.* Perhaps even oblivious to the niceties of "ownership" of artistic creation (copyright, etc.), Tarantino uses what he will, as long as he sees it appropriate to the *new* work he is in the process of creating.*

"It's a heist film. . . . It all leads to violence and blood, but it ends up being black, gallows humor,"[7] says Tarantino. *Reservoir Dogs,* at the most basic level, certainly is also an example of another type within the gangster genre, one using a formula going back at least to *The Gangsters and the Girl* (Scott Sidney, 1914), which, according to William Everson, "anticipates the basic storyline . . . of having the detective hero masquerade as a gangster and work from the inside to bring about the downfall of the gang, collecting evidence and alerting police for the final showdown."[8] Common to the gangster film—see *T-Men* (Anthony Mann, 1947) as just one example—this formula can be found in other genres, including the Western—see John Wayne's *The Man from Utah* (Robert Bradbury, 1934). However, even here Tarantino takes the old and does something new with it: the undercover agent is ineffective and then helpless, finally serving a different purpose than can be found in earlier examples of this type of gangster film. As a heist film, too, it moves away from any formula, ending up, as Tarantino says, as something else. Ending up, in many respects, a tragedy.

Working as a revitalizer, Tarantino is, of course, an imitator but one in a positive tradition of the concept going as far back as Aristotle: "the instinct of imitation is implanted in man from childhood, one difference between him and other animals being that he is the most imitative of living creatures, and through imitation learns his earliest lessons."[9] Imitation is both the basis for the quest for perfection and the base on which knowledge grows. It follows, for Aristotle, that something as foundational as imitation would be enjoyed in art as well as education: "And no less universal is the pleasure he takes in seeing things imitated. We have evidence of this in the facts of experience. Objects which in themselves we view with pain, we delight to contemplate when reproduced with minute fidelity: such as the forms of the most ignoble animals and of dead bodies."[10] Yet, imitation, in the Aristotelian sense of *mimesis,* isn't generally what comes to mind when Tarantino uses older films to make his own—or depicts (imitates) the unpleasant facts (the "ignoble animals" and "dead bodies") of the world. That is often seen today, unfortunately, as a sign of the second rate, the derivative. Put downs of the director for not being original, then, simply result from acceptance of a cultural milieu in which originality alone, unfortunately, is often seen as the hallmark of creativity, in which not creating something that has never been seen before is relegated to the realm of paint-by-numbers.

One who understands the limitations inherent in such contemporary attitudes favoring "originality" might respond, "I don't see what the big deal

---

*Experience may have taught Tarantino caution; before making *Inglourious Basterds,* he bought the rights to *Inglorious Bastards* (Enzo Castellari, 1978).

is. Everybody steals from everybody; that's movies." That line, from *Swingers* (Doug Liman, 1996), comes just as homage to *Reservoir Dogs* commences in the movie and comes with reason. Though the "if everybody does it, it must be OK" logic might be a little strained, the sentiment from *Swingers* still has substance. It's not even the purpose of movies to be original, after all, but to be entertaining (one reason it took so long for them to be considered art). Additionally, if one is willing to take "purpose" back to Aristotle and early attempts to analyze entertainment (and to explore "genre"), one recognizes that to imitate (even in the modern sense in which "imitation" is more associated with stealing from other works than with representation) is to attempt to reproduce certain laudatory effects. What is wrong with that? To be entertaining, one must work with (or against) audience expectations, which means working with (or against) the successes of the past, with or against (essentially) genre. Instead of creating something new, one must react against the old or make the old new—itself now an old piece of advice: "Make it new," ordered Ezra Pound several generations ago, revitalize.[11] That, we see from Aristotle (for whom imitation is an attempt, in part, to achieve perfection) on, is where art lies.

Still, it might be slightly counterintuitive to posit *Reservoir Dogs* as a contemporary version of a Greek tragedy. After all, the characters don't exhibit the Aristotelian requirement that they must be good—or don't seem to initially. Vincent Canby, although he admired the film, in reviewing *Reservoir Dogs* for *The New York Times* snidely declared that its "dimensions are not exactly those of Greek tragedy."[12] If one studies the film carefully, however, it is possible to come to the conclusion that the film's dimensions are exactly that. Furthermore, as Arthur Danto says, speaking generally but with an eye to the Aristotelian tradition, works such as *Reservoir Dogs* (though he doesn't refer to it even indirectly) do "what works of art have always done—externalizing a way of viewing the world, expressing the interior of a cultural period, offering itself as a mirror to catch the conscience of our kings."[13] Even if *Reservoir Dogs* starts from any specific genre, even the heist film, an argument can be made for it also arising from the sort of tragedy Aristotle described than from any other. Furthermore, it belongs to art in the broader sense, and Western views of art, as Danto implies, rest on the Greeks.

Though Friedrich Nietzsche's *The Birth of Tragedy* has never been seen as a definitive work of any sort (it is an exploration, not an arrival), it does provide an apparatus useful in clarifying just what it is *Reservoir Dogs* attempts and why the movie warrants sustained discussion beyond questions of innovation and beyond its role as a cultural marker. Put most simply, Nietzsche argues that true dramatic tragedy arises from the symbiosis of what he calls the Dionysiac and the Apolline. The former, taken from Dionysus, Greek god of ecstasy (among other things), deals with the uninstantiated universal, truth outside of the experiential world, best recognized (in Nietzsche's view) through music. The latter, taken from Apollo, Greek god of truth (among other things), deals with the instantiated particular, reality that we can experience and imitate, best recognized through sculpture. Nietzsche argues that the tension between the Dionysiac and the Apolline are what allow for the creation of classical tragedy: "These two very different tendencies walk side by side, usually in violent opposition to one another, inciting one another to ever more powerful births."[14] The two, together, are the parents of art, neither able to work without the other, the opposition between the two unbridgeable except through that child, art.

Aristotle's *Poetics* describes six parts of tragedy as a dramatic genre, the quality of each contributing to any determination of a work's status as tragedy: plot, character, verbal style, thought, spectacle, and music. The plot of a tragedy must be complex, focusing on change, furthered by reversal or recognition or both. The central relationship in *Reservoir Dogs,* that of Mr. Orange (Tim Roth) and Mr. White (Harvey Keitel), revolves around reversal in White's fortune (it had been Mr. Orange who was shot and Mr. White simply the savior) and around his recognition that the man he was attempting to save had betrayed him and the rest of the gang. This couples with Mr. Orange's story, which is composed to a classic Aristotelian complication and unraveling, the complication, or back story, being told in flashbacks, the unraveling in the movie's "real time." The plot is one of betrayal and trust; the various relationships are all defined by actions on different bases for trust—or lack thereof, and the dénouement is made possible by both trust and broken trust. This fits well into Aristotle's basic depiction of tragedy as "an imitation, not of men, but of action. . . . And life consists in action, and its end is a mode of activity, not a quality. . . . Dramatic action, therefore, is not with a view to the representation of character. . . . Hence the incidents and the plot are the end of a tragedy; and the end is the chief thing of all."[15] Though it isn't fully a tragedy in the Greek mold (Tarantino's films never stick to a single genre or pattern but use such things simply as starting points for his artistic explorations), everything in *Reservoir Dogs* is calculated to support the ending, which focuses on the tragic destruction of a good man through his own good impulses and of a bad man—through *his* good impulses. Thomas Leitch claims that "Aristotle sees a tragic action as distinct from other events, freely chosen, logically consequential, but ultimately limited by a final end."[16] The confession leading to the death of Mr. Orange fits this, absolutely; the action, in response, of Mr. White does too.

The plot of a tragedy is constructed solely to illuminate the ending and, being so built, serves not to illuminate life but to support the point that ending makes. The primacy of the plot and the action over character, even, results from this. Nothing haphazard happens in tragedy; chance has nothing to do with it, unless "chance" becomes a tool for the unfolding of the plot. Even then, the author must stick to the probable and necessary. Plots center on an approach to change, which is a reversal or some sort of recognition, "a change from ignorance to knowledge, producing love or hate between the persons destined by the poet for good or bad fortune"[17] producing "either pity or fear; and actions producing these effects are those which, by our definition, Tragedy represents."[18] Important to the plot, for it furthers understanding of the point the author is making, is suffering, "a destructive or painful action, such as a death on the stage, bodily agony, wounds, and the like."[19]

Except for that of Mr. Orange, the undercover police officer, and Mr. White, who shows dogged loyalty to his wounded "colleague," the characters of the movie fail to reach any level of true audience esteem, leaving it to Orange and White to serve as the principals of the drama (in Aristotelian terms at least)—which may seem strange, for Orange spends most of the movie (except the flashbacks) bleeding to death on the warehouse floor, hardly moving or contributing and, at the beginning of the movie, seems one of the most verbally helpless of the bunch—and White is a career criminal. Yet Orange proves more than simply honorable, even becoming heroic, unable to let White, the man who has been trying to save him, who has now sacrificed himself to keep the cop from being shot again, die without knowing the truth about him—even though he recognizes that this will lead to his own death. He is "a man who is not eminently good and just, yet whose misfortune is brought about not by vice or depravity, but by some error or frailty."[20] Orange's initial injury comes about through error, resulting in his being shot by a woman whose car he tries to commandeer. White's failing is that he realizes too late that he has too much honor to survive among thieves. He has learned that he is not the simple criminal he thought he was, both a tragic realization and triumphant: "the Dionysiac reveler sees himself as a satyr, *and it is as a satyr that he looks upon the god:* in his transformation he sees a new vision outside himself, the Apolline complement of his state."[21]

Verbal style, it might be argued, is the one of Aristotle's parts of tragedy ignored by Tarantino, at least in terms of rising above the ordinary, but Tarantino has become something of the poet of the ordinary, creating dialogue that, though sounding mundane, raises the quotidian to the level of poetry, as the first scene of the movie manages to do, becoming song itself, sung to the dance of the camera about the table in the diner and including exchanges such as the following, between Joe Cabot (Lawrence Tierney), Mr. White, and Mr. Blonde:

Mr. White: For the past fifteen minutes now, you've just been droning on with names. "Toby . . . Toby . . . Toby . . . Toby Wong . . . Toby Wong . . . Toby Chung . . . fuckin' Charlie Chan." I got Madonna's big dick coming outta my left ear, and Toby the Jap I-don't-know-what, coming outta my right.

Joe: Give me my book.

Mr. White: Are you gonna put it away?

Joe: I'm gonna do whatever the fuck I wanna do with it.

Mr. White: Well, then, I'm afraid I'm gonna have to keep it.

Mr. Blonde: Hey, Joe, you want me to shoot this guy?

Mr. White: Shit, you shoot me in a dream, you better wake up and apologize.

Like poetry, this has a strong rhythmic structure, and it uses repetition throughout to hold the lines together again in poetic fashion. Though it seems mundane, and even a thoughtless use of language, it's actually a carefully orchestrated conversation—even more so, when the camera work is added in and it is seen within the context of the scene and then the movie as a whole. Not only that, but it ends with an image that reverberates with the history of drama and fictional representation, and even with discussion of violence in art, tying the snippet together as firmly as the last lines of a sonnet.

Hiding a sophisticated language structure and usage in the putative mundane has a long history in literature and in movies, but it has rarely included the profanity that is so liberally sprinkled in contemporary American English usage. Stephen Crane, Theodore Dreiser, Tennessee Williams, Eugene O'Neill, and Budd Schulberg all long ago reflected the language of "the streets," but none reaches quite as far or accurately as Tarantino does, the "fug" that Norman Mailer had to resort to in *The Naked and the Dead* no longer being a necessary convention. Profanity, in other words, does not now negate the artistry or the quality of the dialogue contemporary artists including Tarantino write. It is simply a demonstration that conventional replacements for profanity are no longer necessary in order for a writer to approach "quality."

In *The Way Hollywood Tells It*, Bordwell suggests that one of the results of the "intensified continuity" that has developed since the fall of the studio system is reliance on editing and camera motion for the dynamics of a conversation-driven scene. Although Tarantino, as often as anyone, does draw attention to the camera here and elsewhere in the film (almost making it a character as much as it is in, say, Tony Richardson's 1963 movie *Tom Jones*, in which it becomes the visual corollary to the voice-over narration), he uses camera motion as only one of his means of constructing a scene, of providing its dynamic. In the commode joke discussion between Mr. Orange and Randy Brooks's Detective Holdaway, Brooks almost dances around the stationary Roth, himself becoming both camera (dancing around the subject) and action . . . a situation somewhat reversed when Roth later rehearses the story before Brooks, who now is still (and still the camera) as Roth moves on an impromptu stage.

Thought, to Aristotle, includes much that is not exposition but is action: "Under Thought is included every effect which has to be produced by speech. . . . Now, it is evident that the dramatic incidents must be treated from the same points of view as the dramatic speeches. . . . The only difference is, that the incidents should speak for themselves without verbal exposition."[22]

In *Reservoir Dogs*, exposition and action are inextricably intertwined (and in a manner in keeping with Aristotelian tragedy), points being made through violence that confirm what we have learned through dialogue—or that advance that knowledge.

One of the problems in understanding *Reservoir Dogs* is that so much attention is paid to the dramatic speeches that it is easy to forget that the point of the movie may be made elsewhere, especially because so much of the action, the incidents of the movie, that do speak for it are extremely violent. What we see, however, is violence used for reasons, to make points. Though he loves words, Tarantino clearly doesn't feel he always needs to use them to illustrate his theses—action does that. He emphasizes this point, even going so far as to use Mr. Blonde (Michael Madsen) to reinforce the idea that words shouldn't be trusted, that they aren't even important: that actions are the thing, even if they don't seem to make sense:

> **Mr. Blonde:** I don't really give a good fuck about what you know or don't know. But I'm gonna torture you anyway, regardless. Not to get information . . . it's amusing to torture a cop. You can say anything you want, because I've heard it before.

In the larger sense of things, this is exactly the situation all of us face in life, and our only escape before death is faith in something we can pray to. What happens to us can appear irrational and unreasonable, and often it is, but it is going to happen, no matter what we do, something even reflected in the movie's presentation: "The film's fractured time scheme heightens the tension: looping, backtracking, spiraling, time encloses the characters as much as the eerily deserted warehouse does. And the nervous, circling camera, which covers space with obsessive back-and-forth movements, as if it is constantly looking over its own 'shoulder,' reflects the dogs' mounting distrust and anxiety."[23] Not to mention our own in the audience.

The horror of the scene, however, isn't in Mr. Blonde's words, in his *claim* of what he is going to do, but in his action, his *joyful* action of destruction without any *deus ex machina* limiting it until, of course, Mr. Orange shoots Mr. Blonde just as he is about to immolate the bound-and-gagged police officer—and even that serves to reinforce the sense that the scene has built, a sense of the fragility of existence.

As if we haven't gotten the point, as if we've been lulled by the reprieve Mr. Orange has bought for the cop, if we're still imagining that all can yet be right with the world, Tarantino later has Nice Guy Eddie (Chris Penn) yell about the still bound policeman, "Who cares what he was gonna do to this fuckin' pig?" and immediately pull out his gun and shoot the officer dead. No amount of exposition can make Tarantino's point more forcefully than this, though few viewers are willing to stand for it or accept it; it offends our expectations. Most viewers react with revulsion, understandably rejecting the point and, often, rejecting the movie, calling it too violent when it is the world, in the view Tarantino is presenting, that really is to blame, that is really too violent.

Spectacle, in *Reservoir Dogs,* is muted, as befits a classical tragedy. The bloodiness so associated with the movie is much more the result of the anticipation of violence surrounding the ear-cutting scene (which, itself, shows no cutting) than of the copious amount of fake blood strewn throughout the warehouse during the movie. Oddly enough, in a visual sense, the most spectacular scene of the movie is probably the understated opening credit sequence, simply slow motion of the group of gangsters walking followed by slow-motion framing of each individually. Though many in an audience may be disappointed that spectacle is lacking, the visual artistry of this film would likely have been lessened had there been budget available for more spectacular sequences.

In addition to using action to show thought in addition to exposition, Tarantino constantly uses music. Peter Romanov writes that "Tarantino's choice of music and its placement also have an uncanny knack of speaking for the characters during instances when they choose not to, or are unable to, speak for themselves. Therefore, the music acts as a signifier of what the character may be feeling at a particular moment in the film."[24] Though song is used in this manner throughout the movie, it is also most certainly a diegetic part of the film and never simply a filler of empty sound-space or a setter of mood. Perhaps it is best understood in the sense Nietzsche posited for music in tragedy and myth, or as an ironic take on it, or both: "Tragedy absorbs the highest musical ecstasies, and thus brings music to a state of true perfection. But then it places alongside it the tragic myth and the tragic hero who then . . . relieves us of its burden. . . . The myth shields us from the music, just as it gives the music its supreme freedom."[25] If, following Nietzsche's expansive vision, we go a step further and define song (in an attempt to better integrate Aristotle into modern drama) as the nonverbal elements of drama whose function is to evoke the sublime, then the camera itself operates on the level of song, as dance does, as well. Certainly, the soundtrack of pop songs well over a decade out of date when *Reservoir Dogs* was made, and not even songs of the top rank from a time of top-40 decline, provides tension to the drama, often ironic tension, while reminding viewers that more is going on "on stage" than an otherwise inattentive viewer might assume. Think of the ear-cutting scene—in fact, think of the whole movie—in light of the following passage from *The Birth of Tragedy:* "Only from the spirit of music can we understand delight in the destruction of the individual. . . . 'We believe in eternal life' is tragedy's cry; while music is the immediate idea of that life."[26] Either ironically or seriously, this passage resonates throughout any attempt at understanding *Reservoir Dogs.*

The rumble at the end of the first act of *West Side Story* (Jerome Robbins and Robert Wise, 1961), in which Riff and Bernardo die; George Balanchine's "Slaughter on Tenth Avenue" from *On Your Toes* (Ray Enright, 1939), with the "death" of a woman and the threat of "real" killing coming from the audience within the film; Gene Kelly's different version of "Slaughter on Tenth Avenue" from *Words and Music* (Norman Taurog, 1948) with its added death; the "Girl Hunt Ballet" from *The Band Wagon* (Vincente Minnelli, 1953), with slaughter aplenty at the end. All of these, from classical Hollywood musicals, are as violent (though without the blood) as anything in *Reservoir Dogs*. Yet they don't get the reactions against the violence that Tarantino does—and they never did. No one says they won't go see a musical because of the violence, yet many refuse *Reservoir Dogs*. But all five of these movies use violence as often as Tarantino does—and dance and music, as Tarantino does also. Though Michael Madsen's Mr. Blonde moves in the amateur way any of us might—and do—to songs on the radio, unlike the professional, choreographed (and distancing) steps of the others, it is dance he performs, quality notwithstanding.

Of course, it is this difference in the dance that creates the impact of the "ear" scene, making reactions to the violence greater than in any of those other movies—on the level of simple and visceral revulsion at least. The fantasy element dance normally represents has been removed—as has the joy of watching skilled artists—stripping away the distancing that we've learned to use to keep comfortable, distancing that provides the excuse for violence when the act is portrayed through art and explicitly as art. Here, the art actually comes through Madsen's use of his character's apparent lack of dancing skill coupled with the apparent artlessness of camera motion. Even so, the presentation has much in common with how dance is filmed in classical Hollywood musicals, with long shots that allow for concentration on the skill of the performer instead of through the quick cuts of montage.

As I have said, all of the older dance numbers are sanitized, presenting the violence in the Hollywood manner *de rigueur* prior to *Bonnie and Clyde* and still influential today. There could not possibly have been a sign of blood in any of them. But that's not the point. All of these older films are stylized, both in terms of dance and of film, using conventions that distance the audience from the subject matter—the opposite of Tarantino's apparent intention of closing that gap. Yet, even with its seeming artlessness, so is *Reservoir Dogs* stylized. Though the language of Tarantino's characters may accurately reflect the way people talked at the end of the twentieth century and the beginning of the twenty-first, there's very little else about this movie that rises to any level of realism, even as practiced in Hollywood. Look at the dress, those suits and ties. Look at the pseudonyms, Misters White, Pink, Orange, Blue, Brown, and Blonde. Look at the plot: the whole heist is preposterous, as is the father/son team behind it. Look again at the plot: it's so well woven that it screams (intentionally screams), "look at me; look at how well crafted I am! No loose ends here!" That's not even a feint toward realism. That's tight artifice—and the movie is proud of it.

Yet there's a lot in the film that appears loose: talk, motion (both of actors and of the camera), body parts, a door latch, and even a balloon on the street. And loose stories are told about the making of the movie after the fact, after the film was complete—stories designed to give an appearance of looseness to the filmmaking. That balloon? Supposedly an accident captured and kept. That door flying open? Simply shows the brilliance of a cast that could keep on going in face of the unexpected and of the quick-thinking of Keitel, who simply walks away from the camera and closes the door as the scene continues. Another story claims that the panning away from the ear cutting was necessitated simply by inability to create a visually realistic image.

All three of these touches are brilliant, no matter their genesis (accident or not), as are numerous others in the film, creating a tension between plan and execution, tightness and looseness, classical structure and a sense of *cinema verité* that's reflected in the action, in the construction, and in the unfolding. Each touch helps create a sense of motion beyond the purposes of that tight plot, adding a counterpoint that reduces the overt significance of any message involving the sort of control found in classical tragedy—a counterpoint that (among other things) allows Madsen to produce a sense of insanity strong enough to make us forget, as we watch the movie, that we are being carefully manipulated by a writer/director with an almost obsessive knowledge of the minutiae of film. At the beginning of the ear sequence, for example, Madsen moves over to Tim Roth's character, who has been lying silent and bleeding for quite some time, reminding us that Roth is still there. Why? Because Roth, Mr. Orange, is going to shoot Mr. Blonde quite soon, and conventional Hollywood continuity requires that the surprise, startling as it may be, immediately connect back in the viewer's mind to a causal agent. Rather than the camera preparing the connection gratuitously, Madsen can do it—gratuitously—and get away with it; since the moment he pulled the straight razor from his boot, our viewer focus has narrowed to him; if nothing else, his extra time with Orange serves to heighten the tension as we wonder just what he is going to do to Officer Nash (Kirk Baltz), who sits tied to a chair and gagged with duct tape.

It is here, in the illusion of loose, almost random motion in a situation highly controlled, that the heightened tension of the violence—or the perception of violence—emerges and the film moves further away from classical tragedy. Along with this comes the power of the scene to evoke viewer reaction more powerfully than do most traditional Hollywood depictions of violence, in which the impact is screened by convention, by dance, or by some other mediating factor. The spinning away from expectation (while actually heightening the expectation), more than the violence itself, generates the shock.

"Hold still, you fuck," says Blonde as he cuts off Nash's ear—but it is the camera that obeys, having glided away from the action. It now centers on the junction of two walls and the ceiling of the warehouse as Blonde completes his cutting, staying still. Blonde then comes back into the frame that had moved away from him, holding his straight razor and the ear, examining both somewhat pensively before walking back out of the picture muttering, "Was that as good for you as it was for me?" After that comes the famous bit of Blonde talking to the ear: "Hey, what's going on?" followed by, "Hear that?" to Nash.

At this point, even those who have been averting their eyes from the screen come back to it, unable to resist watching the macabre humor of Blonde. They may also be a little comforted, realizing that the camera has done what they did (or wanted to do), has looked away from an action that our morbid fascination draws us to, but our humane sensibilities abhor. Unlike John Waters who, in *Pink Flamingos* (1972), forces his camera (if not his audience) to follow every bit of Divine's eating dog excrement in such a way that it is clear it is *actual* dog excrement, Tarantino shows sympathy for the less iron stomached of his viewers.

The "ear" scene, which runs about six minutes, has a long average shot length (ASL) of 15 seconds, a number that would be longer still were it not for a couple of shot/reverse sequences showing the reactions of Officer Nash to Mr. Blonde's antics. The longest shot is the nearly a minute and a half of Blonde retrieving a gas can from his car after the cutting. The shortest is just 1 second.

From the start of Blonde's dance to his speaking to the ear, we only have nine shots, mostly shot/reverse between Blonde and Nash, wide on Blonde as he dances, close on Nash's face as he watches (and as we watch with him). The longest shot is the hold on the blank walls as the ear comes off, nearly 30 seconds. As Peter Romanov writes, "The scene is choreographed so well with the music that it plays out like a music video,"[27] the emphasis on choreography, and not on editing, being significant. Romanov continues:

> After Mr. Blonde finishes taunting the cop with his own severed ear, he throws it down and then tells the cop he'll be right back. The music continues to speak for the cop, 'Trying to make sense of it all /But I can see there makes no sense at all/Is it cool to go to sleep on the floor/I don't think that I can take any more.' Mr. Blonde proceeds to walk out of the warehouse and closes the door behind him. The music stops playing and the happenings of the outside world, such as traffic in the distance, kids laughing, and a car alarm blaring, suddenly begin to be heard.[28]

This contrast is almost as stark as that between the violence and the blank wall.

The blank wall also foreshadows the final shot of the movie, in which Harvey Keitel's Mr. White slides out of the frame, which is held still once he is shot. And it is in these two empty frames, perhaps, that an understanding of Nietzsche can help in coming to terms with just what Tarantino is doing, with just what his point might be: "Dionysiac art . . . wishes to convince us of the eternal delight of existence—but we are to seek that delight not in phenomena themselves but behind phenomena."[29] This passage, as well as any possibly can, expresses one of the main points of the movie, that life itself and alone is only going to provide pain. If we want more, we are going to have to look behind life. Nietzsche goes on to say that what we need to recognize through art is that there is no satisfaction available, ultimately, in the temporal, only in the eternal, which is the "primal essence" behind the experiential. The only way we can reach that, can experience that, is through art, he claims. The tragedy remains; there's nothing we can do about that. But art transcends.

Step back for a moment, so we can set up the role of the camera and its motion, a Max Ophüls sort of role, and its importance here as a moving spectator—as one of the characters in the film, a Mr. Clear, if you will or, perhaps, a Greek chorus. There's no action at the start of *Reservoir Dogs,* though there's plenty of movement—by the camera, that is, taking the audience along for the ride. In that scene in the diner, it circles the table, showing the backs of heads as well as faces, eventually resolving into a shot/reverse sequence when Joe Cabot and Mr. White squabble over the address book and then again when the question of the tip is discussed, the camera having already started to pounce on the traits that will be associated with each member of the group, all but two identified by color-related pseu-donyms, and all but those two dressed in black suits, white shirts, and thin black ties. Traits we get anyway: Mr. Blonde, devoted to Joe Cabot yet exhibiting a strain of happy, charismatic menace; Mr. White, sure of himself enough to be willing to risk the wrath of his boss Cabot and strong enough to have gained Cabot's respect—quite empathetic and emotional, he could be the perfect husband; Mr. Orange, quizzical, quiet, somehow out of place, a wife in need of protection, his arm, at one point, draped on the back of Mr. White's chair; Mr. Pink (Steve Buscemi), with little sympathy for others, strong willed, but willing to put aside his own ideas to work as a team player; Nice Guy Eddie Cabot, strong but none too bright. Also present are Mr. Brown (Quentin Tarantino) and Mr. Blue (Eddie Bunker), but one talks stupidly and the other not at all—both clearly to be dismissed by the viewer as ultimately insignificant to story and plot. This, if Nietzsche is correct, reflects the pure opening structure of classical tragedy: "In their opening scenes Aeschylus and Sophocles employed the subtlest devices to give the spectator, as if by chance, all the threads that he would need for a complete understanding; a feature which preserves the noble artistry that masks the *necessary* formal element, making it look accidental."[30]

Leitch argues that the Hollywood action film in general has moved away from Aristotle, reducing the importance of character and changing the protagonist from actor to reactor. He writes, "What was peripheral in Aristotelian action has become central, what was central has become vestigial."[31] The action film, he believes, relies on spectacle to an extent unimagined by Aristotle and (though he doesn't say so) completely at odds with *Reservoir Dogs,* a film muted in set, costume, and visual activity. Leitch writes:

> What is most distinctive, and most disturbing, about the contemporary action film is not its problematic justification of their ultimate power but its staging of that power as violent spectacle. . . . The recasting of action films towards violent spectacle is only the most obvious symptom of contemporary moviegoers' growing taste for spectacle over Aristotelian action in all genres of popular entertainment. . . . Unlike the Athenian theater that staged dramatic action as an invitation to its audience to contemplate the problematic nature of action itself, Hollywood has turned action into a spectacle at once frightening and entertaining.[32]

In this sense, Tarantino's film is a return to an older, Aristotelian vision of action, one in which the act itself is less important than the action in context of both the play itself and the audience, for it is through the combination of these that any cathartic effect can be realized, though, as Leitch asserts, "Even the most spectacular action films retain the association . . . between represented action and the purposive, morally consequential human agency of characters and audiences,"[33] even as almost anything else besides the set pieces of action recedes into the background.

What happens is that the character in most action films does not initiate the central actions of the film, but reacts to what others have done, a significant movement away from Aristotle's model and distinct from the situation of Mr. Orange, who acts freely on his own and not in a reactive or retaliatory fashion, and of Mr. White, who though he does react and retaliate, acts solely out of principle and without hope or possibility of any sort of success, especially the sort audiences of action movies have come to expect. If Mr. Orange is an Aristotelian hero, perhaps Mr. White is an existential one, Tarantino once more expanding away from any one genre.

The movies, like classical Greek tragedies (speaking most generally), are all about motion, about action—about violence. And about audience. And, as Aristotle makes clear for the much older Greek drama, about relationships between parts in relation to the needs of storytelling and its ends. Tarantino sees things no differently; think of that "commode" scene in *Reservoir Dogs.* We have a story on paper, an exposition of how the story should be told, a rehearsal, the telling, and the showing—all with motion and interaction between tellers and a variety of audiences. We have story and audience, a drama and a movie.

Almost a century ago, the psychologist Hugo Münsterberg described the viewer of film, "the motion which he sees appears to be a true motion, and yet is created by his own mind."[34] Good liars know this, and use it, as do storytellers. Good filmmakers, people such as Edwin S. Porter, Mack Sennett, and D. W. Griffith, already knew this even as Münsterberg was writing, of course, as did dramatists, though working without quite the same "accurate" representational context. And we audience members do know this, too, recognizing (when we wish to) that the motion we *see* not only *appears* to be a true motion, but is the *capture* or *representation* of a true motion, even while it is created in our own minds. We never (unless we are extremely naïve viewers) mistake the screen, the stage, or even the picture frame for a window onto something *real*.

If we don't trust our own experience, we can easily go back to Sergei Eisenstein, to his early discussion of montage,[35] to confirm this divide. Filmic motion is a *creation* of motion, a dance, a depiction itself in motion or an illusion that the audience helps produce through its assumptions. Münsterberg explains how these assumptions work: "Everybody knows how difficult it is to read proofs. We overlook the misprints, that is, we replace the wrong letters which are actually in our field of vision by imaginary right letters which correspond to our expectations. Are we not also familiar with the experience of supplying by our fancy the associative image of a movement when only the starting point and the end point are given, if a skillful suggestion influences our mind."[36] Clearly, adding the viewer to an already complex weave of filmmaking can get you, to mix a metaphor, pied type. Untangling it, or managing to return the letters to their appropriate compartments in the job case, begins to feel as unlikely as solving Rubik's cube. The motion we see in movies comes not just from the filmmaker or the film, after all, but from the viewer, making even broad attempts at outlining it dangerous.

Complexity, convolution of this sort, is just the sort of thing Tarantino apparently loves, for it allows him to use film to make points having nothing to do with film, but concerning people and their interactions. Raveling and unraveling, and doing both at the same time, he plays with the audience— in all senses of the term—not just the film. He plays with dance, motion and violence, with plot and character, speech and thought—with all of Aristotle's parts of tragedy. Not to mention that he play with the conventions both of film viewing and filmmaking. As a result, oddly enough, he ends up constructing movies that become not like toys, but like ships solid enough to withstand just about any wind blown toward them, with anchors lowering deep within the traditions of filmmaking in Hollywood and France, in particular. He never does, however, fall into the trap of believing he is *showing* reality. He certainly talks about it, though, through all the tools at his disposal.

In many senses, Tarantino is an extremely conservative entertainer. That is, his emphasis does not fall on the new but on making the old new, on bringing what was into the context of what is—and this, as we've seen, extends even to Aristotle's views of tragedy in his *Poetics.* If *Reservoir Dogs* is an Aristotelian tragedy at all, it is unusual for its time, for the pattern away from Aristotle that Leitch identifies is real—and not only for action movies.

Aristotle claims that tragedy "is an imitation of an action that is serious, complete, and of a certain magnitude; in language embellished with every kind of artistic ornament, the several kinds being found in separate parts of the play; in the form of action, not of narrative; through pity and fear effecting the proper purification of these emotions."[37] Not only can this description be applied accurately to *Reservoir Dogs,* but Aristotle's prescribed and nuanced relation between action and character is scrupulously maintained. The beauty of Tarantino's plot is that the action is seamlessly buttressed by character without strain and without character ever superseding action or plot for, in the Aristotelian view, character plays a supporting role in relation to action. However, one should not diminish the importance of character as this support and justification for action, and Tarantino, in his heavily character-driven "action" plot, certainly does not. *Reservoir Dogs* follows closely the Aristotelian prescription that "tragedy is an imitation not only of a complete action, but of events inspiring fear or pity. Such an effect is best produced when the events come on us by surprise and when, at the same time, they follow cause and effect."[38] The "cause and effect" within *Reservoir Dogs* relies heavily on character, and the two most dramatic moments of the movie, the slicing of the ear and the final scene, rely heavily on fear (in the first instance) and on pity (in the second) for their effect.

Tarantino is a storyteller in a sense pre-dating modernism and movie classicism. Though some viewers don't see it—and it is easy to lose things in a Tarantino movie, for so much is always going on—there's always a point he's trying to make, or a number of them. In *Reservoir Dogs,* he explores the thin line between the professional and the psychotic and the relations between each of these and the personal. His characters, in other words, aren't simply devices for furthering his plot; his plot, here and elsewhere, furthers understanding of character—and not just these individuals, but of human character in general—and understanding of intimacy. The same is true of his use of motion: it's not there simply for showing off directorial skill, but to increase focus on the characters, their actions, and their interrelations.

In Nietzsche's vision, in the Apolline "dream state" (in representational art), "the daylight world is veiled and a new world, more distinct, comprehensible and affecting than the other and yet more shadowy, is constantly reborn before our eyes."[39] Art affects the dynamic of our knowledge of the world, highlighting it through its clarity but obfuscating at the same time through the constant expansion and change it engenders. The strength of tragedy, to Nietzsche, is that it does not try to make the world understandable through simplification; it is kept from such temptation by the tension between the Apolline and the Dionysiac. He writes: "Dionysiac excitement is

capable of communicating to a whole crowd of people the artistic gift of seeing itself surrounded by a host of spirits with which it knows itself to be profoundly united. . . . This is . . . an abandonment of individuality by entering
another character."[40] The most profound moment of *Reservoir Dogs* comes
when Mr. Orange admits to Mr. White that he is a cop. As an audience sympathetic to both men, we are suddenly cast into a situation with no possible
positive resolution, from our point of view, a classic tragic situation. Add that
to "the Apolline [that] wrests us from the Dionysiac universality. . . . With
the tremendous impact of image, concept, ethical teaching and sympathetic
stirrings, the Apolline lifts man out of his orgiastic self-destruction, and
deceives him about the universality of the Dionysiac event, deluding him into
the idea that he can see only a single image of the world."[41]

Nietzsche believes that there is a "metaphysical consolation"[42] in tragedy,
the idea that no matter what mutable life may bring, it is only a patina over
a joyful and powerful core. This may seem to be at odds with the ending of
Reservoir Dogs, but the glimpse of the abyss (to again use one of Nietzsche's
phrases[43]) provided by the film allows the audience to leave the theater reinforced in its own recognition of the value of life and of experience—and of
the commonality of existence. It is, as Warshow has commented, the necessary opposite of optimism: "Even within the area of mass culture, there
always exists a current of opposition, seeking to express by whatever means
are available to it that sense of desperation and inevitable failure which
optimism itself helps to create."[44] Leaving the theater:

> we should see the condition of individuation as the source and origin of all
> suffering and hence as something reprehensible. . . . In these ideas we already
> have all the component parts of a profound and pessimistic view of the world,
> and at the same time the *mystery doctrine of tragedy:* the basic understanding of
> the unity of all things, individuation seen as the primal source of evil, art as the
> joyful hope that the spell of individuation can be broken, as a presentiment of
> a restored oneness.[45]

We understand a little more fully both the bad of our individual egoism and
the good that can be built through our relationships.

The carefully built rationalizations presented by the individuals within the
movie, arguments making their actions "professional" while others
(Mr. Blonde) act unpredictably, try to build a sense of logic into their
actions. Mr. White, speaking to Mr. Pink about Mr. Blonde and the unnecessary killings the latter performed during the botched robbery, says, "What
you're supposed to do is act like a fucking professional. A psychopath is not
a professional. You can't work with a psychopath, 'cause you don't know
what those sick assholes are gonna do next." Mr. Pink, in a later and heated
exchange with Mr. White, says, "I didn't create this situation, I'm just
dealing with it. You're acting like a first-year fucking thief. I'm acting like a

professional." And that's not the only time. He shouts to White and Blonde: "I don't believe this shit, both of you got ten years on me, and I'm the only one acting like a professional."

It is this warped idea of professionalism that sets the criminals here, and in the gangster genre in general, apart from the rest of us. In them, "the quality of irrational brutality and the quality of rational enterprise become one. . . . Thus brutality itself becomes at once the means to success and the content of success,"[46] the basic problem faced by Pink and White as they try to deal with Blonde.

The "professional" concept isn't used only by the gang. Detective Holdaway, in talking to Freddy Newendyke (Mr. Orange), says, "These guys are professionals. We're professionals. It's a risk, but I think it's a calculated risk." During the Mexican standoff close to the end of the movie, Mr. Pink pleads, "C'mon, guys; nobody wants this. We're supposed to be fucking professionals!" Put into a Nietzschean framework, the "professional" stands in for the scholar, the theoretical man, the person who has replaced emotion with logic, making ratiocination the center or existence yet unable to recognize the falsity of accepted axioms: "theoretical man takes fright as his consequences, and in his dissatisfaction no longer dares to hurl himself into the terrible icy current of existence, but runs nervously up and down on the bank. He no longer wants anything whole, with all the natural cruelty that adheres to things, so coddled has he been by optimism."[47] In *Reservoir Dogs,* both Mr. White and Mr. Orange manage to rise above this meager vision of one's relationship to the world, to move into the broader Dionysiac reality, though it means their deaths.

Tarantino, of course, can't leave the film on such a note, but has to break the mood for the sake of the audience—and to do so in a fashion in keeping with the point he is making about the importance of emotion (the Dionysiac) and the weakness of logic (the Apolline). Romanov writes:

> The lyrics and the sedative tone of the music bring a profound close to the film. The silliness of the song's refrain ("You put de lime in de coconut, you drank 'em bot' up") along with the comedic tone, releases the tension of the film's final few moments. In this instance, Tarantino uses music much differently than he does in other scenes throughout the film. Here, the music accompanies the credits rising over a black screen. There are no visual connections to any of the characters in the film, only a brief aural allusion to Mr. Orange's painful gut injury as Nilsson sings, "Doctor, ain't there nothin' I can take?/I said Doctor, to relieve this belly ache." The music acts as a therapeutic device more than anything. Tarantino is allowing the audience to distance themselves from the film in order to get them to realize that what they have just seen is a reflection of life and not life itself. Without the influence of visuals here, one can also draw their own conclusions about the character's fate and whether it was justified in the film.[48]

Perhaps the most instructive scenes in *Reservoir* Dogs, at least in coming to an understanding of both Tarantino and the movie, are those where Detective Holdaway, Freddy Newendyke's coach and handler, preps Newendyke for his role as Mr. Orange by teaching him how to tell that story "commode" story mentioned earlier, leading to scenes that show the telling of the story—even to the extent of visualizing it within the movie. At one point, Holdaway tells Newendyke:

> The things you gotta remember are the details. It's the details that sell your story. Now this particular story takes place in a men's room. So you gotta know the details about the men's room. You gotta know if they got paper towels or a blower to dry your hands. You gotta know if the stalls ain't got no doors or not, man. . . . You gotta know every detail there is to know about this commode. So what you gotta do is take all them details and make them your own.

Tarantino's rules for storytelling, in one easy lesson. As writer and director, he wants his audience to have confidence in him—not to believe the story he's telling, but to believe in him, in the idea that he is a trustworthy guide, which is what Holdaway is trying to teach Newendyke to manage, as well. The story Holdaway has Newendyke learn to tell even has a point—though it's not the one that's meant to be clear to the gang (that Newendyke is really one and the same as they are). The point is that you *can't* trust the storyteller—though you can still learn something from the story, if you pay attention and if try hard enough.

5

Pulp Fiction: Comedy, Structure, and Consequence

After completing *Reservoir Dogs,* Quentin Tarantino, attuned to the American movie viewer, probably realized that his next movie had to start with that which is familiar to his audience if he was to retain and expand that audience. Speaking with Manohla Dargis, he said he "wanted to start with the oldest chestnuts in the world. You've seen them a zillion times. You don't need to be caught up with the story because you already know it."[1] At this point in his career, he *needed* the familiar, even if he were going to use it differently. So, as would prove to be a pattern, he once again constructed his film on a well-known genre foundation. And his intention, as we see from *Pulp Fiction* itself, *was* once more to move away from the genre base within the movie. The result is that, as Marsha Kinder writes, "By constructing a violent nonlinear narrative full of ellipses, Tarantino cracks open traditional genres to show how original variations can still be generated within the gaps."[2] In this way, what is not shown (and not used) becomes as useful as what is, in *Pulp Fiction,* especially when the elided later becomes part of the shown, though generally within the context of another story.

With this relatively rare (in film—it is much more common in literature) structure in mind, Tarantino initially envisioned *Pulp Fiction* as building from "a crime film anthology. . . . The stories are completely separate, and they're the same stories you've heard a million times. You know, the staples of the genre, but hopefully taken where you've never seen them taken before."[3] Like the results of the movements past all of his starting points, that's not where *Pulp Fiction* ends up: the stories are *not* "completely separate." They are a tangled web of loss, public and private horror, and redemption set against backdrops of human attitudes and actions that, though real, are rarely faced—not, at least, in the movies or in life. And they all work together to a single, simple point: actions have consequences, so know what you are doing.

Jeff Dawson describes the starting point of *Pulp Fiction* as referring "generally to the crime stories from the 1930s and 1940s, the cheap, garishly illustrated news-stand publications . . . a hard-boiled world of footsore private investigators, two-bit hoods, corrupt cops and, of course, black widows."[4] The film, of course, moves on to become something else altogether, something never seen in *Black Mask* or any other pulp magazine. Certainly, it does use the old and once-familiar crime anthology format for accessibility, but *Pulp Fiction* is also a satiric comedy of a subtle sort rare in Hollywood, where the point of the movie, in the tradition and convention of the industry, is expected to be obvious. It addresses attitudes toward race, ethnicity, and gender without overtly judging them, simply presenting them as the actual and active parts of society that they are (the judgment, Tarantino implies, should be on society as a whole, not on these or any other of its parts alone and certainly not on the messenger, the director who presents them); it acknowledges aspects of domestic life generally delicately elided (bathrooms and bathrobes, for example—and even the actual chewing of food); and it accepts that violence, often unexpected and ever shattering, is an integral part of life and has consequences on levels great and small. And it does all of this without insulting or pandering to its audience or reducing itself simply to spectacle, to shock for shock's sake.

If it remains only one thing throughout its runtime, *Pulp Fiction* most certainly retains its position as comedy. As Jessica Milner Davis observes, "This is a film which, despite its apparent realism in setting and characterization, challenges the viewer with its determination to marshal violence into the recognizably familiar patterns of humor."[5] Yet there's no happy ending (if there is an ending at all), there's hardly a joke in the movie, and none of the actors is primarily associated with comedy in his or her prior work. Jerome Charyn points out that, "Horrors abound in the film—Vincent [John Travolta] accidentally shoots one of the yuppie dealers in the face, Marcellus [Ving Rhames] is raped by a redneck, Marcellus shoots the same redneck in the groin after Butch [Bruce Willis] rescues him by slicing the redneck's accomplice with a samurai sword, Vincent has to stab Mia [Uma Thurman] in the chest with a needle of adrenaline that looks like a knife— but we never seem to stray far from comedy."[6] Geoff King writes, "potentially unsettling implications are subordinated to the use of violence as stylish flourish, an effect underpinned to a large extent by the use of deadpan comedy."[7] Ultimately, though, attitudes that we, in the audience, might expect to see condemned in comedy never are; poetic justice, a mainstay of comedic genres, rarely occurs overtly. And the violence, though not extolled, is never rued, something unusual to film comedy outside of slapstick and farce, though farce itself is certainly a part of *Pulp Fiction*. The use of farce conventions in setting up Coolidge's unexpected rescue of Marsellus Wallace, for example, with the two sitting side by side, bound and gagged, allows for the depiction of Coolidge's (and then Wallace's) violent retribution on the rapists to pass without much viewer shock.

The lack of clear and moral judgment shown within the movie on its portrayed actions can be jarring to audience members who have grown up in a tradition in which overt judgmental narrative moral stances are generally needed if a director is to present certain types of attitudes or actions without approbation. The audience cannot be left to assume that a racist attitude, for example, could possibly reflect that of the director. But that happens here: "Tarantino . . . appears to be deeply disturbed by barely repressed, ambivalent feelings about race in general, black masculinity in particular, and the issues of violence, miscegenation, and sex."[8] It's the society Tarantino portrays that is disturbed (and disturbing), not necessarily the director, whose intention is, in part, to bring attention to those aspects of society the audience rarely wants to face, such as real racial attitudes, but to do so without judging *for* the audience.

Race isn't the only area in which Tarantino gets himself into trouble. He breaks the implicit agreement to avoid recognition of the reality of the need to release bodily waste and so is accused of making his presentation of the bathroom anchor "a dense nexus that connects blood and violence to anal eroticism and smearing."[9] Perhaps, and more likely, Tarantino is just tired of the old decorum and sees a chance to wake people up, to make them pay closer attention to the conventions of their lives by breaking this one in film. In these and other cases, any director runs the risk of his public "blaming the messenger" rather than facing within themselves attitudes concerning areas that they might find uncomfortable. But that's a risk that Tarantino has never been averse to taking.

Though it is known as a violent film (the starting assumption about all of Tarantino's movies), the actual acts of violence in *Pulp Fiction* are, as Roger Ebert points out, not as great as one might remember from a single viewing. "As I saw it a second and third time, I realized it wasn't as violent as I thought—certainly not by the standards of modern action movies. It seems more violent because it often delays a payoff with humorous dialogue, toying with us."[10] He finds only nine deaths in all, rather a small number by comparison to the run-of-the-mill contemporary action drama. And, though these deaths are sometimes bloody, they are not presented in any sort of exploitative fashion: "One thing we kept noticing during our shot-by-shot odyssey is that much of the violence is offscreen. When the guys in the apartment are shot, the camera is on Jules or Vincent, not on the victims. When the hypodermic needle goes into Mia's chest, the camera cuts away at the last instant to a reaction shot. . . . The gunshot in the back seat of the car is offscreen. The violence in the pawn shot is graphic, but within the boundaries of standard movie fights."[11]

As befits a comedy, the violence is often played for laughs, not gore—though Tarantino clearly saw no reason to stint on the blood. At the same time, according to special effects specialist (and worker on *Pulp Fiction*) Greg Nicotero, "for Quentin, the physical violence is not as important as the actors' performances, anyway. Certain directors would want to show everything, but not him. . . . What was driving the film was the characters' reactions to the violence, not the violence itself."[12] In regard to *Pulp Fiction* and *Natural Born Killers* (Oliver Stone, 1994), with screenplay by Tarantino, Kinder writes that, "both carry the orchestrated violence and comic exuberance to a new level of stylization, hybridity, and reflexiveness and increasingly address the social consequences of living with violent representation"[13]—this last, important point being something often forgotten in discussions of Tarantino, who so often layers comedy and violence over any commentary, deliberately obscuring his point about consequences.

Still, even the blood serves a real purpose, keeping Tarantino's audience just enough off balance for him to accomplish his ends without seeming to preach. As Janet Maslin wrote on reviewing the film for *The New York Times,* "Suspending his viewers' moral judgments makes it that much easier for Mr. Tarantino to sustain his film's startling tone. When he offsets violent events with unexpected laughter, the contrast of moods becomes liberating, calling attention to the real choices the characters make. Far from amoral or cavalier, these tactics force the viewer to abandon all preconceptions while under the film's spell."[14] And though that spell, the basis for the success of the movie, is based on comedy of a particular and pointed sort, it is also designed to lead audiences not only toward examination of the point of the movie, but to the point of themselves.

Of course, comedy can be defined in numerous fashions,[15] with focus sometimes on the gag, sometimes on the comedian, sometimes on the specific structure, and sometimes on its relation to society. James Agee, writing 60 years ago, defined it through the laugh, claiming that one could chart the descent of comedy to the time of his essay through the loss of laughter: "Even those who have never seen anything better must occasionally have the feeling, as they watch the current run or, rather, trickle of screen comedy, that they are having to make a little cause for laughter go an awfully long way."[16] The odd thing about this excellent essay, which brought new attention to the work of four of the greatest comedians of the silent era, is that its penultimate discussion concerns Charles Chaplin's *Monsieur Verdoux* (1947), a comedy in which Chaplin plays his first completely speaking role, as Verdoux, a role *designed* to raise only a titter or two at most, yet it is a film that Agee calls "the greatest of talking comedies though so cold and savage that it had to find its public in grimly experienced Europe."[17] Reaction to the movie (and to Chaplin, who had stirred American rancor with his political views and personal life) was negative, even causing United Artists to withdraw it from distribution for a time.

Though quite popular, *Pulp Fiction* has also drawn its share of criticism. Foster Hirsch, along with many of those who dismiss it, finds the film trivial: "A ribald, audacious juxtaposition of violence with black comedy populated by a gallery of disarming rogues, *Pulp Fiction* is a rich guilty pleasure, the movie equivalent of junk food. Powerful but, both the short run and in the final analysis, pointless."[18] Yet, 15 years after its release, it still engenders spirited discussion and holds on to a huge number of fans, hardly something that would happen to a "pointless" film. It holds as number five on the open voting top 250 films of the Internet Movie Database (www.imdb.com), not a rank a "junk food" movie could likely reach, let along sustain.

Like *Monsieur Verdoux, Pulp Fiction* is a comedy "cold and savage"— what came to be known by the 1960s as "black comedy." And both movies were nominated for screenplay Oscars, though only Tarantino (with Roger Avary) won, Chaplin having been beaten out by Sidney Sheldon for *The Bachelor and the Bobby-Soxer* (Irving Reis, 1947). Both movies present sympathetic villains; it is hard to dislike Chaplin (all one has to do is remember the tramp) in any character, and as Hirsch notes, "Absentminded Vincent tints his violence with comedy: how can the viewer dislike a hit man in the guise of such an appealing bumbler?"[19] How indeed—especially when played by John Travolta. Both movies divided audiences, even furthering the motion (in Chaplin's case) toward eventual abandonment of the United States. Both were seen by many as in bad taste, though it could even be said for *Pulp Fiction* what Agee said for the Chaplin film in his three-part review of it for *The Nation:* "*Verdoux* is in bad taste if death is, as so many Americans feel; and if it is in bad taste to treat a serious matter seriously, and to make comedy cut to the bone."[20] For both movies do cut right to the bone.

Though there were plenty of "black comedies" made between the times of the two films, a look at *Pulp Fiction* through the lens of Agee's review of *Monsieur Verdoux* sheds more light on the newer film than can comparison with any of the excellent black comedies made over the intervening decades—in part, because those comedies tend to be overtly political, something neither *Monsieur Verdoux* nor *Pulp Fiction* essays to be. This is not because the Chaplin and Tarantino movies are so similar—they aren't—but because they aim for similar social points in a particular way, and each culminates in a character's presentation of what can seem a peculiar moral stance, one casting societal assumptions under a glaring and unfiltered light.

Just as overtly as *The Godfather* (Francis Ford Coppola, 1972) does, both films play on the idea of crime as "business," but for comedic reasons foreign to the Mafia film. In each case, almost all else in life (in terms of human endeavor) is left out, as Agee writes: "The significant omissions are farmers and industrial workers; the world of *Verdoux* is the world of gain, gotten ill, by chance, by heritage, by crime."[21] Just so, the only traditionally employed important character in *Pulp Fiction* is Bonnie Dimmick (Venessia Valentino), Jules Winnfield's (Samuel Jackson) friend Jimmie's (Quentin Tarantino) wife. Though we only see her for a second, and from the back, she motivates the action of an entire chapter of the movie. Because of her, someone with a real job in the "world" most of us live in, evidence of a crime has to be disposed of, and quickly. Like most of the women in the movie, Bonnie is the factor motivating the action of the chapter involving her, which is called, appropriately enough, "The Bonnie Situation." Arguably, here and in the rest of the movie, according to D. K. Holm, "women rule the roost."[22] Though this may be stretching things, it does remain true that one of the primary tensions in the movie is between the needs of "business" and the demands of relationships, represented in the movie by the female characters.

The stories of *Pulp Fiction* and *Monsieur Verdoux* are not of work, or progress, or even of creativity. They are stories of worlds in which "business" has become criminal and completely extramoral, in which even murder isn't a statement of dislike but only a matter of business—worlds such as that shown in *The Godfather,* in which, when Sal Tessio (Abe Vigoda) realizes his betrayal has been discovered by Michael Corleone (Al Pacino) and that he is to be taken away and killed, he says, "Tell Mike it was only business. I always liked him." Just so, "Verdoux is a business realist; in terms of that realism the only difference between free enterprise in murder and free enterprise in the sale of elastic stockings is the difference in legal liability and in net income."[23] Like Marlon Brando's Vito Corleone in *The Godfather,* millionaire crime boss Marsellus Wallace is shown, in *Pulp Fiction,* as powerful (even when bound and gagged; even when raped), not repugnant.

In neither case, however, does the refusal to provide overt moral guidance (for either characters or audience) mean that the film does not take a moral stance. Both films do so, often in different ways, but just as often toward the same basic points about good, evil, and human responsibility. For example, Agee claims that Chaplin's film "is a manifesto against a kind of vulgarity in which Hollywood is drowned—the attempt to disguise emptiness with sumptuousness. . . . Like the casting and acting and directing it is poetic, not naturalistic, though naturalistic elements are finely used poetically. Verdoux's France is a highly intelligent paraphrase, far more persuasive of its place—half in the real world, half in the mind—than most films are of their supposed place, foreign, native, or imaginary."[24] Much the same could be said of Tarantino's film, which through an apparent embrasure of attempts "to disguise emptiness with sumptuousness," makes the film nostalgia restaurant Jack Rabbit Slim's, for example, the precedent to a near-fatal drug overdose.

Like Chaplin, Tarantino uses naturalistic imagery, but the film never tries (as Chaplin's did not) to create any on-screen illusion of reality. Far from it. In both cases, drawing conclusions and making parallels to the "real" world is a job they leave for the viewer—until the very end of each movie. For the most part, the job the directors undertake is to provide, through poetic presentations that keep audience attention, the questions they believe the audience members should be facing—if not answering. Neither black comedy really provides solutions or remedies for the problems they point out—answers are not, after all, what the genre is about. As Agee writes, "For answers to why and how criminality can be avoided, we can look inward more profitably than at the film; for all that is suggested in the film is oper-ant in each of us."[25]

Both Chaplin and Tarantino, whose masteries of cinema stem in part from clear understandings of the role and activity of film viewing as well as of the genres they are working within, recognize the danger of doing for, or preaching to, their audiences. They know that, ultimately, they can do little more than *suggest* that viewers look inside themselves. As do the directors of all successful black comedies, from James Whale (*The Old Dark House,* 1932) to Ethan and Joel Coen (*Burn After Reading,* 2008), both suggest *only* this, though in no uncertain terms. The recognition of "truisms" and the turning of them to the film's own purposes is one of the hallmarks of black comedy; both Chaplin and Tarantino show that they are masters of the utilization of cliché for new purposes.

However, both directors also understand the weakness of black comedy, which is the weakness of the moralist—no matter how well it is hidden in the film, no matter how much is asked of the audience, the necessary moral stance can quickly date the film and may also reduce the complexity of extreme situations. That is, the world of a black comedy is necessarily pre-sented in simplistic, black-and-white terms, and the audience is asked—no, commanded—to incorporate this view into their own (more complex, one would hope) philosophies. In adding an extra level of moral complexity, both Chaplin and Tarantino step beyond the supposed and simplistic ironies of other examples of the genre, each using exposition near the end of the film to make clear their positions that the world is not so simple and that any answers to its problems lie within the viewer, not the filmmaker, anyway. Agee writes:

> Chaplin's theme, the greatest and the most appropriate of its time that he has yet undertaken, is the bare problem of surviving at all in a world such as this. . . . Verdoux is so much nearer and darker that we can hardly bear to recognize ourselves in him. He is the committed, dedicated soul, and this soul is not intact: we watch its death agonies. And this tragic process is only the more dreadful because it is depicted not gravely but briskly, with a cold savage gaiety; the self-destroying soul is rarely aware of its own predicament.
>
> The problem of survival: the Responsible Man. Chaplin develops his terri-ble theme chiefly as a metaphor for business. . . . But it is even more remark-able and fascinating as a study of the relationship between ends and means, a metaphor for the modern personality—that is, a typical "responsible" person-ality reacting to contemporary pressures according to the logic of contempo-rary ethics.[26]

Tarantino's theme, too, is one of survival and responsibility—and even the *meaning* of responsibility and its impact.

The two most heroic acts in *Pulp Fiction* are Vincent Vega's saving of Mia Wallace after her overdose and Butch Coolidge's rescue of Marcellus Wallace from his rapists. Significantly, in both cases agreement is later made between the principals that the incidents will never be mentioned. For whatever reason, both Vega and Coolidge take on responsibility for another person and cede subsequent involvement in the lives they've saved. In the former case, Vega gains, at most, a day or so of life (he is later killed by Coolidge, in an incident unrelated to his date with Mrs. Wallace), whereas in the latter, Coolidge retains his life and the ability to spend his new wealth without living in constant fear. The point is, responsibility, if taken on seriously, is private and is based on a personal moral code having to do only with those directly involved and having nothing at all to do with consequence. The point, however, is also that actions do have consequences, and they can be positive; Vega acts out of fear, but his fears are not realized because he *does* act. Though he later dies, that happens through carelessness and is not connected to the Mia Wallace story. Coolidge acts out of compassion. As a result, he profits, Wallace reaching a quick accord with him upon completion of the rescue.

One irony is that Verdoux takes on private responsibility for others as well, committing his crimes in order to care for a young son and a wife in a wheelchair. Once they are gone, he withdraws from his pattern of robbery and murder—and then accepts his fate when he is recognized by members of one victim's family. The privacy of his motivation being important to him, he does not use his family, even in the end, to justify his actions. In fact, he never does try to justify himself or defend himself on a purely individual basis.

Not only does Verdoux withdraw himself from crime by the end of the movie, but he is withdrawn from scenes of domesticity. Much of the movie takes place in the private space of the home—or homes, in this case—offset by a few café and shop scenes and Verdoux's furniture warehouse/store. In *Pulp Fiction,* domestic space also appears in significant fashion and also serves as a contrast to "business." In fact, as Edward Gallafant, notes, the "three domestic spaces of the film that are given extended attention are always associated with the married state, as the script establishes in each case,"[27] and it is the married state that necessitates "business," even though, as "The Bonnie Situation" makes clear, the two worlds are to be kept apart. As a result of this distinction in both films, the directors are able to use the movement from private to public space and back again to emphasize the related points they are making about good and evil and human responsibility.

Except for Jules Winnfield, never do the characters in *Pulp Fiction* reject crime, nor do they (even Winnfield) withdraw from it with any moral aversion. None of these characters is a sweetheart, and all of them act (at times) in ways most in the audience should likely find repugnant, something that sometimes leads to flawed readings of the film. Todd Onderdonk, for example, sees in the movie a "focus on the dynamics of male loyalty and betrayal . . . *Pulp Fiction* illustrates how women, and by extension, the institutions of marriage and the family, are granted no more than an instrumental function in the norms of a society that places most of its emphasis on male roles in the hierarchy."[28] Tarantino, however, does not really ever focus on questions revolving around male bonding any more than does the society he is commenting on through the movie, though such questions are involved in both. Here again, as with race and bathrooms, presentation is mistaken for advocacy. By contrast, as in *Monsieur Verdoux,* strong family and couple relationships (even between men) are keys to the movie, both thematically and in terms of plot development.

In both movies, relationships (signified by family, for the most part, but not exclusively) become the excuse for crime, for business, as is also true in *The Godfather.* Protecting one's own, acting as a shepherd in an aggressively evil world, becomes rationalization for much of the action, though the situations and relationships are a great deal more complex in *Pulp Fiction* (and in *The Godfather,* for that matter) than they are in *Monsieur Verdoux.* Butch Coolidge endangers his life because of his love for Fabienne (Maria de Medeiros), desiring to provide for her in the future, and then does so a second time, to retrieve a watch that had belonged to four generations of his family. Fabienne has left it behind. Vincent Vega's panicked rescue of the dying Mia Wallace stems from a story about her husband (though Mia denies its truth) Marsellus having had another man thrown out of a fourth-floor window simply for having given her a foot massage. That same Marsellus respects Jimmie Dimmick's overriding desire to protect his marriage and acts at considerable expense to ensure that this is done.

These and other examples set the groundwork for Jules Winnfield's words at the end of the movie, the climactic speech of the film. In much the same way, Verdoux's relations both with his family and with the girl he had planned on killing as an experiment (he does not, when he discovers that she, like he, would kill for love), and his reaction to the later loss of his family set up his own last comments.

Winnfield has developed something of a trademark in conducting his business, quoting (cobbling together several passages inaccurately, actually) what he believes is scripture when about to kill a cornered victim. His passage concerns the righteous man surrounded by the tyranny of evil, who shepherds the weak through darkness, followed by a threat of vengeance from the Lord. He follows with this:

> **Jules:** I been saying that shit for years. And if you heard it, it meant your ass. I never gave much thought to what it meant. I just thought it was a cold-blooded shit to say to a motherfucker before I popped a cap in his ass. But I saw some shit this morning made me think twice. See, now I'm thinking, maybe it means you're the evil man. And I'm the righteous man. And Mr. Nine Millimeter here, he's the shepherd protecting my righteous ass in the valley of darkness. Or is could mean you're the righteous man and I'm the shepherd and it's the world that's evil and selfish. I'd like that. But that shit ain't the truth. The truth is you're the weak. And I'm the tyranny of evil men. But I'm trying, Ringo. I'm trying real hard to be the shepherd.

"Ringo" is the character played by Tim Roth and called "Pumpkin" by Yolanda (Amanda Plummer), whom he calls "Honey Bunny." They have made the mistake of trying to rob the restaurant where Vega and Winnfield, much more deadly, are having breakfast after an extremely rough morning. Because of what he characterizes as a miracle (a man unloaded a gun at the two of them, missing with each shot), Winnfield has decided to leave "the life" and wander "like Caine in *Kung Fu,* just walk from town to town, meet people, get in adventures." Vega hears this differently: "So you decided to be a bum?" What Jules imagines as the heroic Caine, Vince sees as more like Chaplin's tramp. Rather than resolving their differences (an impossibility), Vega excuses himself to go to the restroom—and the robbery commences when he's away. Winnfield has taken control of the situation by the time Vega returns, speaking the above lines just before letting the robbers leave with their loot—including $1,500 of his own money.

What we have in these lines is the crux of the movie, the explanation for it, though it provides no answers. Good and bad, the putative Bible passage states, are distinct entities, knowable by humans and defined by God. And the responsibility of the enlightened individual is to watch out for those who have not attained knowledge, who are, as yet, unable to find the path to righteousness for themselves. The problem is, as Winnfield has come to realize, that it is almost impossible to tell who really is—or should be—the shepherd and who the flock. Or it has been, for him, until the revelation coming as a result of the supposed miracle, a revelation arriving, as he tells Vega, as "I was just sitting here drinking my coffee, eating my muffin, playing the incident in my head, when I had what alcoholics refer to as a 'moment of clarity.'" He recognizes for the first time that he's the evil, even though he wants to be the shepherd, and that he had been fooling himself into thinking that he was simply an instrument of a kind of greater justice—but, as he says, he is trying to change. Maybe for the first time in his life, he has been faced by the three strikingly different visions he describes of the same situation and has had to decide between them. Kelly Ritter outlines his position:

> If Jules is righteous, and Pumpkin, the petty thief, is evil, then the gun (violence) becomes a justification for Jules. If Pumpkin is righteous, and Jules in the shepherd, then the gun disappears as agent, and it is the world that has made the two men the way they are, both men are blameless. Finally, though, Pumpkin is "the weak" and Jules is "the tyranny of evil men," but Jules is "tryin' real hard" to be the shepherd. This changes the scheme of all actions before this, because if Jules is evil but capable of redemption vis-à-vis rhetoric, then there is no justification in continuing violence, and Jules must walk away—he must try harder—and so he decides to give up his life of crime.[29]

Verdoux also recognizes his culpability, but he is able to square it with his shepherding in a way that Winnfield cannot yet do, or is no longer willing to do. To the bitter end, he excuses himself where Winnfield has begun to question—

the crucial difference in the points of the movies, making *Pulp Fiction,* ultimately, the more optimistic of the two: as long as the evil can recognize their evil and try to be good, there is hope in the world—though it may be that Tarantino recognizes "the futility of Jules's words and actions and thus ends the film with Jules in a position of ignorance, as a vessel of regurgitation."[30] Both Winnfield and Verdoux go off to their fates with unwarranted self-assurance, though neither has proven to be the moral compass they imagine.

Unlike Winnfield, Verdoux keeps on the blinders of "business" to the very end. In court, after being convicted and sentenced, he is allowed a final word, calling what he has done a business and then comparing himself to the builders of weapons of mass destruction:

> **Verdoux**: As a mass killer, I am an amateur by comparison. However, I do not wish to lose my temper because very shortly I shall lose my head. Nevertheless, upon leaving this spark of earthly existence, I have this to say: I shall see you all very soon.

He, and Chaplin through him, is saying we are all the same, that everybody does it, that it's only a matter of degree that separates the average person from him and him from national leaders. All are killers; all will meet in hell. This is a much grimmer message than that which Tarantino presents, though Tarantino, too, wants his audience to turn its gaze inward, seeing that neither evil nor culpability solely belong to others.

Before we see Verdoux for the last time, we are shown the antechamber to his cell, where reporters wait to be rotated in for final interviews. One comes out; another speaks to him, asking about his state:

> **Max**: He's nuts. . . . Twists everything with a lot of half truths. Says you can't have good without evil. Something about evil being the shadows cast from the sun.

Blithely cynical, Verdoux is. If evil exists, there's nothing wrong with being evil. It's simply part of life. Taking his turn, the reporter enters the cell where Verdoux reclines, awaiting his executors, and asks Verdoux about good and evil:

> **Verdoux**: Arbitrary forces, my good fellow. Too much of either will destroy us all.
>
> **Reporter**: We can never have too much good in the world.
>
> **Verdoux**: Trouble is, we've never had enough. . . .
>
> **Verdoux**: I don't see how anyone can be an example in these criminal times.
>
> **Reporter**: Well, you certainly are, robbing and murdering people.
>
> **Verdoux**: That's business.

Verdoux's point, left unsaid (for it has been made clear already) is the callousness of "business." In fact, it is the hypocrisy of so much of humanity that is behind the anger Chaplin expresses so gently through the film. So it is, when a priest appears and asks Verdoux if he has made his peace with God, that Verdoux responds:

Verdoux: I am at peace with God. My conflict is with Man.

Father Ferro: Have you no remorse for your sins?

Verdoux: Who knows what sin is?

This self-serving response avoids the real question, the one that Winnfield, after the end of *Pulp Fiction,* will now seek to answer as he wanders, a seeker or a bum—or both.

Though they approach the question of personal culpability in differing fashions—Winnfield realizes that, at least, it is a legitimate question for the individual to face and answer whereas Verdoux casts it upon society—the purpose, again, of both movies is to ask audience members to consider the question for themselves and within themselves, not to provide answers. Both movies resolutely refuse to provide a simple segregation of the good and the bad, instead lumping all of humanity together and demonstrating (or trying to) that evil and good are only matters of degree and perception. Unlike most black comedies, where the moral stance and even outrage is unmistakable, no high ground is taken in any obvious way by either Chaplin or Tarantino. They are entertainers first, after all, and preachers second. They want revelation to come from within their viewers—perhaps while drinking coffee and eating muffins—and not because it was forced on them by an external agent, not even if that agent is their own child, their movie.

Though Agee was unable to successfully protect Chaplin from the storm of protest that came his way, the case he makes for the importance of *Monsieur Verdoux* can convince a reader of the value of the movie even today. What he provides is more than a review, but is something of a new way of looking at film—or so Agee must have hoped. He writes: "the art of moving pictures has been so sick, for so long, that the most it can do for itself is to shift unceasingly from one bedsore to the next. Chaplin, by contrast, obviously believes that if you can invent something worth watching, the camera should hold still and clear, so that you can watch it."[31] It is the story, he implies, that is the heart of a good movie, along with the performance. For all the technical developments and pyrotechnics introduced over the intervening decades, attitudes like his toward film have not disappeared, nor has gloom about the state of the American film industry. Writing at the time of *Pulp Fiction*'s release, Jake Horsley said that "the film was possibly the most over-hyped and prematurely celebrated movie ever released, and its reception is more significant as evidence of the total dearth of quality filmmaking in America today, I think, than of the film's actual merits."[32] Yet the film, as I have said, remains not only popular but influential (whereas *Monsieur Verdoux,* alas, was relatively forgotten with a few years of its release and hardly receives a mention today).

Tarantino, of course, is a different filmmaker from Chaplin. The latter could focus his work on the talent of the most popular entertainer of his time, building his films around a proven screen presence and using the sort of "realism" (as opposed to "montage") Agee points out, in which the camera acts as something of a window onto the action, and the creation of the film is primarily through that window rather than in the techniques applied afterward. Though Tarantino prefers a modified "realist" approach (he doesn't care for computer generated imagery, CGI, and uses its possibilities sparingly), he can't build his films around a single popular character. However, what he does do, instead, shows that he does, like Chaplin, indeed recognize the power actors bring to each new project from past successes. He may not have a Chaplin to work with, but he knew, when casting *Pulp Fiction,* exactly what John Travolta, among others, could do on screen and what he brought with him from previous successes. There are few hints, in *Monsieur Verdoux,* of the tramp who made Chaplin the most recognizable figure in the world. Just so, references to Tony Manero, Travolta's character in the hugely popular *Saturday Night Fever* (John Badham, 1977), in *Pulp Fiction* only appear in the dance contest at Jack Rabbit Slim's—and only tangentially. Both directors recognize the power of the past (Tarantino more overtly, especially in the *mise-en-scène*), but neither is willing to make it the focus as they construct their films.

If Agee was the champion of Chaplin and *Monsieur Verdoux,* then Roger Ebert certainly can lay claim to having played the same role in relation to Tarantino and (like *Reservoir Dogs* before it) *Pulp Fiction.* Though *Pulp Fiction* was certainly profitable, Ebert notes, "It is possibly the most unpopular movie ever to gross $100 million at the American box office."[33] If for the reason of profit alone, it never faced the prospect of being withdrawn from distribution or of being ignored by a large number of those who write on film. Yet it, too, has need of a champion. By not making its point clear but instead asking the audience to participate in consideration of the questions raised, *Pulp Fiction,* again like *Monsieur Verdoux,* runs the risk, as we have seen, of appearing amoral, with superficial viewings leading people to see it as a pointless advocacy of violence and the violent.

Yet, as Ebert claims, "each of the main stories ends with some form of redemption,"[34] a pattern alien to hardboiled pulp stories by the likes of Raymond Chandler and Dashiell Hammett, making this something other than a movie version of a pulp magazine, making the movie more *Reader's Digest* than *Black Mask.* Even so, Tarantino follows the "cardinal principle" that Joseph Shaw, founding editor of *Black Mask,* expressed in his introduction to an anthology of stories from the magazine published in 1946. The magazine's writers, he claimed,

did not make their characters act and talk tough; they allowed them to. They gave the stories over to their characters, and kept themselves off the stage, as every writer of fiction should. Otherwise, as Raymond Chandler puts it, that most powerful factor, melodrama, becomes "used as a bludgeon and not as an art"—and loses ten-fold its effectiveness.

They did not themselves state that a situation was dangerous or exciting; they did not describe their characters as giants, dead-shots, or infallible men. They permitted the actors in the story to demonstrate all that to the extent of their particular and human capabilities. Moreover, as they attained their skill, they wrote with greater and greater restraint, careful of over-exaggeration in a world of their own where text demanded their descriptive contribution, adhering to the sound principle that whatever arouses the incredulity of a reader—no matter how true to life—has exactly the same effect as that which could not possibly happen.[35]

This, a familiar pattern moving from the pulp magazines to *film noir* and beyond, provided a structural base in character that allows Tarantino to move into something new (or, at least, unusual in film), into his disjointed narrative structure and into his comedy, without losing his viewers. It allows him (as it did for Chandler and Hammett) to make his point with a subtlety that is generally absent from black comedy and purposely at odds with the surface violence and language of his presentation.

In contrast to Chaplin, who concentrated on facial expression and body motion, Tarantino humanizes his characters through dialogue, but dialogue with a difference from the plot-driving phrases that make up so much of contemporary film. One of his great skills is ability to create for the screen conversations that appear as mundane, even as pointless, as those all of us participate in daily (a style anticipated, as Hirsch points out,[36] by François Truffaut in his 1960 film *Tirez sur le pianiste*). Even so, as Ebert declares, Tarantino's "dialogue is always load-bearing."[37] That is, the dialogue consistently serves a purpose, even though that purpose isn't always to move the plot along directly. Even here, there's an echo of Chaplin, as well as a contrast with him. Never dialogue-dependent (of course), Chaplin also proved able to use words with more flexibility and nuance than most other directors could manage. Chaplin hesitated to turn to "talkies," not because they were different from what he knew, but because accent on dialogue diminished other aspects of his filmmaking, other skills, and he always wished to keep these front and center—and did, even once he had added sound and then dialogue to his films.

At its best, dialogue in sound films not only advances or aids the plot but provides play and texture, allowing fullness to the movie, making for character more than caricature—even leaving audiences gasping with delight, as in the great screwball comedies of the 1930s and 1940s. At the same time, however, dialogue can shove other aspects of the filmmaker's craft aside, making it seem too easy to get by with sloppy sets, lighting, movement, continuity, and more.

Though he drives his dialogue hard in *Pulp Fiction*, asking it to serve plot, character, a sense of naturalism in conversation, *and* to convey real poetry,

Tarantino is one of the few contemporary directors whose skills range nearly as extensively as Chaplin's (he can't match Chaplin in front of the camera, of course, but who can?). No, he's not a composer, as Chaplin was, but he does understand the use of music, both extradiegetically and as a part of the *mise-en-scène*. As *Pulp Fiction* showed the film-going world, Tarantino is completely in control of every aspect of his filmmaking and to a degree that only a few other directors have even approached. The range of his skills is the essence of his success. The degree of screenwriting craft is evident, for example, in his uses of repetitions and echoic behavior and the nature of the movements within the narrative.

As D. K. Holm writes, *Pulp Fiction*

> has three screaming awakenings from sleep, three home invasions (Brett's, Lance's, and Jimmie's, two of them found in bathrobes), and there are three "deals" in the film, the first between Butch and Marcellus (which Butch breaks), then between Mia and Vincent (to keep their night a secret), and another between Butch and Marcellus. The film is also structured around transitions—from outdoors to indoors, from room to room—and arrivals and departures.[38]

The episodic nature of the movie is contained by the circularity hinted at by these trios (and, of course, by the circling back to the beginning at the end) and the linearity of these movements.

According to Horsley,

> The most interesting and innovative thing about *Pulp Fiction* is the structure: the film is divided into three sections, each of which is—or could be—a self-contained story unto itself, but all arranged in a nonlinear fashion, overlapping slightly in their respective time frames. . . . If *Pulp Fiction* were arranged in the "correct" order it would indeed be a very different film, almost assuredly a less effective one, and certainly less satisfying—seeing as the last episode is the best, and seeing as Tarantino's new order expressly serves to resurrect Travolta's Vince, who is killed off in the second section. But it would be interesting to see how well the film stands up without the "audacity" and trickery of this largely gratuitous reshuffling, because Tarantino rearranges the order of the scenes in much the same way a good lawyer shuffles the evidence: not for coherence but for resonance; for effect.[39]

But a good courtroom lawyer is also a good storyteller, and effect is an important part of any successful narrative. Tarantino, understanding this, would never denigrate the importance of "effect," as Horsley does.

Charyn, much more impressed with Tarantino's filmmaking, uses the dialogue at the start of *Pulp Fiction* as a way of pointing out that Tarantino is not "lost within a world of film, like some ostrich trapped in the dark."[40] That Tarantino picks up on (and uses) such a trivial fact that McDonald's has to use a different name for its Quarter Pounder in Europe, thanks to the metric system, shows, to Charyn, that Tarantino never loses his focus on the "real" world even as he structures his fictional movie world. That Tarantino also uses the cheeseburger as a structural connector within the story to a scene slightly later in the film shows that Tarantino also never loses sight of the needs of his story. If his coherence is not going to be a clear narrative line, it has to rest on something else. For the most part, Tarantino rests it on character and conversation and their echoes, keeping *these* as the linear elements of his structure, allowing him to weave the temporal elements around them.

The result of Tarantino's personal attention to the details of so many of the areas of filmmaking is that he creates movies of unusual depth and texture, movies that can be watched at a number of different levels. This allows scenes of deceiving simplicity, such as when Mia Wallace dances alone in Vincent Vega's coat to Urge Overkill's version of Neil Diamond's "Girl, You'll Be a Woman Soon," in which the camera draws back and lets the character move almost as though unwatched, from behind, but not in a voyeuristic manner (thanks to the coat). Unknown to her, she carries in the coat the heroin that will soon almost kill her, making her not become a woman, but nearly a corpse. This attention to detail also allows for people to miss Tarantino's point completely, mistaking a passion for detail with a passion for the particular items detailed. It is drugs that almost kill Mrs. Wallace, so drugs must be of interest to Tarantino. But no, like race, bathrooms, and male bonding, drugs are only another of the aspects of the world that he uses to make other points.

Rather than a pastiche (or even a work of decoupage) of stories about life in some postmodern moment, *Pulp Fiction* is an extremely old-fashioned and moral movie, distinguished only by the particulars of its storytelling and direction from any number of movies from the past. *Monsieur Verdoux* is only one of dozens of excellent movies with which it could be compared, each dealing with possibilities of redemption, its lack, or even its possibility or necessity. Each movie dealing with the reality of consequences, their relevance to action, and their place in the planning of our lives. The characters of *Pulp Fiction* may be lowlifes, but they are still human and deserve, in Tarantino's presentation, to be treated as carefully as any real shepherd would, as anyone would, who has become what Winnfield claims he now wants to be.

Jackie Brown: Music, Metadiegesis, and Meaning

When you mean to buy an apple and end up walking away with an orange, you are bound to be disappointed in the vendor. Just so, Quentin Tarantino disappointed many of those who rushed to see *Jackie Brown* only to discover that the movie, though grounded in the "caper" genre, was something else again, and something unlike what was expected from Tarantino. It is a movie, as Edwin Page says, "about texture, not plot. It is also the subtle telling of a love story."[1] Its violence, though present, in no way goes beyond that found in common television crime dramas. Its narration unfolds in ways differing from Tarantino's two earlier films, and the director uses his raw material in manners new to his work but more in keeping with the specific purposes of this movie. Perhaps he now thought he was established enough to break the pattern he had established through *Reservoir Dogs* and *Pulp Fiction*.

Though Tarantino uses music in all of his films, both from within the diegesis of the narrative and without (extradiegetic), as well as allowing it to flow between the two (becoming "metadiagetic," to use Claudia Gorbman's term), he actually makes it a more integral part of his discourse in *Jackie Brown* than elsewhere, integrating it with the visual components of the movie to create a whole that neither could sustain alone.

> Significantly, the only element of filmic discourse that appears extensively in nondiegetic as well as diegetic contexts, and often freely crosses the boundary line in between, is music. Once we understand the flexibility that music enjoys with respect to the film's diegesis, we begin to recognize how many different kinds of functions it can have: temporal, spatial, dramatic, structural, denotative, connotative—both in the diachronic flow of a film and at various interpretive levels simultaneously.[2]

The flexibility of music in film allows Tarantino to create a more cohesive argument than would be possible were he simply to concentrate on the visual and only use music to accent what he shows, which, for a long time, was the way music was conceived in relation to film, at least on the part of a number of scholars. The reality of music usage is somewhat different. As the best directors always have known, Tarantino realizes that, to use composer George Burt's words:

> Music has the power to open the frame of reference to a story and to reveal its inner life in a way that could not have been as fully articulated in any other way. In an instant, music can deepen the effect of a scene or bring an aspect of the story into sharper focus. It can have a telling effect on how the characters in the story come across—how we perceive what they are feeling or thinking— and it can reveal or expand upon subjective aspects and values associated with places and ideas intrinsic to the drama.[3]

The effect of music in *Reservoir Dogs* is shocking. In *Pulp Fiction*, it paces the film. In *Jackie Brown*, Tarantino takes it a step further, making the music an integral part of the narrative, using it exactly to the ends Burt describes.

Gorbman, reacting specifically to Siegfried Kracauer's description of film music as operating either parallel to onscreen moods and actions or in counterpoint, also argues that what we really have is a much more complex relationship: "If we must summarize music-image and music-narrative relationships in two words or less, *mutual implication* is more accurate, especially with respect to films of any narrative complexity. The notions of parallel and counterpoint erroneously assume that the image is autonomous. Further, it is debatable that information conveyed by disparate media can justifiably be called the same or different."[4] No simple dualism can contain the fluid and subtle dynamic between sight and sound in film.

Certainly, in *Jackie Brown*, music and image are not autonomous, and the "information conveyed" through symbiosis is greater than the sum of the two. Gorbman perfectly encapsulates the way music is used in *Jackie Brown:* "Music in film *mediates*. Its nonverbal and nondenotative status allows it to cross all varieties of 'borders': between levels of narration (diegetic/nondiegetic), between narrating agencies (objective/subjective narrators), between viewing time and psychological time, between points in diegetic space and time (as narrative transition)."[5] It also enlivens. Without its musical component, a movie such as *Jackie Brown* would be a flat narrative of movement without humanity; it would be an impossibly boring film.

The French composer Michel Chion, like Gorbman (who translates his work into English) a student of the relationship between sound and image in film, writes that the "space that sound defines . . . is not the same as the one . . . constructed by the image. Even though it is so full of detail, and even though it is polyphonic, the contours and borders of its acoustic space are still hazy. Sound . . . does away with the notion of a localizable point of view."[6] Among its other functions, music plays exactly this role of moving from the local and particular in *Jackie Brown*. In fact, this very aspect of the movie becomes part of the foreground of meaning of the film from the beginning, allowing music to play an aggressive and assertive role in presentation of the movie's rather universal messages. Later in his book *Film, A Sound Art,* Chion states that "film is a work of a particular kind, an assemblage of pieces whose divisions are rarely distinct or watertight (unlike the movements of a musical work, the acts of a play, the stanzas of a poem, or the paragraphs of a prose fiction work), so that whatever crosses over these implicit borders and partitions foregrounds the partitioning process itself."[7] The plasticity (if you will) of sound makes music perfect for crossing such borders.

Though it presents itself as a caper film (with extensive homage to the blaxploitation genre), *Jackie Brown* becomes, in large part through its soundtrack, a great deal more than that—it becomes a film about the limitations of individuals hemmed in by racial, cultural, and legal barriers and about the possibility and difficulty of successfully fighting against them—and about the wisdom of even trying to do so. It also becomes a film about relationships across boundaries, about how wishes, like those Janis Ian expressed in her 1966 song "Society's Child" (concerning an interracial relationship stopped because of family pressures), remained, generally, wistful and unfulfilled when the film was released 31 years later. Ian's narrator, having given up her boyfriend of another race, rationalizes her act, imagining that she will do things differently in the future:

> One of these days I'm gonna stop my listening,
> Gonna raise my head up high.

Max Cherry (Robert Forster), as he watches Jackie Brown (Pam Grier) drive away at the end of the movie, might have had these lines in his head—though he may also realize that, for him, it is too late for wishful thinking. It is Brown who raises her head up high. We in the audience don't know what Cherry may be thinking, however: it's the soundtrack to Jackie Brown's life, appropriately, that we now start to hear again, not his. He has given up; she, though in her mid-forties, is just starting to spread her wings and fly (something of an irony for a former airline cabin attendant).

To understand just how important the music is to this movie, one need only look at the parallel car scenes in the movie's chapter called "Money Exchange: For Real This Time." In it (as is frequently the case in *Jackie Brown*), sound is used for delineation, support for images, and the shifting between them—or so it seems (the music, for example, which stays the same at one point in the chapter while the image shifts, may be indicating that what we are seeing is simply what one character is thinking). Jackie Brown drives to the mall where all of the characters in on the caper are to converge while listening to Randy Crawford with the Crusaders performing "Street Life," playing metadiegetically, it seems, for the shot shifts to Max Cherry driving, without alteration of music. He is, in this way, clearly connected to the lines of the song now heard, as is Brown, when the images switches back to her—and, in both instances, the lines do reflect *her* thoughts, both about herself and about Cherry. As the tone, the sound, is better than one would expect from the radio or cassette player in the little subcompact Honda she is driving, the audience has already assumed that the music, if not solely in her head, comes from more than just the car stereo.

Max Cherry we find when we see him parking, has not been listening to "Street Life," but to the Delfonics' "Didn't I (Blow Your Mind This Time)," appropriately a song that reminds *him* of *her,* for she is the one who had introduced him to the song and the artists. By contrast, in the third car, Melanie Ralston (Bridget Fonda) and Louis Gara (Robert De Niro) bicker to the Grass Roots' "Midnight Confession," clearly a diegetic component of the scene, as the quality of the sound reproduction isn't that good and as the volume of the music is the source of their argument.

As Jackie Brown is first seen driving, it is the opening lyrics to "Street Life" that are heard, mostly over a close-up of her in profile, talking about living the street life of necessity, implying that one does what one must and what one can. The song continues even as the scene shifts to Max Cherry's car. We hear the following lines as the picture cuts closer to *his* face (from the front) as he drives, switching back to Jackie Brown only on the last word, "superstar." Very quickly, through the music, we in the audience grasp that the song is being used to inform us about just how strong the connection between the two had grown, and is reflected in Brown's thoughts. It is not simply highlighting what we already know, but is emphasizing for us the requited nature of the affection that Cherry's phone message indicated in an earlier scene through its series of phone and beeper numbers telling Brown how to reach him and the sense it carries that he did not want to hang up. Unnecessary exposition is avoided; the film moves forward, the point made.

The Melanie/Louis part in the "Money Transfer" chapter starts with Melanie in the bathroom, Louis pounding on the door as lyrics to "Undun" by The Guess Who play: "when she found out she couldn't fly/It was too late." Here, the music functions somewhat differently, setting up the series of events that will lead to Melanie's death—caused, in Louis's mind, at least—by her going too far.

As they ride to the mall, Melanie dances in her seat (slapping her thighs slightly off the beat) to "Midnight Confessions," another choice obliquely foreshadowing what will happen later: "But a little gold ring you wear on your hand makes me understand." Melanie doesn't belong to Louis, never will, yet she nags him like the worst sort of life partner. Still, he feels tied to her, though she "belongs" to someone else, to Ordell Robbie (Samuel Jackson): even though she has had sex with Louis, she is Robbie's "little surfer girl."

Chion divides film music into two basic (though nonexclusive and nonlimiting) categories, pit music, the extradiegetic music coming from beyond the world within the film, and screen music, diegetic music clearly originating from instruments or devices within the *mise-en-scène*. A third category, on-the-air music, covers that which, like "Street Life" in the scene described above, isn't clearly in either category (it *could* be coming from Jackie Brown's car radio, merely augmented for the film). He further identifies four categories of film music, categories of "semantic and emotive interaction,"[8] all significant to understanding not only this scene but *Jackie Brown* as a whole. The first is empathetic music, generally pit music, that intertwines with the other emotional aspects of the scene. "Street Life" serves that purpose, here.

Next comes anempathetic music, generally screen music continuing as if oblivious to the unfolding events. "Undun" plays behind the first instance of Gara/Ralston bickering, missing not a beat even when Gara smashes down the bathroom door to hurry her. Third is didactic counterpoint, screen music once more, found in the lyrics of "Undun" and even "Midnight Confession." Ralston will "come undone" quite soon, of course, a fact signified by the lyrics without any emotion or the irony that can be present in anempathetic music. Finally comes an unspecified catch-all category for those instances not fitting within any other category. This is where, perhaps, one would have to locate the snippet of "Didn't I (Blow Your Mind this Time)" when Cherry gets out of his car at the mall.

Chion's point is that music operates integrally in film, not as something tacked on as an afterthought. In the instance of Tarantino, he is exactly right. What may, at times, look like nothing more than editing room flourishes prove to be results of a constant attention to the total impact of the film, giving precedence to no single feature, manipulating each to create the whole. The music, often built on pastiche (as has been the case with film music ever since the local pianist provided bits of popular tunes to go with "silent" films), creates a network within the film, with other films, and with the aspects of society integrated into the film's themes.

Tarantino clearly had a focus in mind for his film that differed from that of Elmore Leonard in the novel *Rum Punch,* on which the film is based. The change of title to the name of the main character, the change in her last name from Burke to Brown (a nod to Pam Grier's past as a blaxploitation star), and an opening that focuses exclusively on the main character makes clear that this is Jackie Brown's movie right from the start. The book, on the other hand, begins with a reprise of two of Leonard's characters from an earlier novel, *The Switch,* lulling the reader into thinking it might be *their* book. Only when we first "see" Jackie Burke do we begin to suspect that we might be wrong. We look at her over the shoulders of two of the other characters, the two lawmen who entrap her, and we soon are invited to share their fascination:

> They watched Jackie Burke come off the Bahamas shuttle in her tan Islands Air uniform, then watched her walk through Customs and Immigration without

opening her bag, a brown nylon case she pulled along behind her on wheels, the kind flight attendants used.

It didn't surprise either of the casual young guys who had Ms. Burke under surveillance . . . Jackie Burke came through here five days a week.

They watched her from a glass-partitioned office in this remote wing of the terminal, Ray Nicolet commenting on Jackie Burke's legs, her neat rear end in the tan skirt, Faron Tyler saying she didn't look forty-four, at least not from here. They watched her bring a pair of sunglasses out of her should bag.[9]

The voyeurism here is clearly also supposed to become the reader's, but it entails a distancing (through the two cops) absent from Tarantino's version, in which it is Jackie Brown and the audience alone.

Even so, the start of *Jackie Brown* operates in much the same way, but immediately, not some time into the narrative, and without the addition of the two intrusive watchers. It also serves to provide a framework and context exclusively for the film and not just the story, echoing the start of *The Graduate* (Mike Nichols, 1967) and placing the movie within a filmmaking continuum, situating the new movie with the old in their examinations of the difficulties of establishing relationships in an uncaring, indeed aggressively destructive, world.

In point of fact, Tarantino's freedom with music, especially popular music, owes a great deal to the earlier film. As K. J. Donnelly points out, "It was with the advent of pop music as a replacement for film music in *The Graduate* (1967) and *Easy Rider* (1969) that the film music paradigm that had been weathered but had persisted since the 1930s was broken."[10] Within a few years, the composite film score, mixing music from diegetic and extradiegetic sources, pulling from disparate popular genres, and adding purpose-composed pieces, became enough of a standard and understood as part of a narrative framework, and not simply as a pastiche, for Tarantino to make it an unobtrusive part of his craft, at times, and in other instances to foreground it. The narratives of the two movies are also of a pattern, starting with the individual struggling to find a place in a world that doesn't seem made for them and ending with the character breaking out.

At the start of both movies, the title character is carried along an airport's sliding walkway, each letting himself or herself be moved without expression while an extradiegetic popular song plays, a song that acts, in some respect, as a theme song for the movie. Whereas these apparently simple and seemingly random parallels can be shrugged off in the newer film as simply an example of postmodern "pastiche," the use of something because it is there (a rejection of "meaning"), or because of its surfaces, doing so begs the question: why choose *this* particular bit to mimic over another of the dozens of movies opening with an airport motif? Simply by making his choice, Tarantino creates a parallel between the two films that sets the stage for the actions and themes of his movie by using those of *The Graduate* as a base.

Something, obviously, about *The Graduate* appealed to Tarantino in relation to the vision he was creating through *Jackie Brown*. It is not sufficient, then, to simply point out the relationship between the two movies as an example of the referentiality imbued in all of Tarantino's movies. One needs to try to understand its function . . . here, and in other similar instances.

Both movies concern the efforts of one individual to take control of his or her life at a pivotal movement; both concern relationships that cross boundaries; both depict worlds that seem to be squeezing their main characters out. In each case, it is the moving sidewalk, at the start, that seems more in control than the individual. In *The Graduate,* the sidewalk is soon replaced by a luggage belt that spits a suitcase into the waiting grip of Ben Braddock (Dustin Hoffman), who is returning home to begin his adult life after finishing college. Dressed in a suit, with his bag now in hand, coat under his arm, clearly in no hurry, Braddock gives a small wave toward someone outside and beside the camera, smiles, and exits the airport through a door that, on the camera's side, says "Use Other Door." Though he seems a willing participant, Braddock has now been deposited and is being met by someone—through little real action of his own.

In contrast to *The Graduate,* in which sounds from the airport and other passengers occasionally intrude, the opening to *Jackie Brown* focuses on Jackie Brown unimpeded, as though, at first, there is nothing else in the world but her, the music, the wall, and the unseen conveyor. Also, the wall behind, dull and uniform in *The Graduate,* is a shifting pattern of pastels in the later movie, serving to draw attention to the bright blue of Brown's uniform (in contrast to Braddock's dark suit). Brown, toward the end, picks up the pace and finally moves quickly and under her own power. She is not, it turns out, exiting the airport, but is hurrying to her job as a flight attendant, running, arriving at the gate just in time to start collecting tickets.

Both characters start their movies within the system, seemingly accepting of their places within it. Both are operating within prescribed roles with limited room for individual action, and they dress for the parts they play or are (in Braddock's case) expected to soon play. In contrast, each, by the ends of the films, will have taken control of situations that, for a large part of each movie, had seemed beyond them. Each, at the ends of the movies, has *really* graduated and is bound for an uncertain future, though each finally trods paths they define themselves—not the mechanical pathways of the films' beginnings. And both endings reprise the songs from the beginnings while the main characters exit automotively—Jackie Brown driving, Ben Braddock (with his "bride") by bus. Both are shown full face at the end, as opposed to the openings, where they are in profile.

In each case, an entire song is played at the start, the scenes tailored and timed to the extradiegetic music, making it another clear marker of directorial intention. "Rather than participating in the action, these theme songs behave somewhat like a Greek chorus, commenting on a narrative temporarily frozen into spectacle."[11] For the older film, the song is Simon and Garfunkel's "The Sounds of Silence"; for Tarantino's, it's Bobby Womack's "Across 110th Street." In the older movie, the song connects the film to a cultural movement that, although implicit in the sensibility of the film, hardly appears—the youth movement of the 1960s. Furthermore, "The Sounds of Silence" was originally recorded with only acoustic instrumentation, the electric backing dubbed in later in a successful attempt to popularize the song, making it signify even more subtly change within a time of change. Written in 1964, "The Sounds of Silence" is also a reaction in lyrics to a time of increasing violence domestically in the United States and through its agents abroad.

"The gilded surfaces of the adults predictably cover empty lives and dead marriages all echoing, in the words of Simon and Garfunkel, the 'sounds of silence.'"[12] There were two Americas apparent to all in the 1960s, that of the World War II generation and that of their children, and they seemed to be drifting apart. The older generation was not yet seen as "the greatest generation" but as a group that had retreated from experience and experimentation in favor of the "gray flannel suit" made famous by the book by Sloan Wilson in *The Man in the Gray Flannel Suit* and the subsequent 1956 Nunnally Johnson movie, the trappings of conformity.

The song is one of disgust at the meek acceptance of the world the singer sees surrounding him, a world to eventually destroy itself and him too. The final lines tell that the truth, the dangers of the situation, of acceptance, of not challenging it, should be plain to see, as long as one is willing to look beyond the mass vision built to deceive oneself and everyone else. When Tarantino made his choice to echo the opening of *The Graduate,* he was certainly aware of "The Sounds of Silence," and not simply of the visual imagery of Nichols's film—after all, he never divorces any aspect of a film from his consideration. Though his own choice of music was necessarily different, then, it was certainly made with Paul Simon's lyrics in mind, with their vision of an urban world (generally a black world) of subways and tenement houses that provides more answers than (by implication) does the white suburbia of *The Graduate.*

Yet the two worlds Tarantino wanted to accent were not the "obvious" ones of the 1960s, but worlds differentiated by a more subtle distinction made up of aspects of class, race, gender, law, and money. Blaxploitation, by contrast to *The Graduate,* the movement in film centering on urban violence, deals with all of these issues, providing a means of introducing the social conflicts underpinning the film. Reference to the genre also allows Tarantino to pay homage to another of the many types of movies he loves.

Like the counterculture movement that many associated with Simon and Garfunkel in the 1960s, blaxploitation movies were more known *about* than experienced by most Americans, even during their heyday in the early 1970s. The Curtis Mayfield song "Superfly" probably reached more ears through the radio than through attendance at the film *Super Fly* (Gordon Parks, 1972); the same could be said for "Theme from *Shaft*" by Isaac Hayes the year before (from a movie also directed by Parks). "Across 110th Street" has probably been heard more often because it was sung and written by Bobby Womack than because of the movie it was composed for, *Across 110th Street* (Barry Shear, 1972). Certainly, as should be clear from any viewing of *Jackie Brown,* Tarantino's use of the song isn't meant to recall particulars of blaxploitation any more than Nichols's use of "The Sounds of Silence" was included to remind people of, say, "the summer of love." In both instances, the cultural situation remains external to the film even though it resonates within it. In both cases, the songs are included as reminders of what's not there and as bows to "realities" outside of the immediate worlds of the characters depicted in the films, but influential upon them, nonetheless.

Tarantino uses other markers for the homage he makes to blaxploitation in *Jackie Brown,* his use of one of its biggest stars (Grier) being one. For the purposes of the film itself, however, the homage isn't homage, but ambiance and background providing understanding of the motivation of the character Jackie Brown, motivation reflected in the lyrics of Womack's song:

Doing whatever I had to do to survive.
I'm not saying what I did was all right,

These are lines right out of Jackie Brown's character—or built into it. As Ken Garner notes, "Far from offering post-modern irony, the homage lays the foundation stone of Jackie's character. In the film *Across 110th Street* Womack's song had accompanied shots of a large black Cadillac driving through rough-looking areas of New York before arriving in Harlem, establishing the environment and world of the film. Tarantino, however, sharpens its focus onto a single character, drawing on the music's cultural associations to locate both his actress's performed past, and her character's background."[13]

Nowhere in Tarantino's various instances of homage is the reference gratuitous, placed simply for the image. Always, the usage has facility in terms of the needs of the film. The only difference here is that the real meaning of the homage is more immediately apparent.

At the end of the movie, as she drives away from Max Cherry's office, Brown listens to Womack's lines before starting to sing along with the chorus. The life of the song, the life of hopelessness, is what she is now driving away from (active, as opposed to the passive movement shown at the film's start), a life every bit as stultifying and unsatisfying as that Braddock flees—more so, in fact, and by far. The real difference between the two situations is that Brown is not able to take her lover along, in part because he never shared in her cultural experience, the life sung about by Womack, and in part because Cherry, unlike Elaine Robinson (Katharine

Ross), isn't willing to cast aside security in favor of passion. Except in his dealings with Brown, Cherry was always on the side of the law, of the "good guys"—the established powers, which had no allure for her. After all, they had threatened to leave her, in her mid 40s, with nothing but a past that negates any gainful future within the straight-and-narrow, just as they had nearly done a few years earlier, when she had previously been caught breaking the law.

Brown's position at that point, significantly, is not unusual. Thousands of people face situations daily that throw them from a tenuous hold on middle-class life down to the very bottom of society. Examples abound: in *Past Due: The End of Easy Money and the Renewal of the American Economy,* Peter Goodman recounts how one woman went from a stable life as a hospital administrator to a homeless shelter—all because she hadn't paid for an auto registration sticker. Her car was towed and, because she was already in credit card debt, she wasn't able to pay to retrieve it. Unable to get to her job, she lost it. Eventually, she wound up in that shelter. Tom Wolfe uses a similar story in his novel *A Man in Full.*

Jackie Brown, at the start of the movie, looks directly into this abyss:

> The best job I could get after my bust was Cabo Air, which is the worst job you can get in this industry. I make about $16,000, with retirement benefits that ain't worth a damn. And now, with this arrest hanging over my head, I'm scared. If I lose my job, I gotta start over again, but I got nothing to start over with.

Her decision to go for her all-or-nothing caper results, as does the confidence built on her success, confidence she exudes at the end of the movie, confidence that comes through even more strongly than her sorrow as she drives away to her new life.

Brown's experiences have prepared her to successfully face a type of life Cherry is not cut out for any longer, a life of danger and intrigue, one with an alien (to him) set of rules. The exchange over the car Brown drives (it belonged to the now-dead Ordell Robbie): Brown now sees it as hers by right of possession, whereas Cherry looks at it solely in terms of law. She has moved into a new conceptual space, one he is unable to enter. In the looks between Cherry and Brown before they part company is a tacit understanding of the words Rick Blaine (Humphrey Bogart) speaks to Ilsa Lund (Ingrid Bergman) in *Casablanca* (Michael Curtiz, 1942), though it is two, rather than three little people, and this time it is the woman's sentiment:

> **Rick**: Where I'm going you can't follow. What I've got to do you can't be any part of. Ilsa, I'm no good at being noble, but it doesn't take much to see that the problems of three little people don't amount to a hill of beans in this crazy world.

Each has to follow his or her own calling, his or her own destiny, and Brown understands in a way that Cherry does not that there is a world of freedom out there for the little person who can act with audacity. She can; he did once, but has decided he is unwilling to again. Though it would certainly make no difference in the larger scheme of things, Brown cannot draw Cherry into either the world of her past or of her future, not for his sake and not for hers. Way too much now separates them, much more than a mutual fondness for the Delfonics can bridge.

There's another parallel to be drawn between *The Graduate* and *Jackie Brown*, one between Jackie Brown and Mrs. Robinson's (Anne Bancroft) daughter, Elaine. Throughout most of each movie, both are about to be trapped, Brown by a society that cares nothing for a middle-aged, single black woman carrying with her what will likely be two serious brushes with the law, and Elaine Robinson by a marriage that will hem her into the love-less life and culture so carefully drawn by the movie. The difference, once more, is that Brown takes matters into her own hands.

Unlike Brown, who created her chance by planning and then action, Elaine Robinson doesn't plan; she simply sees her chance and jumps—a chance her mother (who has said to her husband, when Braddock started screaming "Elaine" and pounding on the glass wall, "He's too late") believes has been removed by the conclusion of the marriage ceremony, an official sealing of her fate. Her next, and last line, said to Elaine as she and Ben turn to flee, is almost a repeat: "Elaine, it's too late." Elaine responds, "Not for me"—exactly what Brown determines, when she decides to work her con. Exactly the attitude that lets Brown take Robbie's car with impunity. Though one plans carefully and the other simply jumps, the sentiment and the result are the same: it is not too late.

None of this could have worked, not even for a director such as Taran-tino, if his casting hadn't been letter perfect, just as Mike Nichols's was with Dustin Hoffman. Casting is no more incidental here than music is, allowing Tarantino to expand his commentaries once more through the personae his actors bring with them to the screen. Pam Grier makes Jackie Brown loom larger than most flight attendants could possibly manage. As M. Keith Booker observes, "The casting of Grier and Forster itself gives the film a nos-talgic flavor, as does the casting of Robert De Niro as Louis Gara, an aging criminal who has decidedly lost his touch."[14]

De Niro, though, is playing against type and is not central to the movie. "Jackie Brown herself *is* the narrative, and so much of Tarantino's magic comes from his devotion to her on the screen, his ability to free her in front of an audience so that she can present herself rather than some performing mask."[15] Another actress, one who did not carry with her status as a genre icon, could never carry off what Tarantino asks of Grier, presenting her out-sized pride along with a real vulnerability (a vulnerability that may stem as much from life experience *after* the heady days of blaxploitation stardom as from acting ability) that makes Brown both believable and likeable. It's appropriate, then, that she starts the movie passively moved on the walkway, but also that she picks the pace up herself, running to get to the gate on time and to start *her* job. It's just as appropriate that the movie ends on her driving, completely in control of her destiny but recognizing (and feeling) the loss that her quest for control has necessitated.

In a certain sense, Grier plays against type as much as De Niro does. Older, of course, than when she played Foxy Brown, Grier's new Brown, Jackie, is not anything of the avenger seen in *Coffy* (Jack Hill, 1973) and in *Foxy Brown* (Jack Hill, 1974) itself. She is not out to set wrongs to right, regardless of her own future, her own well-being. Instead, she is a much more considered and subtly jaded character, one who knows the futility of revenge—at least in terms of changing "the system." She knows that the cheers for Coffy and for Foxy Brown (essentially, the same character) are, for all the good feelings they bring, cheers for failure, for the pimps and dealers defeated will only be replaced by others just as bad. The oppressive culture will continue its destructive ways, hardly even noticing that a few of its tools have been blunted. She can see the failure of such success, so takes another route, the personal one, checking out rather than fighting back.

The importance of the casting of Robert Forster, though noted less frequently, almost equals that of Grier. Though not the star of the movie and having nothing of the iconic power Grier carries from her blaxploitation past, Forster nevertheless had starred in *Medium Cool* (Haskel Wexler, 1969), a movie whose themes inform not only his Max Cherry character but that can help viewers focus on what Tarantino is trying to do through this movie. In the earlier film, Forster plays a news cameraman who uses his camera as a barrier between the world and his person. At the end, the world intrudes on him—roughly—showing the fiction of the barrier and the danger of believing in it. Of course, Max Cherry in *Jackie Brown* manages to maintain a distance that the earlier character, John Cassellis, cannot, but he loses the possibility of a new, self-determined life.

The observer and the observed can never be separated, certainly not in the ways the news media, represented by Cassellis, sometimes believe. *Medium Cool* highlights the interweave between film (of all sorts) and reality, making the point that one cannot live apart from the world, certainly not simply because one is recording the world—or even creating a fictional story. By the same token, movies cannot be seen as simply about the world, or about movies themselves. They are part of the world, part of how people view and construct their lives. Though they don't directly shape reality, they shape our conceptions of reality and so, through that, do play a role in reality and not just in what we conceive.

If nothing else, the casting of Forster is an oblique criticism of those who have claimed that Tarantino makes movies about nothing more than movies. As the movies Tarantino putatively makes movies about are, of course, about something else in the first place, so must be his own films. And the fact that movies (either from audience or creator points of view) cannot insulate one from reality, as *Medium Cool* attempts to show, trivializes attempts to create a movie/reality distinction that does not, at the same time, recognize that, whereas movies are always part of reality, reality is never simply a small part of the movies.

There is a certain postmodern assumption, one finding that a work composed with a postmodern sensibility cannot sustain the type of "close reading" demanded by *Jackie Brown,* not only through its music and casting, but through its insistent referentiality in all areas. Music, as we have seen, is an important part of the movie's referentiality, as it is in all of Tarantino's films, and it can certainly stand close reading. In general, as Alan Barnes and Marcus Hearnes write, a key factor in all of Tarantino's films is "the unrivalled precedence he grants music in the creative process. . . . Tarantino has created some of his most successful sequences by deciding on the right tracks before shooting, or even scripting, has begun."[16] The warp and woof of Tarantino's movies is never accidental, each element having been carefully chosen for the way it will influence each other one in the final cut of the film. There is never a simplistic or even complex postmodern nostalgic pastiche in his movies, though that has become something of the received wisdom of the past few years.[17]

Though it begins as a caper film and as an explicit tribute to the blaxploitation films of Tarantino's preteen years, *Jackie Brown,* soon in the watching, establishes itself as the director's first character-driven movie (and one certainly much more character focused than the source novel, Elmore Leonard's *Rum Punch*). Though he does try to stick to his pared-down version of Leonard's plot, Tarantino doesn't seem able to focus on anything but the relationship between his title character and the bail bondsman Cherry— and probably doesn't want to, anyway. In fact, he adds close to 200 words of dialogue onto the end of the film, taking it beyond Leonard's closing— and he follows that with what is primarily a close-up of Brown driving and then beginning to appear to sing along with Bobby Womack's "Across 110th Street," as we have seen, the movie's real theme song, for an additional 105 seconds.

The Womack song was written for the film *Across 110th Street,* a film whose plot centers on attempts to "secure" a large amount of crime money—just as *Jackie Brown*'s does. The films, however, have very little in common, though they both do follow a certain blaxploitation pattern, one suggested by the lyrics of the song, as Robert Miklitsch writes, of doing "whatever she has to do, whether it's 'alright' or not, to survive, to 'break out' of the ghetto-like circumstances she's found herself in,"[18] a pattern that Novotny Lawrence identifies as key to blaxploitation: "Often times, blaxploitation heroes and heroines use any means necessary to overcome the oppressive establishment. Therefore, the films also feature excessive violence, necessary and significant to the plot. . . . Whether the violence stems from the characters' occupations or emerges as a form of revenge, the motive is always justified by the protagonists' standard of living."[19] 110th Street represents a divide, in the older film, between black and Italian gangs; here, it's the gulf between the white bail bondsman and the black airline hostess.

It is also the line between those with the freedom to make "correct" moral choices and those who believe (often with good reason) that they act from a necessity superseding morality. The latter group is generally composed of individuals representing oppressed minorities, genders, or classes. It is the line between these people and those with what might be called "the luxury of moral choice" that Cherry is unable to cross, at the end.

Though Tarantino clearly wants his main characters to be seen as individuals, they also do represent social positionings. Cherry, a former cop, recognizes the divide and, though he is not willing to step over it, becoming a part of the renegade world, he does have sympathy for it—which is probably why he is a successful bail bondsman in the first place. Like Sam Spade (Humphrey Bogart) in *The Maltese Falcon* (John Huston, 1941), Cherry has enough sympathy for the other side to be able to fall in love with an individual living there (Mary Astor's character Brigid O'Shaughnessey in the older film) but enough sense of himself to know he could not join her there—and survive.

The end of *Jackie Brown*, then, evokes Humphrey Bogart in two roles, Richard Blaine and Sam Spade. Both of these characters are able to control their emotions sufficiently to make the hard choice that they believe, ethically, they must—and they do it with a minimum of fuss, emotion coming more from their eyes than from their actions. Cherry is much the same as they, almost a perfect hardboiled character. Like them, he is willing to bend the rules, but like them, he has a personal moral center that he will not move away from. So it is that Spade's explanation at the end of *The Maltese Falcon* enlightens the ending of *Jackie Brown*:

Spade: I've no earthly reason to think I can trust you. If I do this and get away with it, you'll have something on me that you can use whenever you want to. Since I've got something on you, I couldn't be sure that you wouldn't put a hole in me someday. All those are on one side. Maybe some of them are unimportant. I won't argue about that. But look at the number of them. What have we got on the other side? All we've got is that maybe you love me and maybe I love you.

O'Shaughnessey: You know whether you love me or not.

Spade: Maybe I do. I'll have some rotten nights after I've sent you over, but that'll pass. If all I've said doesn't mean anything to you, then forget it and we'll make it just this: I won't, because all of me wants to regardless of consequences and because you've counted on it the same as you counted on it with all the others. Would you have done this if the falcon were real and you got your money? Don't be too sure I'm as crooked as I'm supposed to be. That sort of reputation might be good business.

The characters of Jackie Brown and Brigid O'Shaughnessey are completely different (O'Shaughnessey is never candid with Spade—in fact, she lies to him often; Brown acts completely in the open with Cherry), but the contrast is significant. Compare the passage above to the following, much more spare exchange, from the end of *Jackie Brown:*

Jackie: I didn't use you, Max.

Max: I didn't say you did.

Jackie: I never lied to you.

Max: I know.

Jackie: We're partners.

Max: I'm fifty-six-years old. I can't blame anybody for anything I do.

Jackie: Do you blame yourself for helping me?

Max shakes his head.

Jackie: I'd feel a whole lot better if you took some more money.

Max: You'll get over that.

Here, it is the woman who is in control in the scene, and not just in a speculative future where the man goes off with the woman. Both Spade and Cherry recognize that they are in love with someone extremely dangerous to them, someone whose power would likely destroy them one day, were they to give in to that love and follow the woman. Lies or honesty on the part of the woman notwithstanding, both men have operated, in relation to these women, with eyes open, knowing exactly who and what they are dealing with. The difference is that Cherry has not only abetted the woman in her scheme (here, the parallel is stronger with Blaine in *Casablanca*), but protects her from police retribution (if only through inaction)—something Spade has not done and will not do.

Jans Wager further explains the parallels between Cherry and Spade:

> Max helps Jackie escape from the economic prison of her existence and takes a fee for doing so. Jackie invites him to go with her to Europe—and for a moment we anticipate he will say yes. Hollywood has firmly indoctrinated us to hope for heterosexual unions at the end of all movies, no matter how unlikely. Perhaps Max ensures his survival by refusing her offer. . . . In the classic film noir *The Maltese Falcon,* Sam Spade (Humphrey Bogart) sends Brigid O'Shaughnessey (Mary Astor) to prison rather than worry about her eventual betrayal of him; Max just lets Jackie go.[20]

In a way, both just let the woman go, though one is headed to prison and the other to Spain. The difference between the women certainly is great, and it does provide the basis for the action Cherry takes that Spade does not:

again, O'Shaughnessey has constantly lied to Spade, so Spade has never had confidence in his position vis-à-vis her or the law. Brown, though she certainly has strung Cherry along (and he knows it—notice, he doesn't agree that she didn't use him, stating only that he had never claimed she did), she has never lied to him—as she asserts and he agrees.

That *Jackie Brown* turns from an Elmore Leonard caper novel into an unrequited love story is certainly clear by the end and through the changes in the ending effected by Tarantino. After the Leonard-penned exchange about using Robbie's car, Tarantino drops Leonard's final lines:

> She walked around to the other side and looked across the low black Mercedes at him. "Come on, Max. I'll take you away from all this."
>
> "Dealing with scum," Max said, "and trying to act respectable." He saw Jackie frown, her nice yes narrowing for a moment. "That's how Ordell described by situation."
>
> "And you like it?" Jackie said.
>
> Max hesitated.
>
> "Where would we go?"
>
> "I don't know," Jackie said, and he saw her eyes begin to smile. "Does it matter?"[21]

For Leonard's characters, the final answer is, probably not. For Tarantino's, it most certainly does matter. In fact, one of the major points of the movie is that it *does* matter, both to Brown and to Cherry—which is why their paths have to split. They are aware, in ways the characters in the book are not, of the consequences of their choices and actions; having made them, they will live by them.

Kill Bill: An Extreme Fairy Tale

Uma Thurman's character, Mia Wallace, in Quentin Tarantino's *Pulp Fiction,* once had a chance for television fame as one of the stars of *Fox Force Five,* a fictional action show about a group of women warriors, each with special talents. Hers were to be knives—and jokes. The pilot didn't fly, not even in fiction, but Tarantino clearly liked the idea of Thurman in such a role. As he explored the possibilities, however, it must have come clear to him that a simple action picture was not going to be enough (a genre never is, for Tarantino, anyway) to encompass what he was beginning to envision.

So he made his movie into, among other things, a fairy tale, perhaps remembering his first experience of *Bambi* (David Hand, 1942) and his youthful desire to bring Bambi's mother back to life. (Something many of us shared. I, too, still remember the shock of her killing; coupled with seeing a drowned boy pulled from the water at about the same time, it profoundly affected my understanding of death—a coupling of a sort Tarantino understands and uses as an underpinning of most of his films.) Jerome Charyn describes what happened:

> *Bambi* broke his heart; it was one of the first films he'd ever seen, together with *Carnal Knowledge* (1971), Mike Nichols's film about a couple of Peter Pans caught in their own juvenile fantasies. Tarantino himself seems stuck between *Bambi* and *Carnal Knowledge.* He had run out of the theater when Bambi's mother died; it marked him as a moviegoer, and froze his sensibility in some crucial way. He's been a griever ever since, mourning Bambi's mom while he's made his films; and his mission has been to turn the 'mother' into a kind of goddess who could bring herself back to life, like Beatrix Kiddo, who rises out of a coma and can only end her carnage *after* she's reunited with her lost child.[1]

As Charyn implies, the influence of the fairy tale and the children's story runs through *Kill Bill.* O-Ren (Lucy Liu), the Tokyo underworld boss, may represent "the revenge of a child on *all* adults,"[2] just as Kiddo (Uma Thurman) herself turns against father figure/lover/pimp Bill.

Whatever generated the idea, it was the idea of the fairy tale (itself often replete with violence), combined with the action genre, that provided Tarantino with the starting point, the vision, for what became *Kill Bill*. Generally speaking, a fairy tale is a story out of folklore concerning impossible creatures (including talking animals) in an ambiguous temporal setting with a happy ending. The action-adventure contains "a propensity for spectacular physical action, a narrative structure involving fights, chases and explosions, and in addition to the deployment of state-of-the-art special effects, an emphasis in performance on athletic feats and stunts."[3] The two are clearly not oppositional, and have been combined many times in cinema, and from its earliest days. The swashbuckling films of Errol Flynn, for example, always had a fairy-tale aspect; both versions of *The Thief of Bagdad* (Raoul Walsh, 1924 and Ludwig Berger, Michael Powell and Tim Whelan, 1940) combine action-adventure and the fairy tale. Other examples are legion.

Stephen Neale claims that "It would be hard to name a New Hollywood action movie that does not overstep the boundaries of reality, or one that does not commingle reality with fantasy. In such films the fantasy elements are consistently situated at the level of the plot, where the violent action takes place, and the dimension of reality (generally tinged with the magic of simplicity) is situated at the level of subplot, where relationships unfold."[4] Why, then, would making another such combination attract Tarantino, a filmmaker who tilts toward the surprising, the different, and not toward the tried and true?

The answer may be that he felt he could use the two genres to explore a creature fairly new to the screen, the action heroine who neither has to be punished for being masculine nor has to twist her femininity into a dominatrix role, a woman who doesn't have to use sex (one way or another) for victory, but who doesn't discard it either. By the time he started thinking seriously about his film, a changing presentation of the heroine was beginning to make its way into Hollywood movies, and this was something Tarantino may have felt he wanted to explore.

In *The Byronic Hero in Film, Fiction, and Television*, published in 2004 just as the *Kill Bill* films were in theaters, Atara Stein posits a change in the view of the female hero that she sees having been growing over the previous decade. After pointing out that there were few genuine female action-movie heroes before Sarah Connor (Linda Hamilton) in the first two *Terminator* (1984, 1991) movies and Ellen Ripley (Sigourney Weaver) of the *Alien* (1979, 1986, 1992, 1997) series, she adds to them Michelle Yeoh's roles in *Tomorrow Never Dies* (1997) and *Crouching Tiger, Hidden Dragon* (2000), Carrie-Ann Moss in the three *Matrix* (1999, 2003, 2003), and Angelina Jolie in *Lara Croft* (2001 and 2003) in addition to the growing number of physically powerful women on television.

Yet it was Connor and Ripley who really set the stage for Beatrix Kiddo. As Jeffrey Brown writes, "Muscular, gun-toting, ass-kicking characters, these women are readily identified as performers of masculinity. Together these two figures have informed . . . the portrayal of subsequence action heroines."[5] They act with men and as men do, pushing away any female characteristics. On the other hand, there are also characters such as the one Pamela Anderson plays in *Barb Wire* (David Hogan, 1996) following a comic book, fetishistic visions of women of impossible bodies and sexual domination. Looking over the range of tough female characters, Brown asks:

> When women are portrayed as tough in contemporary film, are they being allowed access to a position of empowerment, or are they merely being further fetishized as dangerous sex objects? . . . On the one hand, she represents a potentially transgressive figure capable of expanding the popular perception of women's roles and abilities; on the other, she runs the risk of reinscribing strict gender binaries and of being nothing more than sexist window-dressing for the predominantly male audience.[6]

Brown goes on, "A central concern for critics has been the common interpretation of the action heroine as simply enacting masculinity rather than providing legitimate examples of female heroism."[7] This became a central concern for Tarantino, too—as both the *Kill Bill* movies and *Death Proof* show. He rejects the male/female duality so accepted in both older film and popular culture and wants to move to another model, one just beginning to appear. In preparing *Kill Bill*, he saw that, in fact, as Brown also claims, the

> action heroine does enact both masculinity and femininity. But rather than swapping a biological identity for a performative one, she personifies a unity of disparate traits in a single figure. She refutes any assumed belief in appropriate gender roles via an exaggerated use of those very roles.[8]

This conception intrigued Tarantino—and he would likely agree with Brown

> that modern action heroines are transgressive characters not only because their toughness allows them to critique normative standards of femininity but because their coexistent sexuality . . . destabilizes the very concept of gender traits as mutually exclusive.[9]

Duality in action-adventure extends beyond sexuality, allowing Tarantino to texture his discussion through story even further. As Theresa Webb and Nick Browne write:

> violence in the action-adventure genre has two faces. One is righteous, enacted to promote the right and the good, whereas the other is malfeasant, enacted to

meet the often-psychotic needs of an evil fiend. The narrative structuring of violence reflects this distinction in a formulaic, and thus largely unambiguous, manner. . . . Final resolution of the problem always involves a violent exchange between the forces of good and evil, during which time the hero unleashes a wrath of restorative violence bringing about the bang before the calm at the film's conclusion.[10]

The end of *Kill Bill,* however, defies such expectations. Once more, Tarantino builds to up one thing and then switches to another. Instead of the expected fight of epic proportions, we see a simple, though lethal, touching.

If it is true that "how the villain meets his end is a direct reflection of his own evildoing in the story,"[11] then the way he dies is a great blow to Bill's (David Carradine) ego as well as being Kiddo's triumph:

> Though ultimately the one-on-one confrontation of the hero and villain offers the most dramatic resolution of the founding conflict, this combat takes place within a network of social relationships that reveals what ultimately is at stake in their opposition. . . . Ultimately, the villains are tyrannical, opportunistic egoists whose helpers distrust one another, often betray each other, and are treated by the villain as expendable. By contrast, the hero maintains a loyal affiliation with partner or family. . . . The action film works to bring its young audience to adhere to a certain picture of society and justice.[12]

When Kiddo kills Bill, she is at once protecting family and destroying it, a dissonance she recognizes, and the reason she kills Bill with simplicity and, yes, tact rather than with clashing steel and the flow of blood. As he is a moralist, as Tarantino does make pictures reflecting a certain take on society and personal responsibility, is this any surprise?

The idea that *Kill Bill* is a fairy tale as well as part of the action-adventure genre is so obvious that it almost goes without saying. As, of course, is true of *Star Wars* (George Lucas, 1977) and its sequels and prequels. Those put off by the violence of Tarantino's story may not want to place it in the same category with that of Lucas. There is plenty of violence, certainly, in *Star Wars,* but it is sanitized, keeping focus away from the gore. Still, one has only to remember the much more explicit violence of many, many fairy tales to see that, if there is a distinction, it is one merely of degree, not of quality of compassion or of some distinct willingness to revel in gore. As we shall see in this chapter, Tarantino clearly meant for his audience to share in the film as fairy tale, on one level or another. He composed a film that certainly does challenge the genre inside out, but it still retains most of the hallmarks of the fairy tale, even though it does also engage in quite a bit of that genre-bending.

Of course, *Kill Bill* is hardly even the first action-adventure fairy tale involving women protagonists. Both the movie *Charlie's Angels* (McG, 2000) and the television show it is based upon explicitly place their stories within a fairy-tale context, each using a voice-over beginning "Once upon a time." As in the *Charlie's Angels* movie, Tarantino makes use of changes in the image of the action-adventure female star's conception within Western culture (no longer is she simply the masculinized woman of a male/female dichotomy). He also recognizes that there has been "a generational shift in understandings of feminism and femininity; it does not simply reproduce traditional feminine identity but instead often renders it campy or excessive"[13]—among other things.

The prologue before the opening credits of *Kill Bill, Volume 1* is dark, dangerous, and tragic—and in black and white. We have the face of a battered woman, breathing painfully, boots walking, a male voice speaking enigmatically to the battered woman (who is lying on what proves to be a bridal veil), and a hand wiping her face with a handkerchief with the word "Bill" clearly embroidered upon it. The voice talks to "Kiddo," but we don't know that's more than a nickname for The Bride until late in *Volume 2*. She then speaks, "Bill, it's your baby," her words cut off by a gunshot.

This is just the sort of start one might expect from the darkest of film noir, raising the questions that will be answered (to some degree) over the course of the film. But, as soon as the credits have finished, the film (now in color) moves to a fairy-tale suburbia where "The Bells" live in a sea-green house with purple trim and a couple of peaked roofs, children's toys in the yard. Into this fantasy land now steps The Bride, no longer battered and certainly not dead (at this point we in the audience don't know for sure that this is not a flashback, but assume it may be) driving up in what we will later see is an out-of-place, garish pick-up truck with "Pussy Wagon" in huge letters on the back gate.

The Bride is going to quickly demolish the paradise—one of Tarantino's ironies, for The Bride proves to be the movie's protagonist—ruining the home and, as is made explicit, warping the future of the little girl whose mother is soon to be killed by The Bride. The parallels between The Bride and Jeanine Bell, also known as Vernita Green (Vivica Fox), become clear as the movie progresses; the life that Green has is the life that had not been allowed for The Bride. Another irony is that it is The Bride who leaves paradise, driving away in the Pussy Wagon, has clearly now killed two of her antagonists, including green, both crossed off a list that (though we can't see them) obviously contains more names.

If this is a fairy tale, it is a fractured one and a layered one, showing that there really is no "good" to come of any of this, merely a favored protagonist whose sins, from the particular point of view of the storytelling, are excusable. Throughout are hints that, from other points of view, other takes concerning the same incidents, it could be The Bride who is seen as the evil one. In fact, at the end, Bill confronts her directly with the fact that she is a killer, implying that she is no better than he—who already has defined himself that way. The killer/hero, however, is no stranger to the fairy tale and is not something that bothers either Kiddo or the audience very much. Jack, for example, kills a giant, whose home he had invaded after climbing the beanstalk, yet he is the one rewarded. The ambiguity and irony of this, however, is very rarely explored in fairy tales.

It is, in film, though. The fluid doubling and dividing of roles seen throughout *Kill Bill* has a long tradition in Hollywood. Perhaps one of the cleverest and most succinct examples comes from *The Lady from Shanghai* (Orson Welles, 1947), in which Arthur Bannister (Everett Sloane) speaks to his wife as they each seek the "right" image to shoot in a hall of mirrors: "You are aiming at me, aren't you? I'm aiming at you, lover. Of course, killing you is killing myself. It's the same thing. But you know, I'm pretty tired of both of us. You know, for a smart girl, you make a lot of mistakes." These very lines could have been inserted in the final scene of *Kill Bill* without alteration—and they also point out the weakness of the old fairy-tale design's simplistic good/evil dichotomy, one that even *Star Wars* has to breach in order to move beyond the mere formulaic.

Though *Kill Bill* does twist fairy-tale conventions, turning them back on themselves and exposing them as vapid and easily perverted, it still follows Vladimir Propp's "morphology" of the fairy tale[14] rather closely. In fact, though such a structural analysis has proven extremely limited in usefulness in criticism generally, a look at *Kill Bill* through Propp's "functions" does shed light on the movie, especially in relation to the rest of Tarantino's films, showing the distinct aspects of this movie and helping the viewer who is put off by the violence of the story understand that this violence is little more than fairy-tale violence (if there is a difference), but from a fairy tale that recognizes the impossibility of the good/evil dichotomy, the naïve views of individuals, families, and groups fostered by such stories. Tarantino takes the structure of the fairy tale to its extremes (the violence and recognition of good/evil doppelgangers, etc.) and then moves beyond, into a self-aware posture demanding examination of all structures and assumptions, along with self-criticism.

Propp considered his "functions" as having important serial placement. That is, one could not come before its place or after. This becomes problematic in dealing with *Kill Bill,* in which the temporal sequencing of the movie is not that of the "actual" events and in which there are actually doubles (even triples) of most of the functions—and the movie could even be seen as the intersection of a number of fairy tales, further clouding attempts at untangling Tarantino's deliberately obscure weave. Still, it is almost eerie how closely *Kill Bill* follows Propp—it makes one suspect that Tarantino may have been exposed to the "morphology" at some point or another and had used it to build his screenplay. Although this is not likely (or even significant), Tarantino certainly must have set out to construct the movie as a fairy tale, even if subconsciously.

The first of Propp's elements is *absentation* (Propp #1), a family member leaving the home. This act has happened prior to the start of the film—with

The Bride having abandoned her life within the Deadly Viper Assassination Squad, turning her back on the people who had become her family, both metaphorically and (in Bill's case) actually (he fathers her child). On the other hand, what seems a "family" here is more akin to a pimp and his string, especially because Bill sends the Vipers out on "jobs." This parallel is explicitly alluded to in *Volume 2,* in which Kiddo visits Estaban Vihaio (Michael Parks), a brothel owner who had been a father figure to Bill.

As is usual with Tarantino, nothing is quite simple or simply one thing. Kiddo's abstention from the Viper family is not the only abstention significant to this movie; what sparks her quest for revenge is realization that her daughter has been taken from her (she doesn't even know if the daughter is alive). The basic story of the movie, of course, is one of a quest for revenge for the destruction/abduction of the daughter and, finally, of rescue.

Of importance is the fracturing of what had seemed a stable grouping— but this sort of "family" is not something that should be made whole again by the protagonist's return, nor does the protagonist want to return. Instead, she wants to destroy the family, for she feels it has destroyed her own—that is, her daughter, her soon-to-be husband, and the community around them she was trying to build—in the incident partially shown at the beginning of the film. This is the irony here and also what makes Bill and the Vipers so angry; The Bride not only has left but has completely rejected the Viper family by disappearing and by starting this new one. So, we have both the fairy tale and its antithesis involved in *Kill Bill,* starting a twinning of the fairy tale and its darker implications that evolves through the film.

It may seem, at first, that because he starts *in medias res,* Tarantino may not be respecting what was, to Propp, an inviolable ordering. But The Bride certainly has already been given an *interdiction* (Propp #2) or warning by Bill. We in the audience just don't know it yet. It is unveiled to us in *Volume 2,* in a flashback to an earlier time, when Bill was clearly the teacher and Beatrix Kiddo the adoring student. He tells the story of a priest named Pai Mei (Chia Hui Liu), who, feeling an insult by a monk from a different order, appears at the other's temple demanding redress. When his demands were not met, the monks of the order were slaughtered. Though the audience does not see this "warning" until after depiction of the deaths in the church, the parallel is clear and the warning pointed: Bill is telling Beatrix that he is not to be crossed, not even accidentally, though he is also and explicitly speaking of Pai Mei, to whom Kiddo will soon be apprenticed. Adding another layer to the scene, the irony Tarantino builds in here is that the killing technique of Pai Mei, the one he used on the monks, is the one that Kiddo will finally use to kill Bill.

Clearly, the wedding rehearsal that starts the movie is one *violation* (Propp #3) of the interdiction, allowing Bill (in the dual role as family head and villain) to enter the picture—though, except for boots, hand, and wrist, he is not yet fully seen or in any way realized. It's significant that this is a rehearsal (as The Bride herself makes clear at the beginning of *Volume 2*) and not the wedding itself. The real wedding, of course, comes at the end, with the death of Bill, uniting the two characters once more through that killing. In a way, the slaughter at the rehearsal occurs because, as Bill's brother Budd says, The Bride has broken "my brother's heart." She has insulted him in a manner that cannot be forgiven—as if any insult to an egoist such as Bill (as any insult to Pai Mei) could be tolerated, intended or not.

Another of the elements encompassed by the back story is *reconnaissance* (Propp #4) by the villain, an act that generally sparks the action of the story. The Bride has disappeared, so Bill and the Vipers have had to set out to find her. When The Bride asks Bill, at the beginning of *Volume 2*, "How did you find me?" he replies, "I'm the man." He may be, but as the movie shows, being "the man" is no longer enough.

"I wasn't trying to track you down," Bill tells Beatrix close to the end of the movie, "I was trying to track down the fucking assholes I thought killed you." This search certainly touches on the necessity of meeting the needs of Propp's recognizance function for the purposes of the story. One of the interesting facets here, of course, is that The Bride herself also becomes a villain, once she comes out of her coma, setting off on her own reconnaissance quite early on, making her own list of people to kill.

In *delivery* (Propp #5), the villain Bill utilizes the information gained in #4. He has discovered the whereabouts of The Bride and now can attempt to kill her, leaving the viewer momentarily sure that he has and that the rest of the movie will be back story. But the real story is of The Bride herself engaging in delivery, getting revenge and retrieving her daughter.

Trickery (Propp #6) is also found in the back story. The Bride has trusted Bill, her love for him blinding her; she never has recognized that he is deceiving her and using her. Taking the baby, after he has "killed" The Bride, becomes one more bit of trickery. Bill earlier tricked Beatrix when he shows up at the wedding, stating that he will try to be nice but with absolutely no intention of being so.

One of the aspects of The Bride's character, as shown in the movie at least, is forthrightness. Her honesty begins when she discovers she is pregnant, after which her only trickery is the fake identity she constructs in El Paso, and that is based solely on desire to protect her daughter. After seeing the results of her pregnancy test, Kiddo tries to get out of the confrontation with Karen Kim (Helen Kim), who has been sent to kill her, without any more killing. She has other concerns now. However, once she has been shot by Bill and her baby either killed or abducted, she is willing to kill again and never denies it. She is clear and open in her intent.

Though she later turns against him, The Bride has been *complicit* (Propp #7) with Bill, becoming an important part of the Vipers, taking willing part in nefarious activities. This is extremely important to the ending of the film, with the idea that, at a certain base level, Kiddo and Bill are the same—even down to the level of wanting to protect and nurture their daughter and not trusting the other to do so. Again, Beatrix Kiddo, even though she is a mother, is a killer, responsible for the deaths of dozens of people. She once *worshipped* Bill (witness the expression on her face as she watches him across the campfire in *Volume 2*) and would have done anything he said—even if it meant being away from him, as happens when he tells her to stay with Pei Mai as his pupil.

The start of the film, the attack on the wedding rehearsal, shows the *villainy* (Propp #8) of Bill through the killing of the entire wedding party—and the near killing of Kiddo. This element is also connected to the *lack* The Bride feels when she wakes from her coma and discovers that she is no longer pregnant . . . and that she does not have her child who, she assumes until discovering differently at the end of the film, did not survive. Bill has both acted in an evil manner and has taken from Beatrix the very thing that had changed her (or so she thought) from a killer into a family-centered and caring person. Because of its importance to the story, it would almost be assumed that a filmmaker such as Tarantino would choose this high point of Bill's villainy to start the film *in medias res.*

After awakening, The Bride realizes what has been done to her by the Vipers, corresponding to Propp #9, *mediation.* This is a key moment in the story, for it is the decision point for the protagonist. In the sequencing of *Kill Bill,* this moment is delayed (as it is temporally delayed by Kiddo's coma), though its result is known immediately after the credits when The Bride attacks and kills Vernita Green—and when, directly after that, her list of those she plans on killing is briefly and partially shown. Chapter 2 is dedicated to developing audience understanding for The Bride's need to mediate the stream of events that has passed her by, making us accepting of—and complicit with—the violence that is going to follow. The progression is useful for each step of the way the audience becomes more attuned to Kiddo and angrier over the outrages against her.

Before she can embark on *counter-action* (Propp #10), The Bride must first will herself into a state of preparedness. She must gain control over her body again and then work out her plan—which will, as we discover, lead her to the gaining of her magic device (a sword, or so it seems) and then to the killing of the people who attacked the wedding party. Even as she struggles to move toes that have been inoperative through the years of her coma, we learn through a voiceover that she is already planning, working out the order of her actions.

The Bride's "home," the clinic where she had been kept while in her coma, is the place she leaves, fulfilling the next function, though she has actually left home earlier, by leaving the Vipers. In both cases, her *departure* (Propp #11) is from a perversion of the concept of the home, making it a place of no safety at all. Safety is what she wants, however, and what she had hoped to created in El Paso (another home she departs from, though she is forcibly removed). Here again, we have Tarantino's layering on the fairy-tale formula.

For The Bride, simply getting her limbs moving again and herself out of the clinic is a *test* (Propp #12), one of many that Kiddo will pass before she is shown worthy of that supposedly magic sword. The last of these comes in her conversation with sword-maker Hattori Hanzo (Sonny Chiba) himself, and that follows an animated (anime) version of the story of O-Ren Ishii, where she too "passes" a test, making her a viable and worthy opponent for The Bride.

The Hanzo test is subtle, taking place in Hanzo's sushi bar. Though both Hanzo and Kiddo recognize that some sort of test is taking place, each keeps up a genial facade. Kiddo, who speaks Japanese, pretends to ignorance of the language, whereas Hanzo, who clearly knows she is hiding something, patronizes her as a tourist:

> **Hanzo**: You say Japanese word like you Japanese.
>
> **Kiddo**: Oh, now you're making fun of me.
>
> **Hanzo**: No, no, no, no: Serious business. Pronunciation very good. You say "arigato" like we say "arigato."

Once it is established that he is the one she has come to see, conversation slips into Japanese, and to a ritualistic-sounding series of questions, ended only when Hanzo switches back into English. A final test comes when Hanzo shows Kiddo his swords and allows her to handle one. He then says it is funny that she likes samurai swords whereas he likes baseball. He then takes a ball from his tunic and, after showing it to her, throws it at her—and she neatly slices it in half in the air, passing his final test. All that is left is for her to reveal (or for him to intuit, as it turns out) the name of the person she wants to fight. That confirmed, he agrees to make a sword for her.

The Bride shows Hanzo, the man who will create it, that she is deserving of the sword through her *reactions* (Propp #13) to that series of small tests, and by Hanzo's reaction, in turn, when he realizes just who it is The Bride wants to set out to kill. Except for the fight with Green, in a way, everything that Kiddo has done up to this point concerns tests, verbal, physical, and psychological.

The Bride *acquires* (Propp #14) the sword from Hanzo, who calls it the finest he has ever made. Now she is prepared for the first of her combats—one that we in the audience know she will win, for we have already seen her succeed in her subsequent combat with Vernita Green.

The sword, as one would expect from Tarantino, doesn't prove to be the only magic device Beatrix gains, if it is magic at all, though it is treated so throughout the first movie and through most of the second. In fact, there is another magic "device"—a skill first mentioned when Bill and Beatrix sit around the campfire and Bill relates the story of Pai Mei. He ends, "and so began the legend of Pai Mei's five-point-palm exploding-heart technique." It is this technique, which we don't "see" Pai Mei teaching Beatrix (and which he did not teach Bill and which Bill assumes was not taught to Beatrix), that is finally used to kill Bill and not the sword. Of course, if there is a real magical "device" in the movie, it is this. Though Kiddo wields it expertly, the sword remains just a sword. Its magic turns out to be metaphorical, stemming from the fact that it has been made at all. It provides a magical aura to she who uses it because it exists, not for its qualities that, though perhaps greater than those of any other sword, are not of a different order.

The Bride next goes from Okinawa to Tokyo to find O-Ren Ishii. She uses the same fictional airline "Air O," her magic carpet that has transported her first to Okinawa and is now taking her to Tokyo. She accepts its *guidance* (Propp #15) of her movement toward her destination as she has, in the past, accepted the guidance of Bill and Pai Mei—and even of Hanzo. The two scenes of purchasing Air O tickets aren't needed, in fact, except to draw attention to the air flights, which are detailed through kitschy reference to the maps and montages used in classical Hollywood films in order to show movement over long distances. The various vehicles Kiddo drives could also be seen in terms of guidance, especially the Pussy Wagon and the Karman Ghia she speaks to the audience from at the start of *Volume 2.*

The most spectacular *struggle* (Propp #16) in the movie is The Bride's fight against O-Ren and what seems at one point to be her endless supply of minions. Nothing in either volume of the film (and nothing in any other Tarantino movie, not even the climactic chaos in *Inglourious Basterds*) matches the extent of the mayhem presented here, yet this is only one of five struggles against the group who destroyed the life she had been trying to build. Of course, in true contrarian fashion, the climactic struggle, the one with Bill himself, proves to be no real physical struggle at all—in comparison, at least, to this one, at the end of *Volume 1.*

The Bride is *branded* (Propp #17) through her wounding by Bill, through the shooting shown at the beginning of *Volume 1.* This changes her, bringing her back to the lethal stance she had abandoned on discovering her pregnancy (significantly, she does not believe that her pregnancy came successfully to term during her coma). That pregnancy, of course, was itself a change-incurring branding, again showing the type of doubling that Tarantino likes so well.

The Bride defeats O-Ren, providing the *victory* (Propp #18) that concludes *Volume 1.* It is this that gives her the confidence she exhibits in her fight with Green—and the overconfidence that leads to her defeat by Budd (Michael Madsen) who, in turn, acts just as foolishly. Instead of killing her, he accedes to Elle Driver's (Daryl Hannah) thirst for torturous revenge (not suspecting that she's not on his side at all) and buries her alive. This also sets up the expectation that there will be an even more spectacular confrontation when Kiddo actually manages to run Bill to ground.

At the very end of *Volume 1*, Bill asks Sofie Fatale (Julie Dreyfus), whom Kiddo has left alive but maimed, what Beatrix had told her. The last line of the movie is his question, "Is she aware her daughter is still alive?" This jolt for the audience is a restorative, a *resolution* (Propp #20) justifying all she has done as a quest (though she doesn't yet know it) to rescue her daughter and making this the central theme of *Volume 2*. In addition, the defeat of O-Ren is itself a message to Bill that his spell over The Bride is conclusively broken. Kiddo leaves Fatale not simply to inform Bill of what has happened but to show him that his power over her is gone. However, through his question about their daughter, Bill is also indicating that he knows differently. It is certainly not the case that he no longer has power over her. He will, as long as their daughter remains with him.

Almost the last scene of *Volume 1* is Kiddo's *return* (Propp #20) to America, again on Air O. There are returns throughout both movies, however, there is indication that no one tale in the movie is simply its own but is an overlay on many others. No "real" tale, after all, follows a simple pattern of beginning, middle, and end but is an amalgam of many tales, one for each character and situation, none ending (except, of course, in death), all evolving.

In a way, the return home, for The Bride, is to Bill and not to their daughter. She cannot go directly there, however, because of her "unfinished business" with Budd and Elle Driver. Budd, however, turns the tables on her, the pursuer becoming the *pursued* (Propp #21) and quickly captured. Overcome by Budd, Kiddo is soon buried alive. Along with everything else, the rebirth motif (the second of the movie, of course—again, Tarantino doesn't build without redundancy) is clear right here, and this also becomes a reiteration of the sequence of gaining one of the magical devices, for here she loses one putative magical device, the sword and then does use lessons from Pai Mei (the source of her second and "real" magical device) to escape the grave. Kiddo only regains the sword during the fight that ensues upon her return to Budd's house-trailer from the grave.

Coming "back from the grave," The Bride leaves Elle Driver for dead after fighting Driver with Budd's sword and gouging out her remaining eye. That sword was also made by Hanzo and had been given to Budd by Bill. In victory, Kiddo reclaims her own sword. Here, in effect, she *rescues* (Propp #22) herself, allowing the movie to regain its "present," coming back to the time of *Volume 2*'s prologue and from Kiddo's voiceover introducing the flashback scenes concerning her confrontations with Budd and Elle Driver.

The Bride, as she talks to the audience, is on her way to Mexico, *arriving unrecognized* (Propp #23) at the brothel of Esteban Vihaio, where she asks for Bill. On hearing her question, Vihaio quietly responds, "Ah, you must be Beatrix," the first time her first name is mentioned, the first overt verbal "recognition" of her as a named individual and not simply a grouping of characteristics.

When, on Vihaio's direction, Kiddo does finally confront Bill, she finds him ever *false* (Propp #24) as he presents his case, making himself out to be the aggrieved party after allowing their daughter, called "B. B.," to be revealed to Beatrix. Not himself trustworthy, he cannot expect another to be, overcoming that problem (as he questions Kiddo) through a truth serum he shoots into her. He then talks about superheroes and alter egos while the serum takes effect . . . talking about how Superman is the only one whose base identity is the superhero . . . for the others, it is the opposite. Clark Kent, in other words, is the disguise, and Superman the real person. His point is that Beatrix could only disguise herself as Mrs. Tommy Plympton, as Arlene Plympton of El Paso, Texas. She would still be Beatrix, that deadly woman/weapon. "I'm calling you a killer, a natural-born killer. You always have been, and you always will be." He batters her with questions she clearly doesn't want to answer.

Then he asks, "Why did you run away from me?" Of course, the fact of being pregnant had changed her outlook and her plans and had forced her to leave both Bill and the violent life he represented. She didn't tell Bill at the time because Bill would have claimed the child, and Beatrix "didn't want that." Bill replies that it had not been her "decision to make." She agrees, but says she made it for her daughter. She says she had to choose and chose her daughter rather than Bill and the life he led.

Trying to find the people who he thought had killed Beatrix, Bill had eventually learned that she was still alive and living in El Paso, living a life completely at odds with that Bill had created for her. Seeing that she was not only alive but pregnant, Bill "overreacted," as he says, taking her rejection of him as the insult it was, as an insult that he doesn't believe had to have been made ("proving" he was right by taking what was clearly good care of the child). "There are consequences to breaking the heart of a murdering bastard. You experienced some of them." He doesn't excuse himself; she knew his nature when she left, just as he knows hers.

Throughout the last chapter, Beatrix is *tasked* (Propp #25) by Bill to prove herself—and to disprove him. His confidence and control place her in a supplicant position, beginning at the time of her entrance into his rooms, where she is confronted by B. B. with a toy gun. The parents talk of competing through Hanzo swords and later do use them briefly, but their real competition has been going on quite a bit longer and is competition over who will have B. B., the "stolen" child—rather, who is worthy of raising B. B.

Though we've known throughout both volumes that the *solution* (Propp #26) to the quest is to kill Bill, the audience has learned (throughout this movie and through knowledge of his past ones) never to trust Tarantino, a storyteller with always at least one more surprise in his bag of tricks. So it is that we don't really know if Bill's death will be the result. When the verbal sparring moves to actual swordplay, what the outcome will be is still up in the air. In the last instance of their conflict, Beatrix literally sheathes Bill's sword (still in his hand) in her scabbard and uses the surprise accompanying that action to avail herself of the "real" magical device, Pai Mei's "five-point-palm exploding-heart technique." The sexual imagery of the sword and scabbard is quite plain—but it is beside the point. Yes, Kiddo uses a symbol of her womanhood to both emasculate Bill (once he is "inside" her, he no longer has any vitality) and to disempower him. She is now free to act for the first time since they've been together—and she does, first with a look of anger and determination, then viewing what she has done with sorrow.

Only now, in the space between the killing act and his actual death, does Bill finally *recognize* (Propp #27) Kiddo:

> **Bill**: Pai Mei taught you the five-point-palm exploding-heart technique?
>
> **Beatrix**: Of course he did.
>
> **Bill**: Why didn't you tell me?
>
> **Beatrix**: I don't know. Because I'm a bad person.
>
> **Bill**: Naw. You're not a bad person. You're a terrific person. You're my favorite person. But, every once in a while, you can be a real cunt.

Which is exactly what she has been and why she has been able to defeat him. She is a full woman, not a stereotype of culturally defined attributes nor their forced opposite. She doesn't need to be judged by the standards of men or of women, but encompasses both, discarding the limiting trappings their culture has provided to each. In other words, she doesn't have to use sex (her own or turning his against him) to defeat him. She can, as her act entrapping his sword shows, but she does not choose to. And she, through the understanding of herself given by him (who is still clearly her mentor), finally reconciles what had appeared to be the contradictions within herself, within her desire for a new life of peace with her daughter and her need for violence. Bill's epithet, considered by many to be the worst word in the English language and the deadliest insult one can make to a woman, becomes here the sign of ultimate empowerment, of a fully realized sexual being beyond stereotypes—and of rejection of limitation due to sexual status. So she smiles, accepting the compliment as Bill meant it.

At the same time as the "revelation" of Kiddo's real being, we have here the *exposure* (Propp #28) of Bill for what *he* is (and certainly not as the equal of Beatrix) and of the evil within both of them. Here again, Tarantino provides the twinning seen so often throughout his films, making it clear through the affection evinced between the two, shown in the moment between the killing action and Bill's death, that these two are, in many ways, the same. The name of their child, B. B., indicates this as well, through its pairing of their identical first initials. Bill has shown that he has a nurturing side—that is why Kiddo has loved him, and that is what has allowed him to succeed so well in raising what is clearly a well-adjusted and happy child. He has been both mother and father to B. B., rising above sexual stereotypes himself. Yet he is not what Kiddo is, can't become that "perfect" being who can put the world to rights, for he is not enough of a woman to do what she has done, to turn the scabbard into a protective device allowing space for use of an "ultimate" weapon.

Throughout this movie, there has been *transfiguration* (Propp #29). The final one, however, comes as Kiddo wipes the tears from her eyes after Bill has collapsed, clearly dead. She is now complete and whole, established into a position in which she can assume her role of mother, as she does, carrying B. B. in her arms out to her car. Embracing her womanhood, her role as a mother, she rises above it, becoming the being who can both cry and laugh, who can understand loss even as she causes it, who can sacrifice and gain. The final title card presents her as a lioness, but she has become more than that, rising far above (though embracing and encapsulating) gendered segregation. Fully equal to anyone, she has not had to sacrifice any aspect of her being, be that called "feminine" or anything else.

Bill has clearly received his *punishment* (Propp #30) by this point, his death. In addition, he is punished by the knowledge of his impending death and the means. Kiddo kills him through a technique he did not know she knew. In his arrogance, the arrogance of a pimp, he has felt he knows everything about her. But she has held back from him in the past, keeping the full extent of her possibilities from him, hiding, first, that she controls a weapon beyond his skill and, second, that earlier deception, that she carried a child she does not want him to have. *She* wants to have the child; he tears that from her, quite literally. To regain her own being as a woman, she has to remedy that situation. Punishing him becomes merely a necessary byproduct of re-establishing the proper order of the world.

When I first considered *Kill Bill* in terms of Propp's functions, I felt that *wedding* (Propp #31) was the only one that is elided. The Bride, remember, never does marry. Significantly, even the massacre at the Two Pines church happens at the rehearsal, not the actual wedding ceremony. But, after going through the film more carefully with Propp in mind, I discovered that Tarantino has, even here, continued his doubling. Bill and Beatrix, of course, are wedded through violence, through his death, and through B. B. And Beatrix does assume her "rightful" place (something the ceremony is meant to establish) as mother or, more accurately, as parent. That last title card makes this (and the fact of fulfilling this last function) clear: "The lioness has rejoined her cub." In other words, the proper order has been re-established; all is right with the world. And this, of course, is what a wedding signifies in fairy-tale worlds.

The proper order or the world, though, is not the one we would expect, is not one of male and female roles as descended to us through Western culture. Instead, it is a much more primal and unlimited order, one based on the person and not on imposed gender roles. A number of women have told me, with slight wonder in their voices, that their teenaged daughters and nieces love this movie, that they watch it again and again. Some have said that they started watching with them and have found themselves drawn in too. The attraction, I think, is that Kiddo can fully realize her identity as a woman without assuming a feminine role defined exclusively by men. She doesn't have to become a dominatrix, for example, though she is an action hero. She doesn't have to flash her feminine attributes through scanty outfits or seductive behavior to somehow "counter" her toughness. Confident in her own being, she doesn't have to fight the sexism around her, defeating it instead through the essence of her own being, not by changing the signs of it or by seeing it through the actions or possessions of others. Take sexual advantage (or any other sort) of her and she may kill you, but if she needs your "Pussy Wagon" or anything else you've got, she will use it, sexist accoutrements notwithstanding.

After all, she is the one who is making their old meanings meaningless. Certainly, she don't need no stinkin' definitions.

Death Proof: Making Movies

In talking about *Grindhouse,* the double feature comprised of his own *Planet Terror* and Quentin Tarantino's *Death Proof,* Robert Rodriguez says, "I was tired of traditional movie formats and wanted to do something new and different."[1] What the two of them did, instead, was make the old new and different. Though the concept did not prove a complete success, it does show that there's much more that could be done with movies than a rigid adherence to convention allows.

Death Proof is the movie many people who have never seen his films or who don't watch them carefully believe Tarantino always makes, a movie exploiting interest in gore, violence, and suspense. A movie about movies. In fact, it is nothing like his other movies, but it has provided a chance for the director and his audience to explore aspects of the lower reaches of his industry with the broader purpose of examining the value in and values of filmmaking. From making the film appear to be much worn and poorly spliced, from casting young people whose parents have recognizable names as actors, from incorporating the conventions of at least two narrow genres, and from making what Carol Clover calls the "Final Girl" into a trio involved with filmmaking, Tarantino develops a way to talk about the entire business of filmmaking through film itself, and then to examine the relation of its products to the "real" world.

This is not a film that did well at the box office. In all of his other movies, Tarantino made storytelling his priority. Here, he focused more on making movies, a distinction likely lost on fans looking for the intricate narrative structures of his earlier films. Had he simply used the language of film to prop up his story in making this movie, adding in the language of filmmaking, he might well have matched his other efforts. But his priorities weren't quite straight; in his other movies he seems to have had something to say first, then develops a story for saying it. Only then does he come up with the way of telling it. Here, though he certainly is saying something, he focuses too immediately on the way of telling it, leaving the story for last. The result is a bifurcated film (both internally and externally as part of the double-bill release *Grindhouse*) that confused viewers in the theater even more than *Pulp Fiction* did but that does not weave and reweave, creating a whole the way the earlier film does. Though perfection was never its purpose—the film is meant to be flawed—*Death Proof* does not make use of its flaws quite deftly enough to establish itself as the movie about movies, the "metamovie" it strives to be.

To see what Tarantino is trying to do, one need only look at the contrast between the two sets of "girls" featured in the film. The first set's members are, by and large, rather frivolous. Dope-smoking, drinking, and somewhat sexually naïve young women, they are not nearly as aware of the rest of the world as they think they are. Sidney Poitier's daughter Sydney plays the leader of the group, "Jungle Julia" Lucai, a hip Austin, Texas, DJ sensation heavily promoted by her station. Cheryl Ladd's daughter (and Alan Ladd's granddaughter) Jordan plays Shanna, another of the trio. In providing Lucai with her DJ profession, Tarantino helps establish his bona fides as a knowledgeable student of the slasher genre that marks the first half of the film, making sly reference to at least two earlier slasher films, *The Fog* (John Carpenter, 1980), in which Stevie Wayne (Adrienne Barbeau) works as a DJ, and *Texas Chainsaw Massacre 2* (Tobe Hooper, 1986), in which Vanita "Stretch" Brock (Caroline Williams) is also a DJ. Both of these, but Brock more forcefully, play Final Girl roles, something that might be expected for Lucai—though, in typical Tarantino fashion, that is not to be.

Supposedly a professional with extremely good knowledge of popular music, Jungle Julia still manages to slightly goof up the name of the 1960s British pop band "Dave Dee, Dozy, Beaky, Mick, and Tich" three times. This drives home the point that she is not quite as knowledgeable and worldly as she might appear. She also, sounding authoritative, makes the preposterous claim that Pete Townshend would have been better off joining that band rather than staying with The Who. As songwriter and guitarist, Townshend pretty much defined The Who, a band with one of the most successful histories in all of rock and roll. As the band's leader, Townshend was able to turn his group toward rock opera, attempting musical explorations much more challenging than he could have done if he had joined an established pop band focused on catchy three-minute hits and with what amounted to its own in-house songwriters. In other words, Jungle Julia doesn't always know what she is talking about.

The "girls" of the second half, on the other hand, know exactly what they are talking about and exactly what they are doing—and just how good they are at it. One of them, the stunt specialist Zoë Bell plays . . . Zoë Bell, a stunt specialist, completing a melding of character and performer important to an understanding of the film's point about female competence. Tarantino got interested in doing more with the stunt community during the making of *Kill Bill,* which overlapped with the making of the documentary *Double Dare* (Amanda Micheli, 2004),[2] a film about stuntwomen Jeannie Epper and Zöe Bell. Bell worked on *Kill Bill,* and part of the *Double Dare* details the process of her hiring and some of her stunts as a double for Uma Thurman on that film.

Bell's inclusion in *Death Proof* signals that this second group of "girls" is meant to represent the "real thing" on all levels; these are not women to be messed with carelessly. Each is a professional, two of them in stunt work, one in makeup, and one as an actress and model. The stress on the significance of professionalism in its own right has already been underscored in the movie, through that casting of the children of famous stars. Both Poitier and Ladd easily show, in *Death Proof,* that they are competent actors, but the facts of their parentage allow the film to use them as an additional offset between the first group of girls and the second, in which it is the seasoned professional, Bell, who leads the group, not the pampered Lucai or someone like her, who probably achieved her position through something other than competence (though she may not even realize it). Certainly, as the film makes clear, Lucai is no expert in her field.

Even Lee Montgomery (Mary Elizabeth Winstead), dressed in her costume as a cheerleader and the least tough of the second group of "girls" (and the only one not present for the chase scenes), is clearly made out to be a confident professional when she sings skillfully along with her iPod and then again when she asks Abernathy Ross (Rosario Dawson) to pick up the new issue of a magazine that has in it pictures she modeled for. The later conversation about sex and men as the four women ride in the car, reflecting back to an earlier one by the "girls" in Austin, also demonstrates a much higher level of sophistication and experience compared to that found in the earlier group.

Stuntman Mike (Kurt Russell), seeing the second group of "girls" by chance and through his perverted sexual prism, doesn't know what he is getting into—though he should have suspected. He follows three of them to the airport to pick up the fourth (Bell) and takes photos of them cavorting in the parking lot as they make their way back to the car. Though they are young and energetic, these are not schoolgirls. Skillful and confident in their movements, and even in their play, they clearly understand their relationships to the world around them and show confidence in their ability to meet any challenge that comes to them. These are not the weak and even foolish females Stuntman Mike has encountered before.

On the other hand, it may just be their enthusiasm and confidence of all the "girls" (somewhat misplaced, in the first of the two groups) that sparks Stuntman Mike's fascination. The five young women he killed in Texas also exhibited a certain *joie de vivre* that Stuntman Mike (whose initials are appropriate for a man who likes to harm others while he is harming himself, though less severely) likely hates, finds threatening, and wants to destroy.

Like everything else here, Stuntman Mike serves a dual function. First, he is an out-and-out psychopath. Texas Ranger Earl McGraw (Michael Parks) describes what he thinks Stuntman Mike is and why he does what he does (though he admits he cannot prove it):

> McGraw: Well, I'd guesstimate it's a sex thing. The only way I can figure it. High-velocity impact, twisted metal, busted glass, all four souls taken exactly the same time. Probably the only way that diabolical degenerate can shoot his goo.

At the same time, Stuntman Mike stands in for a society not yet comfortable with young, confident (again, a little overconfident, for the first group) women—be they in process toward reaching their self-assured maturity or having arrived there already.

Rather than psychoanalyzing Stuntman Mike, however, it might be best to look at him, his car, and the two groups of girls within the framework of the "slasher" subgenre that Tarantino is using here as his launching pad: "At the very bottom, down in the cinematic underbrush," writes Clover, "lies—horror of horrors—the slasher (or splatter or shocker) film: the immensely generative story of a psycho killer who slashes to death a string of mostly female victims, one by one, until he is himself subdued."[3] The one who does that is, generally, that Final Girl. This is a type of movie better known of than known and whose more mainstream cousins generally change some of the rules, moving themselves out of the genre and into something more palatable to general audiences. Yet *Death Proof* is not a slasher movie either, not really, for it is a bit too self-conscious for that, and as usual for Tarantino, it contains things completely alien to the genre. But it does start from the genre and does hold to quite a number of its basic tenets. Tarantino recognizes the importance of a standard formula to that genre and knew he would bend it:

> The thing that makes the slasher film work so well is how similar all the films are to each other. I mean, that's actually one of the comforting things about the genre. That's why you can write about it with a very big picture—because so many movies fit.
>
> It's such a specific thing that if you try to fuck up that balance, you might not be fucking it up to a good effect—you're just kind of fucking it up. I just realized, oh man, this is just going to be too reflective. If I try to do it as a real slasher movie, it's just going to be too early 1980s reflective, and that's not what I do—even though people accuse me of doing that. That is not what I do; I reinvent.[4]

Tarantino and Clover clearly agree about the slasher movie, Clover providing what could be seen as amplification to Tarantino's comments: "Students of folklore or early literature recognize in the slasher film the hallmarks of oral story: the free exchange of themes and motifs, the archetypal characters and situations, the accumulation of sequels, remakes, imitations. This is a field in which there is in some sense no original, no real or right text, but only variants, a world in which, therefore, the meaning of the individual example lies outside itself."[5] By wanting to reinvent only, as he is aware, Tarantino takes his work out of the slasher subgenre and into his own metagenre storytelling scheme. That doesn't bother him, though; he never intended to make a slasher film in the first place, only to draw attention to the subgenre in the course of exploring in film his own thoughts about film.

Clover, who sees the subgenre as descending quite directly from *Psycho* (Alfred Hitchcock, 1960), identifies five necessary and similarly shaped components to the slasher film: the killer, the locale, the weapons, the victims, and shock effects. As important as any of these (more important, perhaps, to Tarantino—for it is not only part of the genesis of this movie but of *Kill Bill*), and discussed extensively by Clover though she doesn't include it on the list in her article, is the Final Girl.

As Clover states, the "notion of a killer propelled by psychosexual fury . . . has proved a durable one."[6] Like Norman Bates (Anthony Perkins) in *Psycho,* such characters move to kill rather than seduce those women who arouse their sexual appetites. The two alternatives rarely exist together in the genre; rape and death as a single event is unseen in the slasher film.

Though the "girls" in the first half of the movie are uneasy with Stuntman Mike, they don't see him as a serious sexual threat. Arlene (Vanessa Ferlito) even provides him with a lap dance to the Coasters' "Down in Mexico," a song that could itself be about a lap dance, though the term itself is probably much newer, for the song contains the line "And then she did a dance that I'd never seen before." Stuntman Mike, old enough to be Arlene's father and worse for the wear, reacts as though there's nothing *he* hasn't seen before. Though the protocol of the lap dance is for the man to do nothing, Stuntman Mike seems even more relaxed than might be expected, more amused than aroused.

In the bar with the girls, Stuntman Mike is every inch the outsider, much older, scarred and weather beaten, certainly different than anyone the girls have encountered before, certainly different than the weak boys they fool around with almost as an afterthought (boys who smirk, in their ignorance, at Stuntman Mike). Stuntman Mike hasn't even much success as a stuntman to brag about. His list of credits doesn't raise a flicker of interest, the shows having disappeared many years previously. He sticks out not just in the bar, but in Austin, a town with a young beat that has passed Stuntman Mike by. So different is he that Vanessa actually makes note of him earlier in the day, when she sees him cruising the street in his muscle car—only to have him speed away with a look-at-me squeal of tires once he's sure she's watching. He's a loner and a misfit, the complete opposite of the crowd-loving, rather standard-issue (though prettier than most) girls.

Clover centers the locale of the slasher movie on a specific "Terrible Place." In this case, that place is a black 1970 Chevrolet Nova—later in the movie, it is replaced by a 1969 Dodge Charger, also black. This is the "death-proof" instrument of death that sparked the film's title. It is death proof for the driver, but not for anyone else—in it, as Pam (Rose McGowan) finds out after she accepts a lift home, or outside of it, as the others in the first group of girls discover minutes later. The car is a moving house of horror.

One of the oddities of slasher films is that guns play a small role in them. Perhaps this is because shooting someone is too quick, and the death, in our movie conventions, is not generally very bloody. Except for knives, few other traditional weapons are favored. Almost anything else, however, becomes a legitimate means for killing, both by the killer and by those he (or she, for it can be either) is trying to murder. In *Death Proof*, Tarantino chooses to make the car the weapon, allowing him to cross genres with the chase movie, reviving the dying use of the car chase and paying tribute to *Vanishing Point* (Richard Sarafian, 1971) and other examples of the early 1970s chase genre. And, of course, allowing him to work with veteran stunt drivers such as Jeff Dashnaw (whose career started back a quarter of a century before *Death Proof*) and Buddy Joe Hooker (who has been around even a decade longer).

Almost the only weapon besides a car in *Death Proof* is Kim's (Tracey Thoms) "roscoe" (perhaps a deliberate bending of the slasher film conventions, especially now that, in the second half of the film, the slasher subgenre has been completely abandoned). Though she does manage to wing Stuntman Mike with it, her real weapon also proves to be the car, a 1970 Dodge Challenger just like the one from *Vanishing Point*. In addition, Bell does attack Stuntman Mike with what appears to be a length of pipe. The only other weapons are the fists of the three girls and Abernathy's foot, which administers the *coup de grace*.

Tarantino says, "By the time you're in the third act of the third act, you're not watching a horror movie anymore, you're watching a balls-out action movie."[7] He keeps it simple, too, concentrating on the chase, on what he shows, not on what he can do with the chase through CGI or editing, not on the peculiar weapons that can show up in a slasher film, but on a straightforward battle between two cars.

Clover comments that almost all of the victims in slasher movies share one quality with Marion Crane (Janet Leigh) in *Psycho*, who she sees as a "sexual transgressor." Intimidated and yet challenged by women who take their sexuality under their own command—as all of the girls in both groups in *Death Proof* do, given their conversations and what little we do see of their interactions with lovers, real and potential—Stuntman Mike finds he cannot make love to them, so he kills them. Or tries to, at least. A risk-taker as a stuntman has to be, he finds satisfaction in risks to himself that lead to the destruction of women, as we see during the final chase sequence. He goes from whimpering self pity to glee and back again as he thinks he has given the girls—who are now chasing him—the slip, and then sees them again, once more on his tail. Earlier, right before Kim wounds him, he laughs with the spirited relief of someone just off a roller-coaster ride. Both cars have stopped, and he even thinks that the girls should join him in appreciation of the thrill of their just-past encounter.

On the other hand, the girls do turn the tables on him even in laughter during that final chase, pulling their car next to his and talking to him, laughing at him. By this time, they have moved from victimhood to "Final Girl" status, one of the holdovers in the second half from slasher conventions. Clover writes that the Final Girl is the one "whom we see scream, stagger, fall, rise, and scream again. She is abject terror personified. . . . She alone looks death in the face; but she alone also finds the strength . . . to kill."[8] In *Death Proof,* as I have said, the Final Girl is a trio, but that doesn't really change the nature of the role.

Clover makes the critical point that the sexual identities of killer and Final Girl are not as simple as they might appear at first: "The Final Girl is boyish, in a word. Just as the killer is not fully masculine, she is not fully feminine."[9] Not, that is, in traditional definitions of gender and gender distinctions . . . which is something of Tarantino's own point in this movie. Stuntman Mike objectifies women and then is infuriated when they don't stick to subjugated type. The standard Final Girl seems both sexually active and sexually reluctant—that is, she generally clams up and shies away when approached with the assumption that she, as the woman, should be the passive partner. She neither needs men nor has to wait for them. When she wants them, she will go and get them. Significantly, in the standard slasher movie, "No male character of any stature lives to tell the tale."[10] It is the Final Girl who triumphs, through a combination of her female nature and the male attributes she has assumed in battle, a combination effectively removing her from older cultural conceptions of sexual difference and distinction.

It may be possible to read too much into the Final Girl, seeing her perhaps as a feminist response to a male-dominated society. On the other hand, she may be "simply an agreed-upon fiction, and the male viewers use of her as a vehicle for his own sadomasochistic fantasies [may be] an act of perhaps timely dishonesty."[11] However, though the audience may be primarily male, there are "also many female viewers who actively like such films, and of course there are women, however few, who script, direct, and produce them. These facts alone oblige us at least to consider the possibility the female fans find a meaning in the text and image of these films that is less inimical to their own interests than the figurative analysis would have us believe."[12]

It might also be that the Final Girl represents the child, the killer the parent, the child moving from a passive (read "female") role to an active (read "male") adult role. One way or another, it may be that "gender is simply being played with, and that part of the thrill lies precisely in the resulting 'intellectual uncertainty' of sexual identity."[13] Tarantino, of course, is interested in all of these concerns, the role of women in perception contrasting the actuality of female experience being something that he can explore but, as a man, never can understand integrally.

One of Clover's most relevant points about the Final Girl, at least in terms of *Death Proof*, is that "she addresses the killer on his own terms."[14] That is, the famous scene from *Raiders of the Lost Ark* (Steven Spielberg, 1981), in which Indiana Jones (Harrison Ford) simply shoots a man threatening him with long knives, would not be found at the end of a slasher movie. Instead, the tables are turned on the killer through the killer's own devices for killing—in this case, through a car.

Generally speaking, Tarantino, like Hitchcock, prefers "the oblique rendition of physical violence"[15] over the specific and graphic. In *Death Proof*, however, he bows to his reputation for violence and gives the viewer exactly what is expected from him (as he does in "The House of Blue Leaves" in *Kill Bill*). In this self-conscious look at movie making, he also makes use of the way in which "the slasher film intersects with the cult film, a genre devoted to such effects [self-parodying horror]."[16] Though the crash that kills the first group of girls is gruesome, it is gruesome in part to show how gruesome Tarantino can be, to comment on the genre and on the skill of moviemakers, in keeping with the themes of the film in general. Though they don't die, the second group of girls, certainly, is used to this same purpose; that is, they are skillful and competent, in part, because of movies. They are better at life because they are so good at movies.

Indeed, as I have said, one of the critical discussions within *Death Proof* centers on questions of competence. By starring a professional stuntwoman (Bell) as a professional stuntwoman, Tarantino highlights that which he is trying to show through the movie, the competence required to make a good film. His attention to detail, starting with Lucai's apartment and continuing through the fake products in the fake Circle A convenience store chain, from the billboards in Austin for Jungle Julia's radio show to that for the fake movie *Potheads Two* outside the convenience store—and more, much more—Tarantino is providing proof of the care he takes in creating a film . . . even when that film is meant to look sloppy and cheap. The juxtaposition of the careful and the slipshod, of course, continues the discussions of the meanings of moviemaking that are the heart of the film. The "mistakes" are not mistakes. Cheap grindhouse movies, for example, could find themselves retitled for a number of reasons, with the change made through a cut-and-splice insertion of a cheap title card, sometimes leaving a few frames of the old title showing—something Tarantino plays with through allowing a few frames of what seems to have been the original title, *Quentin Tarantino's Thunder Bolt,* to show just before a much cheaper title card appears, saying simply, in white on black, "Death Proof." "Making" such mistakes is Tarantino's own proof of his skill and his appreciation of (and knowledge of) a type of movie presentation that has disappeared through the rise of home viewing.

No longer can films develop the "aesthetic" of the grindhouse, prints scratched and worn through too many showings, reels switched, sometimes between different color films processed differently, sometimes even between black-and-white and color. Films repaired, often in odd fashion or incompletely. Tarantino loves the result:

> The aesthetic I was really going for was the aesthetic of watching old prints I own. A lot of these prints are little Frankenstein monsters, as far as how they've been compiled over maybe a couple of different prints. So one reel's washed out, another is red, another one is in Technicolor, and then a reel change happens—boom—and all of a sudden it looks gorgeous. I really got into that aesthetic. Into the idea that it was not us, the filmmakers doing it, trying to create this artistic palate, but that it's an actual print itself that's this quality. Without really even realizing it, our film just ended up going that way because it seemed natural to me.[17]

In ripping up his film to approximate this accidental aesthetic, Tarantino had to be careful not to make every degeneration meaningful. The stretch of black and white right at the beginning of the second half of the movie may or may not have significance. Certainly, finding something of meaning for every bit like that would ruin the effect.

In most slasher movies, the Final Girl is present from the start. In *Death Proof,* Tarantino doesn't allow this, killing off his first group of girls completely, effectively splitting his movie in two, connecting them only through the killer. The second group of girls, then, bridges the gap between characters such as Marion Crane and Stretch Brock, the former dying and the latter managing to survive and even kill. In *Death Proof,* Tarantino doesn't even need to show a change in the girls, from feminized personae to masculinized ones, for he has replaced the one sort with the other after the first group dies. Nevertheless, this missing change, for Clover, is critical: "The Final Girl (1) undergoes agonizing trials and (2) virtually or actually destroys the antagonist and saves herself. By the lights of folk tradition, she is not a heroine . . . saved by someone else, but a hero, who rises to the occasion and defeats the adversary with his own wit and hands."[18] Saved, that is, by turning the killer's own methods and weapons against that killer.

Clover's distinction between "heroine" and "hero," and her implied rejection of gender identification with either term, is central to any understanding of what may have been happening through the slasher films of the

1970s and of what certainly has happened regarding female action heroes at least since the turn of the century. Strong as they may be, the heroines of most of the last century nearly always stand with a rescuer, generally a man—an almost all-encompassing situation whose ubiquity is reflected in the popular feminist slogan coined by Irina Dunn in the early 1970s in disgusted repudiation: "a woman needs a man is like a fish needs a bicycle." Feminism notwithstanding, strong Princess Leia (Carrie Fisher) stands with Han Solo (Harrison Ford) in *Star Wars* (George Lucas, 1977), and Rose Bukater (Kate Winslet) survives because of Jack Dawson (Leonardo DiCaprio) in *Titanic* (James Cameron, 1997), two of the most popular movies of their times. It wasn't until slasher sensibilities began to seep into the mainstream, perhaps starting with Sigourney Weaver's Ripley in *Alien* (Ridley Scott, 1979), that women really began to take on genuine "hero" roles in significant numbers. Even two decades after that, Sherrie Inness's comment that "the association between men and toughness, which the media help to perpetuate, serves to keep women as second-class citizens"[19] remains absolutely true. This is one of the points Tarantino tries to make through *Death Proof,* just as he tries to do through *Kill Bill.*

Against expectations from outside the genre, in slasher films "the female exercise of scopic control results not in her annihilation, in the manner of classic cinema, but in her triumph."[20] Since the time of Clover's article, we've seen the rise of the Final Girl from her birthplace in a generally ignored genre and up toward the mainstream through phenomena such as Joss Whedon's television show based on the movie he wrote, *Buffy the Vampire Slayer* (Fran Kuzui, 1992) and even through Tarantino's own *Kill Bill.* This is a distinct change from mainstream presentations of the past: "The idea of a female who out-smarts, much less outfights—or outgazes—her assailant is unthinkable in the films of [Brian] De Palma and Hitchcock. Although the slasher film's victims may be sexual teases, they are not in addition simple-minded, scheming, physically incompetent, and morally deficient in the manner of these filmmakers' female victims."[21] Though having surface similarities with the slasher genre, their attitude toward women is significantly different, and different from what was to come or, in De Palma's case, from what was being done on the fringes of his field. Whedon's express purpose in creating Buffy was, as Sara Crosby notes, "to undo the equation between woman and weakness by establishing one between women and toughness."[22]

It may be, then, that the slasher film has had more impact on Hollywood as a whole than has been generally recognized, setting the stage for a new presentation of women, one not based on the old ideas equating the feminine with the passive, the male with the active, but showing that a woman can erase such boundaries. It may be that Tarantino, in presenting his tribute to the slasher film, is also providing a broader picture of what lay behind the choices he made in creating *Kill Bill,* where Zoë Bell was the stunt double for Uma Thurman. As he always does, Tarantino lays down thick (though often obtuse) hints to his purpose in *Death Proof*. Among these are the images interspersed with the final credits, cut to the beat of April March's version of "Laisse tomber les filles," both in English ("Chick Habit") and in French. The song, with lyrics like:

You're gonna see the reason why
When they're spitting in your eye

and the chorus line, "Hang up the chick habit," make clear that the song is directed at the Stuntman Mike character and, through him, at all the men (and women) who can't see women as other than simply female—and female as defined through generations of dichotomy, of opposition to the vision of what men supposedly are. The chick habit is as deeply engrained in feminists as in traditionalists. Both need, in the view Tarantino puts forward in this movie, to get over it, to forget about the barriers, the differences they have concocted between men and women. To recognize, as Inness writes, that we "have been told a lie. The media have supported the myth that men are tough heroes—or predators—and women are frail victims—or prey. Despite what the media might suggest, women have *always* been tough, both in literature and in real life."[23] Again, that, perhaps, is what Tarantino wants viewers to take away from his movie.

The end credits allow Tarantino to do a little more, here, just as in *Reservoir Dogs,* in which he uses the Harry Nilsson song "Coconut" to emphasize the absurdity of the situation just portrayed, the difficulty of assigning responsibility, and the circularity of human error. Nilsson's apparently silly (but catchy) little song deals with stupid action—followed by asking for help by telephoning the doctor and waking him up. The remedy proposed, though, is exactly the action of the initial instance and the doctor doesn't want to deal with it anyway. The song seems to say, "You did what you did, now let me sleep!" Few of us want to get involved in the stupidity of others; we would rather turn inward than explore the implications of actions we can't do anything about anyway. We are the doctor, with responsibility for our patient—yet we do nothing but tell the patient to do what the patient has already been doing, an action, in the song, clearly in no one's best interest. At the end of *Death Proof,* the song is once more addressed to the audience as a whole, to a culture whose "chick habit" really is an objectification of women.

One of the signs of a truly literate person is the way that person handles a book. He or she will look at the whole of it and seek signs in it illuminating any reading of the text, signs well beyond the putative demarcations between word and presentation. Front matter, including date of publication, place, and publisher, will be noted, as will any material on the writer herself or himself. The back matter, if there is any, will be considered, as will dedication (back at the front again) and acknowledgements. Any introduction will be read, though it may not be "necessary" to the body of the work. Binding, paper quality, and design will be judged—often without the person doing so even consciously knowing it. A great deal goes on concerning a book that is not in the primary text itself, much of it recognized almost unconsciously by the examiner.

The same is true of movies. Tarantino knows so and in *Death Proof* wants to make sure his audience does too, so he creates his own "self-aware" movie by playing with its physical aspects, by drawing attention to them. This is not a new conceit, not in film, and certainly not in literature. In the eighteenth century, Laurence Sterne "intruded" on his text *The Life and Opinions of Tristram Shandy, Gentleman* through pieces normally used as part of the surrounding presentation (among other techniques), putting marbled endpaper, for example, amidst the text and not simply around it. One of the points is that no part of the work, not even its housing, should be ignored. Included among this are the end credits. Michel Chion writes about *their* importance:

> The movie screening proposes . . . a new ritual that we should not take lightly: in a world that rarely allows us time to take stock of things, here is a moment that has been left open, a sort of airlock between the temporality of the film and that of daily life. A precious moment it is, even if it is sometimes purely formal as in the old Catholic mass in Latin when the priest would say '*Ite Missa est*' ('The mass has been spoken'), even though we knew it was not quite over, that we'd have to wait a bit more before leaving, but this waiting also had human value. We would exit from church to the all-embracing tones of the great organ, and this leaving became all the more significant.[24]

In a movie theater, one can tell the difference between the "literate" filmgoer and those whose interest extends no farther than the moment by their reactions to the start of the final credits. Those who just get up and leave think the movie is over, that there is nothing left. Those who watch know that the film contains more, even if it is only the rolling list of names, for even that, as Chion tells us, is an opportunity provided by the film itself for clearer understanding or, at least, for reflection before returning to the world.

The juxtaposition of "Chick Habit" with both the credits and with a series of interspersed images that, for the most part, objectify women (even here Tarantino does not act so simply to just one point) provides a commentary on the film that is properly seen as part of the film. One short video clip (most are stills) shows Vanessa sitting in a car, winking at the camera. She has died, of course, much earlier in the film: is this, then, something akin to the "blooper" credit that was so popular for a while? Or is Tarantino talking through the wink? We don't know for sure, for Tarantino lets his movies

speak without real amplification from him. But we do get the point: objectification is a waste.

Because of its slasher and grindhouse surfaces, it is easy to dismiss *Death
Proof* as simply a pointless in-group homage, *Rocky Horror Picture Show* (Jim
Sharman, 1975) without the music or the humor, a cult film looking for a
cult, such as *The Adventures of Buckaroo Banzai Across the 8th Dimension*
(W. D. Richter, 1984). But a careful viewing, as we have seen here, shows
that it clearly does more, taking themes from slasher films and presenting
them with a little more clarity and sophistication than might be found within
the subgenre itself. Beyond that, it is also an exploration of the importance
of the less skillful (and, frankly, less moneyed) end of the filmmaking business by one of the most skilled and knowledgeable directors in the business,
showing that the best know that the bottom end shouldn't be ignored simply because it lacks the resources found at the top. The creativity in slasher
films comes in doing more with less, in making films that can find their audiences even while watching every penny.

At the same time, Tarantino, whose ego has never been in danger of disappearing, demonstrates what *he* could do with this genre, as he had already
shown (of course) in relation to a number of others. By the time he came to
make *Death Proof,* his reputation was such that even an old Hollywood hand
such as Hooker could say, "It's quite an opportunity to work with Quentin
because I've been a fan of his from day one. He comes from the same school
as I come from: CGI, computer-generated stuff—throw that out. He likes
to work in real time, and that's what we like."[25] Though a comparative
youngster, Tarantino is an old-school director in quite a number of ways,
including in this reluctance to rely on montage and computer-generated
imagery.

Though not a strict film "realist" by any means, Tarantino recognizes the
importance of approaching his projects without an assumption that he can
rely on montage, that mistakes can be fixed in the editing room. Speaking of
Le Ballon Rouge (Albert Lamorisse, 1956) and the balloon's recorded movements, André Bazin identifies one of the main differentiations between realism and montage: "Of course there is a trick in it, but it is not one that
belongs to cinema as such. Illusion is created here, as in conjuring, out of
reality itself."[26] Bazin calls this important for, in montage, the balloon need
not ever have existed. In realism, it must have: "If the film is to fulfill itself
aesthetically we need to believe in the reality of what is happening while
knowing it to be tricked."[27] Today, this strikes most film viewers as irrelevant;
the ontology of the objects portrayed in a movie interest them not at all. It
remains important to the filmmaker such as Tarantino, however, for in the
making, the ontology does have an impact. When "fix it later" is no option,
closer attention is paid to the *mise-en-scène* and the precision of the acting
and the action. Closer cooperation is also possible, in ways not available
in the editing room or CGI studio, between actors, director, director of

photography, stunt people, make-up artists, and all of the others involved in the actual shoot. The range of input is naturally going to be greatest here, for the group encompasses a greater range of skills than will likely be found together later.

Sergei Eisenstein, the first major proponent in film theory of montage as prime methodology, claims that, "If montage is to be compared with something, then a phalanx of montage pieces, of shots, should be compared to the series of explosions of an internal combustion engine, driving forward its automobile or tractor: for, similarly, the dynamics of montage serve as impulses driving forward the total film."[28] If montage is the explosion, though, realism provides the air, the gas, and the electrical spark that combine to allow it. All films, of course, do contain elements of both realism and montage, but it is realism that provides the tools for all but animation (and even here the claim is questionable) and abstract film.

CGI is philosophically related to montage as a filmmaking technique in that the real work comes after the shoot, not before the camera, as in realism. One advantage to the latter approach is that it forces careful preparation on the part of the filmmaker before the first take. Again, "We can always fix it in editing or with the computer" is not an option. This means every detail has to be worked out in advance—and *that* requires knowing *why* that detail needs to be there. Take, for example, the poster of the record sleeve from Buffy Saint-Marie's "Soldier Blue" in Lucai's apartment at the beginning of *Death Proof:* this is not only homage to a violent and controversial movie from the past, in this case to *Soldier Blue* (Ralph Nelson, 1970), but it also foreshadows Stuntman Mike and his perverse and murderous way of "loving." The chorus of the song is addressed to the troops of the movie, but it might as well be talking to Stuntman Mike:

> Soldier blue, soldier blue, soldier blue:
> Can't you see there's another way to love her.

The earlier film, made during the Vietnam War and amid the controversy of such actions by U.S. military as the My Lai massacre, told of an even earlier massacre, one against Native Americans, mainly women and children, at Sand Creek, Colorado Territory, in 1864, while the Civil War was still going on. Several hundred people, most all of them noncombatants, were killed.

The other significant work of art chosen by Tarantino for Lucai's apartment is a huge poster of Bridgitte Bardot, who had starred in *Contempt,* a 1963 film by Tarantino's hero, Jean-Luc Godard—just one among the dozens of films that had established her as one of the sexiest women in the world. Lucai is specifically linked to Bardot by reclining on a couch beneath the picture in exactly the same feet-up pose, though holding a marijuana pipe rather than a drink. The accent is on legs and on feet, both important to Stuntman Mike's perversion and its results. It would be difficult (though not impossible) to pull off the juxtaposition through computers or editing. Done via realism, it seems both natural and accidental.

As in all of Tarantino's films, there's an element of nostalgia in *Death Proof*, though it does not dominate the film and runs deeper than a cultish fascination with those genres subsumed in the technological tsunami of the 1990s. The mainstream of American culture manages to engulf every successful "counterculture" experiment or deviation from the primary path, destroying each but bringing the pieces along as part of the continuing onslaught. Thomas Doherty writes, for example, of the "gentrification of the teenpic" of the 1950s as a result of the growing influence of the baby boomers in the 1960s coming on top of the replacement of the early "subversive" teenpics with the "clean teens" of the early 1960s.[29] He goes on to contrast *Easy Rider* (Dennis Hopper, 1969), a movie embraced on its own by youth culture, with *Zabriskie Point* (Michelangelo Antonioni, 1970), an attempt to cash in youth culture "on a par with the record industry's campaign to sell polka music to 1950s rock 'n' rollers."[30] It was becoming more and more difficult for anyone to carve out a contemporary genre that wouldn't be immediately subsumed by the larger culture had it any success at all.

In response, some film viewers turned to nostalgia, to finding the films that Hollywood forgot in its quest for financial return. Others embraced movies that, they thought, could never find their way into the mainstream— the slasher film being a subgenre of this type. Unlike people whose agenda becomes, in effect, a rejection of the mainstream, Tarantino has developed a different aesthetic. Like the one he describes that developed out of the accidental couplings and changes in the 1970s B-films he collects, it embraces change, difference, and accident. He loves all films, the forgotten, the shunned, and the mainstream. He loves them, in part, because all of them have an impact on the culture surrounding them, as slasher films, with their development of a real female hero type that has since started to become part of the mainstream, show.

Tarantino's reaction to film has been to embrace nostalgia, to embrace genre, to embrace every aspect of the movie world. His reaction to movies has been to make them his own, to become, of course, a filmmaker so that he can share his love with the world.

9

Inglourious Basterds:
Spelling It Out

A theory, I've contended, is only valid as long as it is useful. Only as long as it helps open up the subject. In other words, when a subject has to be twisted and squeezed to fit the theory, it's the theory that should go. This same "rule" pertains to the value of any one way of trying to make sense of film. The same *certainly* pertains to any single attempt to try to make sense of *Inglourious Basterds*. It is tempting to try to twist the movie to fit our preconceived notions concerning Tarantino, filmmaking, violence in society, and the place of film in society—and I am sure we all do so, to a degree.

The movie itself makes that easy to do. It's an attack, after all, on preconceptions and expectations, but one that *uses* preconceptions and expectations as major parts of its argument. In some ways, it is something of a romp—when it is not a criticism of the shallowness of the romp. In other ways, it is satire, but it hates the deadly seriousness of satire and its moral smugness. It screams to us that a movie is just a movie, not history, not anything with any weight at all, yet it has an intelligent and deadly point to make about what we mean by "history" and about the modern world, a point as significant as any in any movie in recent memory, though the film does seem to hide it. Right out in the open, of course. It's a movie, then, that we should talk about with care, for it is made to tempt us into carelessness—and, fortunately, to lure us back again.

There is more: classical Hollywood style, based on genre and continuity—on expectation—finds itself shot, stabbed, bludgeoned, choked, and blown up in *Inglourious Basterds*. Furthermore, if any of Tarantino's movies deserves the descriptor "postmodern," it is this one. Instead of extending from past process, here Tarantino gleefully turns on it, mocking it severely. Yet, while turning Hollywood norms (among others) on their heads, he continues to show mastery of those very norms, making a movie whose accessibility is achieved through accepted industry and audience channels, through the very things he mocks. And, though he makes an intelligent and "self-aware" film, he continues his distain for the remaining avant-garde, if there is one, for an avant-garde that still believes popular art is cheap and naïve art, if it is even art at all. He continues it by making his cheap and naïve art that is never cheap or naïve.

Just look at the movie's title: "deviant" spellings. But the meaning comes through. And, after all, the spelling of "basterds" is closer to American pronunciation than is "bastards." So what's to complain about? What is the point, Tarantino seems to be asking, of our spelling conventions when they aren't needed for clarity or for understanding? This is a fundamental challenge that few but dialect writers ignore. Why doesn't spelling change with the times? Why not spell something as we want, even if spelling conventions don't change? What's the point of judging people by their spelling anyway? The want of hard-and-fast spelling rules didn't hurt the language of the sixteenth and seventeenth centuries, after all. If Shakespeare wanted to spell his name differently at different times (as he did), more power to him. And if Milton wanted to spell "he" as "hee," who are we to question him? No less than George Orwell, in "Why I Write," says he once found youthful pleasure in reading Milton's "hee." Why shouldn't Tarantino aspire to similar artistic freedom? Simply because of the tyranny of the dictionary, a constraint that has grown since Milton's time and that most every one of us, today, takes for granted?

Whatever his secret reasons for the idiosyncratic spellings in his title, Tarantino, known for his weak command of conventional spelling (he spells "soldier" "soirjer" in his sketch for an apartment for *Death Proof*[1]), doesn't turn defensive about it. Instead, he attacks the mindless conventionality and judgmentalism of insistence on standardization—and makes this one of the themes of the film more generally as well. The strength of spelling conventions is incalculable, logic and usage notwithstanding, and the audacity of attacking them in the title of a major film should not be underestimated.

Tarantino, by snubbing conventions that are used as much for weeding out those who just don't make society's grade as for keeping the language from chaos, shows right from the start of *Inglourious Basterds* that something unusual is going on here, that this is a movie that is not going to follow rules or worry about consequences. It's an impudent movie and daring. That doesn't mean it's a great movie or even a good one; such judgment rests on other grounds. It means, instead, that this film steps willfully beyond boundaries. But it is never experimental, distaining the elitism that word implies, relying instead on the tried and true, though the "tried" in new ways and the "true" only insofar as it never attempts to fool anyone.

History this is not, though Tarantino does work to reproduce the feel of an era half a century past. In this, he works in a New Hollywood tradition, one growing from the explosion of home viewing—and re-viewing—that began with the birth of the VCR in the 1970s. One result of this is that, today, anachronisms chase filmmakers across the Internet, haunting them for years. Fearful directors (and even ones as confident as Tarantino) spend long hours getting little details right—even when they are playing fast and loose with historical probability and possibility, as Tarantino most certainly does.

This is a voluntary restraint on the directors, of course, a convention such as that surrounding the way sound effects are used, not realistically, but meeting audience expectations developed over generations. Some deviations are acceptable, others not. But constraints, of course, can even be one of the tools of the filmmaker. In *Modern Times* (Charles Chaplin, 1936), Chaplin only allows recognizable speech to intrude through electronic devices, diegetic parts of the movie. This allows him to keep to *his* old constraint, eliding conversation as a narrational device. In this way, his movie retains features and strengths of the silent cinema while still making use of a soundtrack for more than effects and score. One way Tarantino also does, in fact, constrain himself in *Inglourious Basterds* is through insistence on a reasonably accurate image of occupied France. Also like Chaplin, he uses an internal electronic device—in this case, a movie projector—to make a point. Where Chaplin made comment on the artifice of sound, Tarantino makes clear the distinction between his picture and what is often called a "war picture," all the while making use of the sensibilities and characteristics of the genre—and making fun of them, as well.

In *The World War II Combat Film: Anatomy of a Genre,* Jeanine Basinger provides a list of the common elements of such films: "The hero, the group of mixed ethnic types (O'Hara, Goldberg, Matowski, etc.) who come from all over the United States (and Brooklyn), the objective they must accomplish, their little mascot, their mail call, their weapons and uniforms."[2] Tarantino is aware of all of these and uses them to some extent in *Inglourious Basterds,* though often as objects for parody. But he is not really making a war picture, for he also recognizes the necessary propaganda aspect of almost every World War II film, combat film or not, something that had such momentum that it carried into films made long after the war was over, even making it difficult to switch directions when Vietnam became a serious film subject. In order to mark his film as different from the World War II movies with their necessary propaganda baggage, Tarantino includes in his movie snippets of a fictional German war film called *Stolz der Nation* (*A Nation's Pride*), a movie meant, among its other purposes in *Inglourious Basterds,* to mock the World War II combat film.

It is easy to fall into the trap of calling this simply another Tarantino movie about movies, of mistaking the language and the medium for the subject and mistaking the creation of a film within the film as simple self-referentiality. But what he is doing by inclusion of *Stolz der Nation,* consciously or not, is following his pattern of undercutting what he is doing in the film to make points that, though relevant to filmmaking, have much more to do with the world beyond movies. Here, among other things, he makes us aware of limitations of combat films as reflection of any real-world experience by removing his film from the genre of combat films even as he uses the conventions of combat films—just as Chaplin was removing *Modern Times* from the realm of the silents while still allowing himself the space to use the techniques of the silents.

World War II, Jewish revenge against Nazis, terrorism, stereotypes, violence, intrigue, comedy, loss, and responsibility; *Inglourious Basterds* deals with all of these, but it is not *about* them. Nor is it, once again, about movies, though that is the stereotypical view is of all of Quentin Tarantino's films. It's about the relationship between movies and the world, about the ways we use movies to develop more fully our understanding of our cultural biases and assumptions. This is clearly the reason for the inclusion of that fictional pet project of Joseph Goebbels, *Stolz der Nation,* a propaganda film—that is, a film explicitly designed to have an impact on the world and not simply as entertainment.

When Shosanna Dreyfus's (Mélanie Laurent) image and voice come through the smoke and flames of the theater at the end of the movie, few in the *real* theater won't recall *The Wizard of Oz* (Victor Fleming, 1939), the wizard's voice coming through smoke and fire surrounding his gigantic and ghostly head, intoning, "I am Oz, the great and powerful." Nor can we forget Dorothy's response, "I am Dorothy, the small and meek." Even so, it is not movies we are supposed to be thinking of as we watch the scene, but of the relationship between the small and meek and the great and powerful. Fleeting recognition of the connection between the two films is all that is called for—if that. After all, the topic is something else, and this is merely one of the images used to build it. Nevertheless, who is it but Dorothy Gale (Judy Garland) who manages to destroy the Wicked Witch of the West (Margaret Hamilton)? Who was it but Shosanna Dreyfus who destroyed Hitler—in this movie, at least? Both have help, but it is the drive of these young women that provides the momentum. This chapter of the movie is called "Revenge of the Giant Face," making sure that audiences recognize the importance of the image that continues to be seen, projected onto the smoke, as the theater burns. Making sure that people will see and understand the significance of the film image and not simply the planning behind its appearance. The burning desire of the small and meek to exact revenge on the great and powerful remains central to the message of the movie. The role of film in making that happen follows close behind.

One of the keys to understanding Tarantino's movies, his relation to them, and his vision of their place in the world is his use of fairy-tale phrasing, as he does, once again, in *Inglourious Basterds,* with the title of his chapter "Once Upon a Time In . . . Nazi-Occupied France." Quite aware that the fairy tale itself has two images, the nice children's tale and the cauldron of horrors, Tarantino uses the traditional fairy-tale beginning here to signal that nothing we'll see is any more one simple thing than is a fairy tale. The first juxtaposition, of course, is right there on the intertitle; the fantasy land is one ravaged by perhaps the most infamous regime in human history. Yet it is followed by an idyllic farmyard scene, the farmer chopping at a stump, a woman hanging sheets on a clothesline. As the wind blows the sheet, we see behind it in the distance a car with two motorcycle outriders approaching. The sheet screens and reveals . . . just as a movie does.

The house and the approach evokes memories of dozens of movies, including *The Searchers* (John Ford, 1956), almost all of them starting with a similarly quiet scene that quickly turns tragic. The audience members, no matter what the specifics of their movie-going experience, are likely to be prepared for ill fortune by their prior viewing experience.

From the very first we see them, the eyes of the Frenchman, Perrier LaPadite (Denis Menochet), convey a sadness and a fatalism that will haunt the surrealism of most of the rest of the movie, providing a sobering framing of absurd activity. Here, though, they provide another jarring contrast—this time to the jovial, almost comic face of Colonel Hans Landa (Christoph Waltz). To make the point of distinction absolutely clear, LaPadite smokes a sedate and common pipe whereas Landa's is a huge calabash that would seem to overdo things even for Sherlock Holmes. LaPadite is tragic, facing a choice that will, he knows, ruin lives, possibly even his own and those of his daughters. Certainly those of the Jewish family he is hiding. Landa, on the other hand, for all his erudition and command of language and verbal gymnastics, is farcical.

In LaPadite's house, and with a bouncy boyishness, Landa asks for milk instead of wine, all the while making it clear to LaPadite that he's an extremely competent and dangerous individual, carefully arranging papers and an inkpot and filling his pen, talking all the while. At one point he asks about a Jewish family, the Dreyfuses, that has not yet been located. LaPadite says only that he has heard rumors. Landa interrupts him:

Col. Landa: I love Rumors! Facts can be so misleading, where rumors, true or false, are often revealing. So, Monsieur LaPadite, what rumors have you heard regarding the Dreyfuses.

As LaPadite knows, as Landa knows he knows, these rumors are meaningless. The Dreyfuses are hiding under the floor of the room where the men sit.

Absurd and surreal or not, Landa makes clear to LaPadite that he must reveal the Dreyfuses or face the loss of his family. The farmer makes the only choice he can, his eyes now sadder, if possible, than ever before.

The Dreyfuses are slaughtered where they hide, only one of them surviving, young Shosanna who Landa, in his arrogance, lets flee. The self-confidence of this clown, though clearly over the top, is also warranted by the deaths he has just instigated. A parody of the worst and most dangerous of the officers of the Third Reich, Landa is also as likeable as a character in farce. The stereotype of the Nazi, he also constantly breaks the stereotype, doing so nearly every time he opens his mouth.

The only character in the movie able to appreciate the full extent of the horror of such a likeable villain is Shosanna Dreyfus, who encounters him again years later, when she is living in Paris under an assumed identity and running a movie theater. Laurent's performance as Dreyfus in that scene is one of the high points of the movie. In the screenplay, Tarantino has the character losing bladder control as she sits with Landa, so traumatic is the meeting with the man who has killed her family. Laurent plays the part to such perfection that the added emphasis concerning her state of mind is clearly not needed. It is not included.

In many ways, as I have indicated, *Inglourious Basterds* can be viewed as an attack on accepted rules of all sorts and on the ways we judge based on rules and externals and not on the thing (or individual) in itself, not even when that person hides behind rules or symbols. Twice in the film, Lt. Aldo Raine (Brad Pitt), for example, makes the point that the uniform doesn't make the man. In the first instance, he is speaking to a captured German private, who says he wants to remove and burn his uniform as soon as the war is over:

> **Lt. Raine**: Yeah, that's what we thought. We don't like that. You see, we like our Nazis in uniforms. That way, you can spot 'em just like that. But you take off that uniform, ain't nobody gonna know you was a Nazi. And that don't sit well with us.

This foreshadows the ultimate scene of the movie, when Raine and Utivich (B. J. Novak), the only other surviving Basterd, have "captured" Col. Landa:

> **Lt. Raine**: I mean, if I had my way, you'd wear that goddamn uniform for the rest of your pecker-suckin' life. But I'm aware that ain't practical. I mean, at some point ya gotta hafta take it off.

What Raine is worried about is that the Nazis will be judged on externals, on what they appear to be, instead on internals, on what they actually are. He sees a fundamental evil in the heart of anyone who wears a uniform of the Third Reich, much as the Nazis felt about Jews. Like the Nazis, who insisted that Jews wear identifying emblems, Raine wants Nazis always identified, so he carves swastikas into their foreheads. He is scared that too many will take the externals as the mark of the man, an attitude of the sort parodied by the satiric verse at the end of the version of "The Streets of Laredo" by the Kingston Trio:

You can see by our outfits that we are both cowboys,
So, get yourself an outfit and be a cowboy, too.

Based on the opposite logic, "once a Nazi, always a Nazi, no matter the clothes," the Basterds carve swastikas on the foreheads of those Nazis they let live—including Col. Landa—who they feel will eventually try to hide their Nazi pasts.

One of the points of the movie, and the ultimate reason for the various juxtapositions it presents, is simply that surface and depth are not the same thing. An inability to attain command of the minutiae of conventional spelling (or even of its broader "principles") does not mean that the thought expressed is similarly chaotic (or, more accurately, similarly rule bound). And the evil underneath is not always reflected in surface appearances. Raine and his men may worry about Nazis "hiding" in civilian clothing, but they themselves hide in Nazi uniforms—in order to kill more effectively. Dreyfus and her lover Marcel (Jackie Ido) use the thug tactics of fascists to get developed the film that will be projected as "the giant face." The question arises: are the Basterds "good" because their real uniform is the American uniform? Are they (and Dreyfus) good because they are Jews (all except for Raine), not Nazis? Does the fact of being Jewish, in other words, carry more weight (on the good/bad scale) than the fact of having worn a Nazi uniform?

Clearly, *Inglourious Basterds* is something more than Eli Roth's depiction, "kosher porn."[3] Yes, there is certainly an aspect of Jewish revenge to the movie, something rarely seen in quite the way presented here, even in *Defiance* (Edward Zwick, 2008), in which the revenge taken is presented as neither gleeful (from a directorial point of view, certainly) nor triumphant. But *Inglourious Basterds,* though recognizing and fulfilling (wishfully) the need for revenge, still does not exonerate the avengers. Even Dreyfus, with the most up-close-and-personal experience of Nazi atrocities, ends on that unnecessary (from the standpoint of killing Nazis) and monomaniacal note of her face on the screen, understandable given what happened to her family but clearly not the result of rational thought and planning. And even she, to get done what she needs to get done, is willing to imperil the innocent; she and Marcel treat the owner of a processing lab as brutally as a Gestapo agent might. Though her "right" to revenge is clear, one wonders if she—or the Basterds, for that matter—is really any better than the Nazis she fights.

In other words, does the right to revenge justify revenge? And what is the effect of thirsting for, and even of gaining, revenge? Might it not make you one and the same with your enemy? Is carving a swastika on a Nazi brow substantially different from forcing a Jew to wear the Star of David? Or is the difference only one of degree? Thinking not of the victim, of guilt or innocence, only thinking of the perpetrator, what is the impact of such imposition on the one doing the imposing? If, as Lt. Raine says at the end of the movie, the swastika he has carved on Col. Landa is his masterpiece, what is left for him? The last line of the screenplay says that he and Utivich "ghoulishly giggle"[4] over the mutilation of Lande. Where does that leave them? Certainly not in the position of moral superiority we imagine for those who vanquished the Nazis, the "greatest generation" as Tom Brokaw named them.

These questions are not new. My own father struggled with them in the aftermath of his service in the Pacific theater of the war. He saw his fellow American soldiers reduced to a level of savagery that shocked him into a pacifism that lasted his entire life. But such questions cannot be dismissed due to age. They have not been answered and possibly cannot be. Perhaps, though, they need to be posed more than answered and posed again for each new generation.

It is when such questions are not considered that humans fall into the belief that violence can actually have salutary effect. Though it may be true that violence is sometimes necessary (I do not share my father's pacifism), the impact of violence on any perpetrator, even one acting for the most noble of reasons, is part of the destruction wrought. We see this brought home, quite literally, in post-traumatic stress disorder. America, though, like most cultures, celebrates the violence of its past, recognizing only the good that came of it, never the damage. In a sense, then, certainly through the final image, *Inglourious Basterds* is a send-up of such attitudes, of what Richard Slotkin calls American belief in "regeneration through violence,"[5] the idea that violence can be a cleansing experience, even redemptive. Tarantino, though known as one of the most violent of directors (though he rarely depicts violence solely for spectacle), may have a more sophisticated understanding of violence than those who criticize him but laud, without reservation, the warriors whose violence they never see. It's not that what the Basterds are doing is itself inherently evil (though it may be), it's the fact that the impact on *them* of what they've done is ignored that needs consideration.

Dreyfus's act, too, merits examination in a context fuller than revenge. Her fully understandable and justifiable thirst for revenge against the system that destroyed her family and her life aside, she condemns her lover to die as well, along with the innocents and fellow travelers who happened to be attending the opening of *Stolz der Nation*. Perhaps things such as that have to be done. Even so, those who benefit need to understand the full aspect of the act, so that it doesn't itself grow further into its own Nazi-like pattern of violence and self-justification. Otherwise, at the very least, such actions grow into mythical representations of violence as positive act that have very little in common with the actual practice.

Slotkin describes such myths, relating specifically to how they appear in American culture, arising from its early days and from settler "interaction" with Native Americans: "As artifacts, myths appear to be built of three basic structural elements: a protagonist or hero, with whom the human audience is presumed to identify in some way; a universe in which the hero may act, which is presumably a reflection of the audience's conception of the world and the gods; and a narrative, in which the interaction of hero and universe is described."[6] *Inglourious Basterds* is a quest to examine such myths by showing that the hero can never be simply a force for good or even worthy of audience identification, by presenting a universe that points out the flaws of the audience's conception of their world, and by unfolding a narrative in which the interaction between hero and universe may be deemed necessary, it can never be simply called "good."

A point of pride for Raine is his combined mountaineer and Native American heritage. The former, in his mind, justifies the corners he cuts and his lack of respect for rules of any sort. The latter leads him to identify his Basterds with Apache warriors and to the scalpings that are among the movie's more gruesome moments. Interestingly, this is an identification with the losers and with the side that, in early American myth, was identified with savagery and not heroism. One would almost expect this to be turned around. After all, as Slotkin writes, Indian wars "pitted the English Puritan colonists against a culture that was antithetical to their own in most significant aspects. They could emphasize their Englishness by setting their civilization against Indian barbarism."[7] Just so, today, Americans often justify American "exceptionalism" through comparison to the evil of the Nazis they defeated.

According to the depictions in *Inglourious Basterds,* however, the Americans aren't really that different from the Germans, something that was also a problem for early European Americans, some of who noticed a similar resemblance between themselves and the Native Americans:

> This resemblance between whites and Indians became more troublesome as time went by. It was at times an embarrassment to Puritan writers and a source of guilt to Puritan soldiers that under the pressures of battle in the tangled and isolated wilderness, white troops often behaved precisely like their Indian enemies.[8]

By further tangling identification, Tarantino leads his audience to the very questions their cultural ancestors raised and, unfortunately, often buried.

Inglourious Basterds is "postmodern." It is "surreal." It is "satire." It is a "celebration of violence."

There is a strong inclination to assume we have understood something once we have named it, allowing us to then drop it from thoughtful consideration. It doesn't matter that the name may be inappropriate or poorly descriptive of the particular case; it is called that; it is that. With this danger in mind, I even hesitate to even use the word "surrealist" in relation to *Inglourious Basterds,* though I certainly do see it as a surrealist movie; I doubt that Tarantino was thinking of André Breton or of his "Surrealist

Manifesto" (though he may well be familiar with both) as he penned the screenplay.

Yet Breton's words bubble up each time I view the movie:

> We are still living under the reign of logic: this, of course, is what I have been driving at. But in this day and age logical methods are applicable only to solving problems of secondary interest. The absolute rationalism that is still in vogue allows us to consider only facts relating directly to our experience. Logical ends, on the contrary, escape us. It is pointless to add that experience itself has found itself increasingly circumscribed. It paces back and forth in a cage from which it is more and more difficult to make it emerge. It too leans for support on what is most immediately expedient, and it is protected by the sentinels of common sense. Under the pretense of civilization and progress, we have managed to banish from the mind everything that may rightly or wrongly be termed superstition, or fancy; forbidden is any kind of search for truth which is not in conformance with accepted practices.[9]

Rather than logic, surrealism stems from something entirely different, from thought, from "the actual functioning of thought. Dictated by the thought, in the absence of any control exercised by reason, exempt from any aesthetic or moral concern."[10] Tarantino steps outside of traditional modes of thought in this movie, using something other than logic to make his point, using movies—an entirely different type of discourse, one rooted in depiction of preconceived notions and in analysis through such depiction.

Surrealism comes into play when logic becomes impossible, when questions become circular, even persistent—or perhaps because they do. What do you do when people complain that your movies are only about movies? How do you explain that movies aren't about movies in the first place, and never were, so movies "about" movies can't "only" be about movies? Interlocutors just look at you like you're crazy. Explanations aren't going to do it; you have to *show* it in a way that opens new visions, new methods of seeing. Which is what Tarantino tries to do in *Inglourious Basterds*. Which is what surrealists have also essayed.

How many ways, in *Inglourious Basterds*, does Tarantino try to show that there are unbreakable bonds between the world and film? At least 10. He shows that:

- Film draws people together.
- Film attracts real-world attention.
- Film violence can hide real violence.
- Film confirms and destroys stereotypes.
- Film can be effective real-world propaganda.
- Film can act in cathartic fashions, but the catharsis is in the real world.

- Film does strive to encompass reality, but reality always encompasses film.
- Film presents fantasy, which is only identified as such through the real world.
- Film, even when talking about film, is talking about the real world at the same time.
- Film stock, especially old nitrate stock, burns extremely easily, making it a real-world danger.

The parallel between the film audience watching *Inglourious Basterds* and the audience watching *Stolz der Nation* within the movie can't be missed. In both cases, people have gathered together to watch a movie, something that hasn't changed. Even with the increased home-viewing possibilities of recent years, enough people show up at the theaters to keep them in operation. As a result, movie theaters have been among the places attractive to terrorists since the 1970s, at least (the first I could find was in a Tel Aviv theater on December 11, 1974, not long after the commencement of modern terrorist activities). In addition, films become the metaphors we use to talk about the world (perhaps Tarantino's most important point throughout all his films), further drawing people together or, at least, into a common discussion.

Since the 1920s, it has been hard to find anything equaling film as a topic of public conversation. Even when they are not the center of the discussion themselves, movies often enter tangentially as the origins for metaphors used in other discussion. So, the best place to hide, Shosanna Dreyfus finds, is where there's the most attention, thinking of herself as something akin to Poe's purloined letter. Her theater hosts "German Nights" of German films, attracting German soldiers—including Fredrick Zoller (Daniel Brühl), himself the star of a German movie about himself. He is said to be the German Sergeant York, but he is more akin to Audie Murphy, whose *To Hell and Back* (Jesse Hibbs, 1955) fictionalizes his story even while he portrays himself. Basinger describes the film and its star:

> In 1955 the merging of historical reality and filmed presentation of historical reality was solidified by the curious case of Audie Murphy. Murphy was officially listed as the most decorated soldier of World War II. An authentic and celebrated war hero, he was credited with killing or capturing 240 German soldiers. He was awarded the Congressional Medal of Honor, along with 27 other medals, among them three Silver Stars, the Distinguished Service Cross, the Legion of Merit, A [sic] Bronze Star, three Purple Hearts, the Victory Medal, the European Theater Medal, the American Theater Medal, the French Legion of Honor, the Croix de Guerre, and, of course, the Good Conduct Medal. . . . *To Hell and Back* . . . was a reenactment (fictionalized) of his own World War II combat experience. The film is a curious mixture of what is presumably Murphy's recollection and actual experience, reenacted, and an

amalgam of what a typical filmgoing audience would accept as "true" combat experience via generic story telling.[11]

Though direct reference to either Murphy or the film within *Inglourious Basterds* itself might have been more of an anachronism than even a Tarantino movie could have borne, alternative history though this one is. Zoller is a hero on Murphy's scale, having killed almost the same number Murphy did. The analogy between the two extends to their boyish charm. No one could look at either and imagine a killer, let alone one with credit for death in such almost unbelievable numbers. Dreyfus's theater attracts enough attention (as she does, from Zoller) to make it the site of the premier of *Stolz der Nation,* the movie starring Zoller and about Zoller.

The importance of the attention paid to movies can be simply demonstrated; today, more people know of Murphy through his movies than through his heroic exploits in Italy and France. The movies, after all, are occasionally shown; the war itself is not.

One of the ironies of contemporary discussions of film violence is that they often take attention away from the problems of physical violence that surround us. In *Inglourious Basterds,* they do this more directly. While the screen shows Zoller shooting and shooting again from his bell tower, Dreyfus shoots *him,* the real man, not the screen man . . . no, the screen man in color, not the screen man in black-and-white. Her gunshots are covered by those from the soundtrack—as are his, only a few seconds later, shooting her. But all of them, of course, are on the soundtrack. The reality is that none of it is real, of course, as filmmakers have made sure we know since the very first movies of the Lumière brothers or Georges Méliès: "It's only a movie."

The thing is, as Tarantino is pounding into our heads in *Inglourious Basterds* (and in his other movies, but not quite so emphatically), it's *not* only a movie. Paradoxically, this is also often the point of those who criticize Tarantino for making movies that are "too violent." Actions have consequences; this is one of Tarantino's most constant themes. Movies are themselves actions (in the sense that they have an impact), so they must have consequences, too. Tarantino might argue that it is the movies, not the violence in the movies, that have consequences, but that might be a distinction without a difference, bringing us back to Sergei Eisenstein's depiction of the motion picture as inherently violent. Or on the other hand, this might be a risk Tarantino has to take, for it might just force us to accept that the movies and what they depict differ on a fundamental level, something that Tarantino is trying to show is not to be the case. He wants to argue that movies are a part of the world, not that certain movies have an impact and others don't.

One of the funniest bits in *Inglourious Basterds* is the scene in which Lt. Aldo Raine introduces himself to the squad of Jewish killers he is going to lead into occupied France. Not only is Raine an over-the-top caricature of the gung-ho American warrior, but his Basterds, when we see them, are all of a type, all stereotypically Jewish rather than of the stereotype of a group of soldiers all of differing racial, ethnic, or class grouping, making up the "real" America.

Raine's talk to his men is one of the more hypocritical uses of stereotypes while showing that one's own self is exactly what one is railing against, an exact evocation of "an eye for an eye."

> **Raine**: The Nazis ain't got no humanity. They're the foot soldiers of a Jew-hatin', mass-murderin' maniac, and they need to be destroyed.

The smug, self-confident attitude of Raine's is every bit as dangerous as that he fights:

> **Raine**: And the German will be sickened by us.
> And the German will talk about us.
> And the German will fear us.
> And when the Germans close their eyes at night and they're tortured by their subconscious for the evil they've done, it will be with thoughts of us they are tortured with.

But we, in the audience, lulled by generations of stereotypes of the Germans who fell under the National Socialist spell, react only with encouragement. The evil of the Nazis is so engrained that anything proposed for fighting them must necessarily be acceptable—even if it carries implications as horrible as German fascism itself.

Stolz der Nation, itself (again) a parody of the Audie Murphy–type war film, also shows the importance placed on wartime propaganda. Propaganda, of course, was an important tool for all sides during the war, but we most often remember it in terms of those who tried to influence the other side, such as Tokyo Rose and Lord Haw-Haw. The winners in a war don't like to think of the entertainment created to buck up the home front (and even the soldiers) as propaganda, but it is, and *Stolz der Nation* clearly evokes the patriotic American movies of the war years, movies such as *Wake Island* (John Farrow, 1942), *Flying Tigers* (David Miller, 1942), *Gung Ho!* (Ray Enright, 1943), and *Thirty Seconds Over Tokyo* (Mervyn LeRoy, 1944), among many others.

If there is any catharsis shown in *Inglourious Basterds,* it is in the sick glee felt by Raine and Private Smithson Utivich as they cackle at the end, looking at the swastika Raine has carved in the forehead of Colonel Landa. Dreyfus dies before she can gain any satisfaction from the chaos she creates in the theater, leaving that to those viewers who can appreciate that "kosher porn" aspect of the film. The movie itself perhaps plays another cathartic role, purging the American filmgoer (at least) of the need to see even one more World

War II movie. By killing Hitler, *Inglourious Basterds* kills the genre. No film about that war, coming after this one, is going to be able to take itself quite as seriously as once it could have—creating a dividing line one would have thought the vapid television show of the 1960s, *Hogan's Heroes,* would have made. For the sake of its place in the history of film, it is a good thing *Defiance,* another story of Jewish resistance to the Nazis, appeared before *Inglourious Basterds.*

The "world" of *Inglourious Basterds* is not a world at all, of course, but a play on the real world as understood by the audience. It goes a step further, though, by playing havoc with the narrative unities we impose on fictional worlds as something of a protection against the vagaries of the real world. The story of British Lieutenant Archie Hicox (Michael Fassbinder), for example, seems to be heading toward some sort of significance of its own, but is cut off in a basement bar, with the Basterds forced to take over the drama. The messiness of the stories of the movie reflects more closely the messiness of real life than is usually allowed in movies, where everything is controlled, a comfort in a world where randomness can and does alter lives forever at a second's whim.

The scene at the climax of the movie, in the movie theater, showing the destruction of Hitler and his top henchmen in 1944, is pure fantasy—the fantasy of Dreyfus, who has put it together out of the horrors brought onto her life by the Third Reich and the films she has devoted her life to since the killing of her family. A second fantasy is that of British professionalism and ability, shown in the interview between Hicox and General Ed Fenech (Mike Myers) while Winston Churchill (Rod Taylor) observes (for the most part). This one even includes a beautiful German movie star turned spy, Bridget von Hammersmark (Diane Kruger).

A third, of course, is the Basterds themselves, the American fantasy of the small group that proves more than a match for any number of Germans. And finally, the fantasy of Landa represents the Nazi ideal of the cultured, smart man, more than a match for any he comes up against, a fantasy symbolized and undercut by that calabash pipe, taken out in the house of LaPadite as Landa flatters himself through his words to LaPadite, essentially teasing him as a lead-up to killing the Jewish family LaPadite has been hiding—the family, of course, of Dreyfus. There are also smaller fantasies, such as that of Zoller, thinking that he can succeed in his quest to seduce Dreyfus, and of Joseph Goebbels (Sylvester Groth), who (as Hicox puts it) "sees himself closer to David O. Selznick."

All of the fantasies interact, of course. The British fantasy, though quickly destroyed, does introduce von Hammersmark, who is then incorporated into the American fantasy. Landa threads his way through them all, providing the final fulfillment of one American fantasy, of locking Nazis forever into their identity, never allowing them to step beyond it. A fantasy based on a belief in the essential, unchanging nature of the individual beneath the outer trappings of uniform, a version of this fantasy proved disastrous in Iraq, when the conquered army and the ruling Ba'ath party were disbanded with no attempt to "rehabilitate" them (and no attempt to permanently identify them, either, as the Basterds are doing to Nazis), a disastrous policy, it turned out, and one at odds with what was done in Germany and Japan in 1945, an older policy of rehabilitation that gave rise to the idea of characters such as Dr. Strangelove (Peter Sellers) in the eponymous 1964 movie directed by Stanley Kubrick. Another small American fantasy might be called the Dick Cheney Fantasy, the belief that torture is effective. When one captured German is beaten to death by a Basterd with a baseball bat, the next immediately provides wanted information.

Again, the ridiculousness of all of these fantasies is shown in the sadness of the eyes of LaPadite in that first scene of the movie, eyes that recognize that it is the imposition of the fantasies of those with power that alter the real—not the fantasy—world, and in ways that the fantasists themselves, so caught up in their stories, cannot and will not recognize. Movies, of course, are the dominant outlet for fantasy in the contemporary world, so it is not surprising that Tarantino, one of today's most brilliant students of film, uses movies to comment on fantasy.

Manohla Dargis ends her *New York Times* review of *Inglourious Basterds* by claiming that the film "is simply another testament to his [Tarantino's] movie love. The problem is that by making the star attraction of his latest film a most delightful Nazi, one whose smooth talk is as lovingly presented as his murderous violence, Mr. Tarantino has polluted that love."[12] Perhaps that is the point; movies aren't something one can love simply for their own sake, for movies aren't static . . . movies do things. Tarantino, in *Inglourious Basterds*, shows just what movies can do in relation to the real world. Instead of holding up a mirror to the world, they let us explore it, using "what if . . ." as a means for learning about ourselves. What if there were a Nazi, one of the worst, who was also an incredible charmer and smart enough to see what the outcome of the war would be? And, what if the Americans were as mean and venal as the archetypal Nazi? The answers to these questions, and they are real questions, asked in *Inglourious Basterds* reflect upon our attitudes toward the world and not toward movies.

Film exists in the world as a physical presence, not simply figuratively, a point that Tarantino uses to bring attention to the importance of film as a cultural artifact, not simply as physical film or, today, digital combinations on a variety of storage devices. It's appropriate that he chooses Paris and World War II to make this point, for it was in Paris during the war that Henri Langlois risked his life over and over for film, famously even moving films to new hiding places in a baby carriage. Without Langlois, without the films he saved and the *Cinémathèque Française* thus nurtured, there would have been no place for Jean-Luc Godard to learn film, probably no *Cahiers du cinema* or André Bazin, no François Truffaut . . . no *nouvelle vague*. No Quentin Tarantino. As I have written elsewhere:

> The Nazis, for the most part, wanted to destroy all films exhibiting ideas anathema to them—and that was most films. With the complicity of at least one understanding German army officer and film enthusiast, Frank Henzel, Langlois was able to collect an astonishingly large number of movies from those the occupiers themselves had sieved—at the same time that he was hiding others from them. . . . He even managed to get films out of Germany, where they were in greater danger, to the relative safety of France.
>
> Perhaps it was his understanding of the role film can play in people's lives that led to Langlois's peripheral role in the *Resistance* during the occupation. Morale, of course, is always critical in war time, and the secret home film showing that Langlois provided were most certainly important to keeping up the spirits.[13]

Langlois and others risked their lives for film. Others still likely lost theirs. They did not do this out of any simple love of movies as movies, but of movies as part of life. That is, life without movies would be diminished, without them we would lose much of the flowering of the twentieth century.

Films, occupy a central place in contemporary cultural activities and discussions, even those ranging far beyond the movies, for they have become a central repository for our metaphors, for what really has become a "postmodern" language of English, at least. Films, always real, are now, Tarantino shows those of us who didn't already know, a major part of the way we even talk about the real.

Conclusion

If there is one consistent theme in Quentin Tarantino's movies, it's that life cannot be lived to its fullest with eyes in blinders. Actions have consequences, and we cannot understand either if we aren't willing to look at the whole of the situation. When we sanitize what we are doing in our own minds—it's only business, as in *Pulp Fiction;* we're acting like professionals, as in *Reservoir Dogs*—we become prone to ill-considered, immoral, and violent action. Our self-serving sanctimony, however, can never excuse us in the long run—as *Inglourious Basterds* shows. We may consider that the end justifies the means in extreme circumstances, but whose actions are justified ultimately? All of the characters in *Inglourious Basterds* are shown to be insane, and they all use violence as an excuse for perpetuating violence. Who is justified?

Our lives and our actions cannot be fully understood when we refuse to consider their full extent, limiting what we will look at. In the *Apology,* Socrates says that the "unexamined life is not worth living"—but it's more than that; the unexamined life (like all lives) affects other lives, and perhaps with more negativity for the lack of examination. By not looking at violence, for example, we perpetuate it, perhaps more strongly than if we were to face it directly.

Film, of course, isn't life, but entertainment. As such, it cannot be enjoyed to its fullest possibility if constrained, for entertainment is also part of life and carries life's necessities. Reality intrudes into entertainment, whether we like it or not. Movies, even if we consider them simply as distractions from reality, are involved in our negotiations with that reality. They are not always going to be likable as a result, any more than life is always what we desire. They are not always going to reflect our biases or our attempts to make life palatable. Part of our larger cultural discussions, ones that do, at times, lead us down paths of false conceptions of reality (consider what happened in Germany in the 1930s), is an attempt to avoid just that, the disfiguration of our public sphere. Art, by drawing attention to the very ways we distort our perceptions, helps us do that, though it is also used to the opposite purpose of making us accept distortion as truth, creating a complicated and even dangerous discussion.

The danger of constricting art, either in our individual choices (though those must be made) or societally, is that it then serves the purpose of confirming bias rather than challenging it, for the world viewed has been previously warped (in depiction) to fit that bias. This is the problem of trying to restrain artists from including violence in their work. No matter how we frame it, what we are doing is attempting to force art to reflect more strongly than it already does our preconceived notions of the world.

It's true that film, like any other art, carries within it bias and myth, altering the ways we look at the world. But it is also the arts, speaking most inclusively, that help keep us from that state of perpetual war, described so famously by Thomas Hobbes centuries ago:

> Whatsoever therefore is consequent to a time of Warre, where every man is Enemy to every man; the same is consequent to the time, wherein men live without other security, than what their own strength, and their own invention shall furnish them withall. In such condition, there is no place for Industry; because the fruit thereof is uncertain; and consequently no Culture of the Earth; no Navigation, nor use of the commodities that may be imported by Sea; no commodious Building; no Instruments of moving, and removing such things as require much force; no Knowledge of the face of the Earth; no account of Time; no Arts; no Letters; no Society; and which is worst of all, continuall feare, and danger of violent death; And the life of man, solitary, poore, nasty, brutish, and short.[1]

And therein lies the conundrum; do we accept the aid of arts, even if they depict the violent, in our attempts to create a world where Hobbes's "no" is turned to "many"? Without them, we will fail; with them, violence continues an ersatz omnipresence that could, itself, make us fail. There's no halfway in this; as we've seen through our centuries-long struggle to impose "propriety" on the arts, doing so also plants seeds of conflict as it works toward eradicating it.

One way or another, clearly, violence is going to be part of our lives . . . is part of our lives. The question is, how do we deal with that fact? And how do we deal with its depictions (which are also going to remain with us)? Violence in art doesn't seem to work as a stand-in for actual violence, so what's the point of it? Does it help us understand violence better? Does it release us, through some sort of catharsis, from pent-up violent tendencies? Or is it something that needs no justification, being a necessary part of effective art *because* it is a part of life, and art is also a part of life?

Perhaps the most gruesome scene in all of Tarantino's work is the head-on collision near the end of the first half of *Death Proof.* There are other scenes of greater violence, certainly, in both *Kill Bill* and *Inglourious Basterds,* but nothing comes close to this in terms of simple ghoulishness. What is its point? Why did Tarantino include it? He could have cut the actual impact out or concentrated on the cars and not the people, the young women, as they are being killed. But he did not.

The scene, like the violence, was planned quite carefully. Tarantino knew what he wanted each of the four women in the car to be doing at the point of impact and how he wanted them each killed. Though as stylized and choreographed as anything in *Kill Bill*'s "house of blue leaves," this scene presents a realism to the violence that is missing in most of the other instances in Tarantino films. Making the "death proof" car into a slicer, a grinder, a crusher, and a thrower (having already served as a hammer), Tarantino creates a different type of death for each of the characters. The one riding in the "death proof" car had been bounced around inside the passenger compartment until bloodied and then killed. The driver of the other car was crushed by the steering wheel. Jungle Julia (Sydney Poitier) had her leg severed (among other trauma). Shanna (Jordan Ladd) is thrown forward from the car, landing like a limp doll. And Arlene (Vanessa Ferlito) has her face opened and her skull splattered by a whirring tire.

The purpose of the graphic nature of the depiction of these deaths? Ultimately, it doesn't really matter any more than does the purpose of any other aspect of a work of art. There's no law that any work of art "must" have an overt point. Still, Tarantino never works through accident (though he will use accident if it suits his purposes). There was something he was trying to do through his presentation of the crash. As special effects coordinator Jon McLeod recalls, "Each girl has a very detailed and choreographed ending to her life that only a guy such as Quentin can put into words."[2] And the end of each is shown in slow-motion replay of that detail of the crash.

The driver of the car, Lanna Frank (Monica Staggs), appears somewhat older than the others (Staggs is a decade older than Ferlito and three and five years older than Poitier and Ladd respectively, both of whom are playing much younger than their real ages), has not been partying all day long (though she did supply the marijuana). She is killed by the driver's tool, the steering wheel, possibly a comment on her responsibility. The tall, long-legged beauty Jungle Julia Lucai, referred to earlier by Shanna as a "baby giraffe," and whose beauty Tarantino has explicitly featured quite lovingly and whose feet have been showcased in an almost fetishistic manner, has her leg severed almost at the hip and thrown onto the highway, perhaps something of a statement on an almost passive reliance on looks for success (she rarely does much in the film aside from lounge). Shanna, the smallest of the group, also seems to be the one who treasures belonging most. She has just reached for the radio to increase the volume when the crash occurs, putting her right in the middle of the group. The crash, of course, propels her out of it, with obvious implications. Arlene, the most sexually aggressive of the group (though she makes it clear that she will go only so far—she's more of a "tease" than a "tramp," to use the rather pejorative and sexist terminology of the past—relies on her looks as Lucai does but lacks the indolent air of her friend. Always the last to join in, always the one needing convincing, hers is also the last death shown. Her body is untouched, virginal; her face, though, is demolished.

What happens, however, is not portrayed as cosmic justice. This is tragedy of a different sort, undeserved. The "girls" may have faults, but these aren't tragic flaws. In their deaths, Tarantino is pointing at who they were, making their destruction even more poignant than it might otherwise be. And he is speaking quickly, through the images of gore, rather than engaging in drawn out explanations. In fact, he is using explicit violence to enhance our understanding of the waste and destruction caused by the insanity of Stuntman Mike (Kirk Russell), to make the deaths real even though stylized, through using them to further create "real" characters, maybe more real in their deaths (which is certainly Tarantino's point) than in the rather silly lives they have been leading.

As they die, the "girls" are listening to Dave Dee, Dozy, Beaky, Mick and Tich's "Hold Tight," a pop hit by a British vocal group that never managed to get much of a hold in the United States (though they were extremely successful in England). As usual for Tarantino, the lyrics of the song say something about the scene:

And hold tight, we will fly,
Swinging low, swinging high.

The "girls," of course, cannot hold on tight enough. Stuntman Mike does fly—right into them, his car swinging high as theirs swings low.

The violence of this scene of *Death Proof,* one of the more explicit and lovingly created bits of mayhem ever brought to the screen that still keeps to a level of realism (most scenes this gory become elaborate, clearly choreographed dances with little relations to "real" violence), cannot be offered as example of violence that would encourage viewers to go out and repeat it. For one thing, though realistic, it *couldn't* be replicated outside of the theater. For another, the risk to the perpetrator is insanely high. *His* car may be "death proof," but few others are—and even his "death proof" vehicle, the second half of the movie shows, is not enough to save his life.

The explicit nature of this crash scene emphasizes the waste that Stuntman Mike's obsession causes. The "girls" may be young, naïve, and foolish, but they are not evil, and they have great prospects, whatever their small failings that the movie shows. Reaction to their deaths should be outrage, and Tarantino makes sure it is through his graphic and bloody depiction. Sanitized, the scene could never have the impact he aims for. Sanitized, it would actually make the deaths more acceptable, as they are in movie after movie. Tarantino is forcing the audience to react: death is "real."

Without the violence of this scene, the movie would be nothing, and the final retribution meted to Stuntman Mike would seem horrendous and uncalled for—as it is, one could argue, given the knowledge of the other group of "girls," none of whom has, of course, any inkling of what Stuntman Mike has done in the past, though they might guess. In their fury, the second "girls" take revenge for a slew of others and not just for what Stuntman Mike has tried to do to them. Abernathy's (Rosario Dawson) death blow to Stuntman Mike's head, just after the credits begin, would seem as horrible as what he, himself, has done in the past, if it weren't for the explicit, gruesome deaths shown earlier (and, quite deliberately, not shown here at the end of the movie).

There is no way that Tarantino could make the movies that he does make without the ability to use violence. The gore is not simply tacked on for the sake of spectacle, but serves integral narrative purposes, as I hope I've shown in the preceding exploration of the scene from *Death Proof*. Every other example of mayhem in Tarantino works in similar fashion, both as spectacle and as part of the narration. All are different, some working as glorious set pieces against which the narrative gains traction, others as narrative projectiles themselves.

When someone complains about the violence of Tarantino's movies, they are complaining about the explicit nature of the violence and not about the violence itself. Or they are complaining that the consequences to violence are not clearly enough delineated for them or for those they wish to protect (children, the less discerning, whoever). They are attempting to define a world for themselves where violence is kept hidden or a world of justice. Neither reflects the experiential world well, and both serve only to restrict understanding, not expand it.

Not yet 50, Tarantino probably has a lot of years of Hollywood left in him and maybe even a few more movies for us to love and to hate. Whatever he does, he'll certainly keep our attention. And he will probably continue to keep us from sinking into the slough of assumption in which our inattention can easily let us drift. Even if we hate his films, we should at least thank him for bringing his enthusiasm into one of America's great art forms.

Whatever he does in the future, it is going to be hard for Tarantino to top a film that starts with intentional misspellings and ends with the death of Hitler a year early—and in Paris, at that—as *Inglourious Basterds* does. But, even though Tarantino doesn't think in terms of what he has already done, he will find a way. He is always looking to what he *might* be able to do, to new types of stories to tell and new ways of presenting them in film.

Though he loves a challenge, Tarantino is also extremely careful. That is, he never sets challenges for himself that are completely beyond his possibility, just as he never challenges his audience without providing a means for meeting it. By starting off from known genres, he places his viewers in a comfortable and confident position, a stable base for reaching up to touch and grab a new form of understanding of, say, narrative, or of the relation between movies and the world. He challenges them to look to the extremes of what they can do and to follow their imaginations, just as he does for himself.

Because he starts low and aims high, Tarantino is often dismissed by those who take a quick glance at his films, seeing only the low. Generally, these are people themselves still mired in a kitsch/avant-garde duality, people who believe that slasher movies, say, are products of low culture and the films of Julian Schnabel of the high—and that never the twain shall meet. Tarantino, though, embraces each, and at once, and sees no reason to distinguish between them, at least not in judgment. Art can be found in both places, and can be found lacking in both. Though he rises out of a Hollywood tradition extending back nearly a century, Tarantino is also the harbinger of a new type of filmmaking, one that refuses ideological barriers and even self-imposed limitations, always mining the past nonjudgmentally for ways of dealing with the new, creating a movement that cannot be encapsulated in definitions or, perhaps, even named.

As has always been the case in Hollywood, these new filmmakers will continue to focus on storytelling, though Tarantino has shown them that they don't need to be restricted by general adherence to traditional narrative forms, as long as they are willing to use their work to teach their viewers how to watch and to understand what they are doing. The movies will be grounded in the world, as Tarantino's are, but will twist presentations of it freely to make the points of the filmmakers. The films will often appear trivial to the older generation, but they will speak loudly to the young and, I suspect, to future generations.

And the joy of storytelling will live on.

Timeline

Year	Directing	Writing	Acting	Producing
1987	*My Best Friend's Birthday* (incomplete and unreleased)	*My Best Friend's Birthday* (incomplete and unreleased)	*My Best Friend's Birthday* (incomplete and unreleased)	*My Best Friend's Birthday* (incomplete and unreleased)
1988				
1989				
1990				
1991		*Past Midnight* (uncredited)		
1992	*Reservoir Dogs*	*Reservoir Dogs*	• *Reservoir Dogs* • *Eddie Presley*	
1993		*True Romance*		
1994	*Pulp Fiction*	• *Pulp Fiction* • *Natural Born Killers*	• *Pulp Fiction* • *Sleep With Me* • *Somebody to Love*	*Killing Zoe*
1995	• Television: "Motherhood" episode for *ER*. • "Man from Hollywood" segment for *Four Rooms*	• "Man from Hollywood" segment for *Four Rooms* • *Dance Me to the End of Love*	• Television: "Pulp Sitcom" episode for *All-American Girl* • *Destiny Turns on the Radio*	• *Four Rooms*

(Continued)

Timeline (Continued)

Year	Directing	Writing	Acting	Producing
	• *Dance Me to the End of Love*	• *Crimson Tide* (uncredited)	• *Desperado* • *Four Rooms* • *Dance Me to the End of Love*	
1996		• *From Dusk Till Dawn* • "Gecko Brothers news report" in *Curdled* (uncredited) • *The Rock* (uncredited)	• *From Dusk Till Dawn* • *Girl 6*	• *From Dusk Till Dawn* • *Curdled*
1997	*Jackie Brown*	*Jackie Brown* (screenplay)	*Jackie Brown*	
1998				*God Said 'Ha'*
1999				• *From Dusk Till Dawn 2: Texas Blood Money* • *From Dusk Till Dawn 3: The Hangman's Daughter*
2000			*Little Nicky*	
2001				*Iron Monkey*
2002			Television: "The Box: Part 1" and "The Box: Part 2" episodes for *Alias*	

Year				
2003	*Kill Bill, vol. 1*	*Kill Bill, vol. 1*		
2004	• *Kill Bill, vol. 2* • Television: 4/20 episode for *Jimmy Kimmel Live*	*Kill Bill, vol. 2*	Television: "After Six" and "Full Disclosure" episodes for *Alias*	*My Name Is Modesty: A Modesty Blaise Adventure*
2005	• "Special Guest Director": *Sin City* • Television: "Grave Danger," parts 1 and 2, episodes for *CSI: Crime Scene Investigation*		Television: "Master and Disaster/All in the Crime Family" episode for *Duck Dodgers*	• *Hostel* • *Daltry Calhoun*
2006				*Freedom's Fury*
2007	*Death Proof* segment, *Grindhouse*	*Death Proof*	• *Death Proof* • *Planet Terror* segment, *Grindhouse* • *Sukiyaki Western Django*	• *Hostel: Part II* • *Planet Terror* segment, *Grindhouse*
2008				
2009	*Inglourious Basterds*	*Inglourious Basterds*		*Hell Ride*

Notes

CHAPTER 1

1. Manohla Dargis, "Movie Review: Inglourious Basterds, Tarantino Avengers in Nazi Movieland," *The New York Times*, August 21, 2009, http://movies.nytimes.com/2009/08/21/movies/21inglourious.html.
2. Quentin Tarantino, quoted in Ciment and Niogret, rpt. Peary, p. 26.
3. D. K. Holm, *Kill Bill*, 6.
4. Jerome Charyn, *Raised by Wolves*, 92.
5. Jerome Charyn, *Raised by Wolves*, 93.
6. Jean Baudrillard, *Simulations*.
7. Catherine Constable, "Postmodernism and film," 44.
8. Catherine Constable, "Postmodernism and film,"44.
9. M. Keith Booker, *Postmodern Hollywood*, xiv.
10. Dwight Macdonald, "A Theory of Mass Culture," 60.
11. Dwight Macdonald, "A Theory of Mass Culture," 60.
12. Clement Greenberg, "Avant-Garde and Kitsch," 99.
13. Clement Greenberg, "Avant-Garde and Kitsch," 102.
14. Clement Greenberg, "Avant-Garde and Kitsch," 102.
15. Noël Carroll, *A Philosophy of Mass Art*, 32–33.
16. Claudia Gorbman in Michel Chion, *Film, A Sound Art*, 474.
17. Noël Carroll, *A Philosophy of Mass Art*.
18. Noël Carroll, *A Philosophy of Mass Art*.
19. Noël Carroll, *A Philosophy of Mass Art*, 196.
20. Noël Carroll, *A Philosophy of Mass Art*, 199.
21. Noël Carroll, *A Philosophy of Mass Art*, 204–205.
22. Noël Carroll, *A Philosophy of Mass Art*, 204–205.
23. Noël Carroll, *A Philosophy of Mass Art*, 205.
24. David Bordwell, *The Classical Hollywood Cinema: Film Style & Mode of Production to 1960*, 3–11.
25. David Bordwell, *The Classical Hollywood Cinema: Film Style & Mode of Production to 1960*, 8.
26. Fredric Jameson, "Postmodernism and the Consumer Society," 112.
27. Christine Gledhill, "Rethinking genre," 223.

28. Alissa Quart, "Networked," 50.
29. M. Keith Booker, *Postmodern Hollywood*, 12.
30. M. Keith Booker, *Postmodern Hollywood*, 12.
31. J. David Slocum, "The 'Film Violence' Trope," 25.
32. Jean-Francois Lyotard, *The Postmodern Condition: A Report on Knowledge*.
33. K. J. Donnelly, "The Hidden Heritage of Film Music," 6.
34. K. J. Donnelly, "The Hidden Heritage of Film Music," 9.
35. K. J. Donnelly, "The Hidden Heritage of Film Music," 3.
36. D. K. Holm, *Kill Bill*, 7.
37. Fredric Jameson, "Postmodernism and the Consumer Society," 113.
38. Fredric Jameson, "Postmodernism and the Consumer Society," 113.
39. Fredric Jameson, "Postmodernism and the Consumer Society," 114.
40. Fredric Jameson, "Postmodernism and the Consumer Society," 115.
41. Quentin Tarantino, quoted in Ciment and Niogret, rpt. Peary, p. 16.
42. Pauline Kael, "Godard Among the Gangsters," *The New Republic*, 9/10/1966, Vol. 155, Issue 11, 27–29.
43. Pauline Kael, "Godard Among the Gangsters," *The New Republic*, 9/10/1966, Vol. 155, Issue 11, 27–29.
44. Pauline Kael, "Review of *Phantom of the Paradise*," in *For Keeps*, 584–585.
45. Jacques Derrida, *Acts of Literature*, 221–252.
46. Stephen Neale, *Genre and Hollywood*, 24.
47. J. David Slocum, "The 'Film Violence' Trope," 27.
48. Rick Altman, "Cinema and Genre," 276.
49. Steve Neale, 2000, *Genre and Hollywood*, 31.
50. Steve Neale, 2000, *Genre and Hollywood*, 23.
51. Quentin Tarantino, quoted in Camille Nevers, "Encounter with Quentin Tarantino," *Cahiers du Cinéma* 457, June 1992, p. 49, trans. T. Jefferson Kline.
52. David Bordwell, David, *The Classical Hollywood Cinema*, 8.

CHAPTER 2

1. Jami Bernard's *Quentin Tarantino: The Man and His Movies*; Jerome Charyn's *Raised by Wolves*; Wensley Clarkson's *The Man, the Myths and His Movies*, Jeff Dawson's *Quentin Tarantino: The Cinema of Cool*; and Paul Woods's *King Pulp: The Wild World of Quentin Tarantino* all have strong biographical elements.
2. David Bordwell, *The Way Hollywood Tells It*, 60.
3. David Bordwell, *The Way Hollywood Tells It*, 196–197. All of the following statistics (except the conversion to 2008 dollars) come from the appendix, "A Hollywood Timeline, 1960–004," of that work.
4. Robert Sklar, *Movie-Made America*, 301.
5. *A Fistful of Dollars* (1964—U.S., 1967), *For a Few Dollars More* (1965—U.S., 1967), *The Good, the Bad, and the Ugly* (1966—U.S., 1967).
6. Leonard Quart and Albert Auster, *American Film and Society Since 1945*, 73.
7. Stephen Prince, *Screening Violence*, 10.
8. See David Bordwell, Kristen Thompson, and Janet Staiger, *The Classical Hollywood Cinema*.
9. Steven Jay Schneider, "Introduction," *New Hollywood Violence*, 7.

10. Robert Sklar, *Movie-Made America*, 289.
11. David Bordwell, *The Way Hollywood Tells It*, 12.
12. Robert Skar, *Movie-Made America*, 293.
13. Robert Skar, *Movie-Made America*, 293.
14. Thomas Doerty, *Teenagers and Teenpics*, chapter 7.
15. http://www.imdb.com/title/tt0061735/business.
16. Leonard Quart and Albert Auster, *American Film and Society Since 1945*, 81.
17. Leonard Quart and Albert Auster, *American Film and Society Since 1945*, 82.
18. Malcolm Gladwell, *Outliers: the story of success*. New York: Little, Brown and Co.
19. Connie Zastoupil, quoted in Wensley Clarkson, *Quentin Tarantino: shooting from the hip*, 12.
20. See Wensley Clarkson, *Quentin Tarantino: shooting from the hip*.
21. Quentin Tarantino in Richard Rodriguez, Quentin Tarantino, and Kurt Volk, *Grindhouse*, 13.
22. Nöel Carroll, *Interpreting the Moving Image*, 244–245.
23. Novotny Lawrence, *Blaxploitation Films of the 1970s*, 19.
24. See my *The DVD Revolution: Movies, Culture, and Technology* for more on this topic.
25. Robert Sklar, *Movie-Made America*, 290.
26. Quentin Tarantino, quoted in Paul Woods, *King Pulp*, 13.
27. Quentin Tarantino, quoted in Paul Woods, *King Pulp*, 15.
28. Quentin Tarantino, quoted in Michel Ciment and Hubert Niogret, "Interview at Cannes," Peary, 11.
29. Jerome Charyn, *Raised by Wolves*, 17.
30. Quentin Tarantino, quoted in Michel Ciment and Hubert Niogret, "Interview at Cannes," Peary, 12.
31. Caylah Eddleblute, quoted in Tarantino and Rodriguez, *Grindhouse*, 162.
32. Vincent LoBrutto, *Martin Scorsese: A Biography*, 130.
33. Nöel Carroll, *Interpreting the Moving Image*, 244–245.
34. Nöel Carroll, *Interpreting the Moving Image*, 244.
35. David Bordwell, *The Way Hollywood Tells It*, 60.
36. Thomas Pynchon, *Gravity's Rainbow*, 63.
37. Jeff Dawson, *Quentin Tarantino: The Cinema of Cool*. New York: Applause. 141.

CHAPTER 3

1. National Highway Traffic Safety Administration (NHTSA) statistics presented at http://www.car-accidents.com/pages/fatal-accident-statistics.html.
2. FBI Web site: Crime in the United States, http://www.fbi.gov/ucr/cius2008/data/table_01.html
3. William Rothman, "Violence and Film," 40.
4. William Rothman, "Violence and Film," 42.
5. J. David Slocum, *Violence and American Cinema*, 9.
6. J. David Slocum, "The 'Film Violence' Trope," 24.
7. Stephen Prince, *Classical Film Violence*, 33.
8. Stephen Prince, *Classical Film Violence*, 258.
9. Leo Charney, "The Violence of a Perfect Moment," 48.

10. Leo Charney, "The Violence of a Perfect Moment," 52.
11. Marsha Kinder, "Violence American Style," 65.
12. Stephen Prince, *Screening Violence*, 9.
13. Peter Kramer, "'Clean, Dependable Slapstick," 113.
14. Sissela Bok, *Mayhem: Violence as Public Entertainment*, 37.
15. Sissela Bok, *Mayhem: Violence as Public Entertainment*, 37.
16. Sissela Bok, *Mayhem: Violence as Public Entertainment*, 33.
17. William Rothman, "Violence and Film," 46.
18. William Rothman, "Violence and Film," 42.
19. Stephen Prince, *Screening Violence*, 27–28.
20. William Rothman, "Violence and Film," 42.
21. William Rothman, "Violence and Film," 43.
22. Sissela Bok, *Mayhem: Violence as Public Entertainment*, 55.
23. Sissela Bok, *Mayhem: Violence as Public Entertainment*, 55.
24. Herbert Gans, "The Creator-Audience Relationship in the Mass Media: An Analysis of Movie Making," 315.
25. Will Brooker and Deborah Jermyn, *The Audience Studies Reader*, 333.
26. William Rothman, "Violence and Film," 38.
27. William Rothman, "Violence and Film," 39.
28. Stephen Prince, *Classical Film Violence*, 30.
29. Pauline Kael, *For Keeps*, 149.
30. Geoff King, "'Killingly Funny,'" 127.
31. J. David Slocum, "The 'Film Violence' Trope," 21.
32. J. David Slocum, "The 'Film Violence' Trope," 21.
33. J. David Slocum, "The 'Film Violence' Trope," 22.
34. J. David Slocum, "The 'Film Violence' Trope," 23.
35. Quentin Tarantino, interview with Elle Taylor, in *Quentin Tarantino Interviews*, 47.
36. J. David Slocum, "The 'Film Violence' Trope," 27.
37. Sissela Bok, *Mayhem: Violence as Public Entertainment*, 41.
38. Jessica Milner Davis, *Farce*, 3.
39. Jessica Milner Davis, *Farce*, 23
40. Jessica Milner Davis, *Farce*, 4.
41. Jessica Milner Davis, *Farce*, 5.
42. Jessica Milner Davis, *Farce*, 6.
43. Jessica Milner Davis, *Farce*, 7.
44. Jessica Milner Davis, *Farce*, 31.
45. Jessica Milner Davis, *Farce*, 16.
46. Geoff King, "'Killingly Funny,'" 131.

CHAPTER 4

1. Nietzsche, *The Birth of Tragedy*, 15.
2. See Travis Anderson, 2007, "Unleashing Nietzsche on the Tragic Infrastructure of Tarantino's *Reservoir Dogs*" in Richard Greene and K. Silem Mohammad, eds., *Quentin Tarantino and Philosophy* (Chicago: Open Court), 21–39.
3. Robert Warshow, "The Gangster as Tragic Hero," 13.

4. Foster Hirsch, *Detours and Lost Highways*, 259–260.

5. Mack Sennett, quoted in James Agee, "Comedy's Greatest Era" (1949), *Agee on Film*, 398.

6. David Bordwell, *The Way Hollywood Tells It*, 63–68.

7. Quentin Tarantino, quoted in David J. Fox, "Hmmm. Let's See. Whose Calls Won't I Return Today?" *Los Angeles Times* Calendar Section, Feb 2, 1992, 22.

8. Everson, *American Silent Film*, 228.

9. Aristotle, *Poetics*, IV, 15

10. Aristotle, *Poetics*, IV, 15

11. See Pound, *Make It New: Essays.*

12. Vincent Canby, "A Caper Goes Wrong, Resoundingly," *The New York Times*, Oct. 23, 1992, http://movies.nytimes.com/movie/review?res=9E0CE6 DD113EF930A15753C1A964958260&scp=1&sq=reservoir%20dogs%20quenti n%20tarantino&st=cse.

13. Danto, *The Transfiguration of the Commonplace*, 208.

14. Nietzsche, *The Birth of Tragedy*, 14.

15. Aristotle, *Poetics*, VI, 27.

16. Thomas Leitch, "Aristotle v. the Action Film," in Schneider, *New Hollywood Violence*, 105

17. Aristotle, *Poetics*, XI, 41.

18. Aristotle, *Poetics*, XI, 41.

19. Aristotle, *Poetics*, XI, 43.

20. Aristotle, *Poetics*, XIII, 45.

21. Nietzsche, *The Birth of Tragedy*, 43.

22. Aristotle, *Poetics*, XIX, 69–70.

23. Foster Hirsch, *Detours and Lost Highways*, 259.

24. Romanov, *Soundtrack: The Significance of Music in the Films Written and Directed by Quentin Tarantino*, 6.

25. Nietzsche, *The Birth of Tragedy*, 100.

26. Nietzsche, *The Birth of Tragedy*, 79–80.

27. Romanov, *Soundtrack: The Significance of Music in the Films Written and Directed by Quentin Tarantino*, 12.

28. Romanov, *Soundtrack: The Significance of Music in the Films Written and Directed by Quentin Tarantino*, 13–14.

29. Nietzsche, *The Birth of Tragedy*, 80.

30. Nietzsche, *The Birth of Tragedy*, 63.

31. Thomas Leitch, "Aristotle v. the Action Film," in Schneider, *New Hollywood Violence*, 109.

32. Thomas Leitch, "Aristotle v. the Action Film," in Schneider, *New Hollywood Violence*, 122.

33. Thoms Leitch, "Aristotle v. the Action Film," in Schneider, *New Hollywood Violence*, 111.

34. Münsterberg *The Photoplay: A Psychological Study*, 70.

35. Sergei Eisenstein, *Film Form*, 3–17.

36. Münsterberg, *The Photoplay: A Psychological Study*, 66.

37. Aristotle, *Poetics*, VI, 23.

38. Aristotle, *Poetics*, IX, 39.

39. Nietzsche, *The Birth of Tragedy*, 45.
40. Nietzsche, *The Birth of Tragedy*, 43.
41. Nietzsche, *The Birth of Tragedy*, 102.
42. Nietzsche, *The Birth of Tragedy*, 39.
43. Nietzsche, *The Birth of Tragedy*, 47.
44. Robert Warshow, "The Gangster as Tragic Hero," 12.
45. Nietzsche, *The Birth of Tragedy*, 52.
46. Robert Warshow, "The Gangster as Tragic Hero," 15.
47. Nietzsche, *The Birth of Tragedy*, 88–89.
48. Romanov, *Soundtrack: The Significance of Music in the Films Written and Directed by Quentin Tarantino*, 14–15.

CHAPTER 5

1. Quentin Tarantino, quoted in Manohla Dargis, "Quentin Tarantino on *Pulp Fiction*," 66.
2. Marsha Kinder, "Violence American Style," 81.
3. Quentin Tarantino, quoted in Ciment and Niogret, rpt. Peary, 25.
4. Jeff Dawson, *Quentin Tarantino: the cinema of cool*, 142.
5. Jessica Milner Davis, *Farce*, 25.
6. Jerome Charyn, *Raised by wolves*, 86.
7. Geoff King, "'Killingly funny': Mixing Modalities in New Hollywood's Comedy-with-Violence," 134.
8. Ed Guerrero, "Black Violence As Cinema," 221.
9. Sharon Willis, "'Style,' Posture, and Idiom," 280.
10. Roger Ebert, "Secrets of Pulp Fiction," 1.
11. Roger Ebert, "Secrets of Pulp Fiction," 1.
12. Greg Nicotero, interview by Laurent Bouzereau, in Bouzereau, *Ultraviolent Movies*, 88.
13. Marsha Kinder, "Violence American Style," 77.
14. Janet Maslin, "Movie Review: Pulp Fiction," *The New York Times*, September 23, 1994. http://movies.nytimes.com/movie/review?res=9B0DE5DA143AF930A1575AC0A962958260&scp=2&sq=janet%20maslin%20pulp%20fiction%20review&st=cse.
15. See Stephen Neale, *Genre and Hollywood*, pages 65-71 for an overview of definitions of the comedy genre.
16. James Agee, *Agee on Film*, 393.
17. James Agee, *Agee on Film*, 410.
18. Foster Hirsch, *Detours and Lost Highways*, 271.
19. Foster Hirsch, *Detours and Lost Highways*, 270.
20. James Agee, *Agee on Film*, 248.
21. James Agee, *Agee on Film*, 249.
22. D. K. Holm, *The Pocket Essential Quentin Tarantino*, 90.
23. James Agee, *Agee on Film*, 256.
24. James Agee, *Agee on Film*, 249.
25. James Agee, *Agee on Film*, 256.
26. James Agee, *Agee on Film*, 251–252.

27. Edward Gallefant, *Quentin Tarantino*, 72.
28. Todd Onderdonk, "Tarantino's Deadly Homosocial," 290.
29. Kelly Ritter, "Postmodern Dialogics in *Pulp Fiction*," 296.
30. Kelly Ritter, "Postmodern Dialogics in *Pulp Fiction*," 299.
31. James Agee, *Agee on Film*, 249–250.
32. Jake Horsley, 1999, *The Blood Poets*, 237.
33. Roger Ebert, "Secrets of Pulp Fiction," 1.
34. Roger Ebert, "Secrets of 'Pulp Fiction,'" 1.
35. Joseph Shaw, *The Hard-boiled Omnibus*, viii.
36. Foster Hirsch, *Detours and Lost Highways*, 90.
37. Roger Ebert, "Pulp Fiction: Great Movies," 5.
38. D. K. Holm, *The Pocket Essential Quentin Tarantino*, 90.
39. Jake Horsley, 1999, *The Blood Poets*, 239.
40. Jerome Charyn, *Raised by Wolves*, 63.

CHAPTER 6

1. Edwin Page, *Quintessential Tarantino*, 169.
2. Gorbman, *Unheard Melodies*, 22.
3. George Burt, *The Art of Film Music*, 3–4.
4. Gorbman, *Unheard Melodies*, 14.
5. Gorbman, *Unheard Melodies*, 30.
6. Michel Chion, *Film, A Sound Art*, 120.
7. Michel Chion, *Film, A Sound Art*, 427.
8. Michel Chion, *Film, A Sound Art*, 430.
9. Elmore Leonard, *Rum Punch*, 39–40.
10. K. J. Donnelly, "*Performance* and the Composite Film Score," 153.
11. Gorbman, *Unheard Melodies*, 20.
12. Quart and Auster, *American Film and Society Since 1945*, 85.
13. Ken Garner, "'Would You Like to Hear Some Music?,'" 193.
14. N. Keith Booker, *Postmodern Hollywood*, 14.
15. Jerome Charyn, *Raised by Wolves*, 126–127.
16. Alan Barnes and Marcus Hearn, *Tarantino A to Zed*, 104.
17. See M. Keith Booker, *Postmodern Hollywood*, 14.
18. Robert Miklitsch, *Roll Over Adorno*, 101.
19. Novotny Lawrence, 2008. *Blaxploitation films of the 1970s*, 19.
20. Jans Wager, *Dames in the Driver's Seat*, 153.
21. Elmore Leonard, *Rum Punch*, 343–344.

CHAPTER 7

1. Jerome Charyn, *Raised by Wolves*, 170–171.
2. Jerome Charyn, *Raised by Wolves*, 137.
3. Stephen Neale, *Genre and Hollywood*, 52.
4. Theresa Webb and Nick Browne, "The Big Impossible," 82.
5. Jeffrey Brown, "Gender, Sexuality, and Toughness," 48.
6. Jeffrey Brown, "Gender, Sexuality, and Toughness," 47–48.

7. Jeffrey Brown, "Gender, Sexuality, and Toughness," 47–48.
8. Jeffrey Brown, "Gender, Sexuality, and Toughness," 49.
9. Jeffrey Brown, "Gender, Sexuality, and Toughness," 50.
10. Theresa Webb and Nick Browne, "The Big Impossible," 90.
11. Theresa Webb and Nick Browne, "The Big Impossible," 91.
12. Theresa Webb and Nick Browne, "The Big Impossible," 96–97.
13. Jacinda Read, "'Once Upon a Time There Were Three Little Girls . . . ,'" 212.
14. Vladimir Propp, *Morphology of the Folktale*.

CHAPTER 8

1. Robert Rodriguez, in Tarantino and Rodriguez, *Grindhouse*, 6.
2. Tarantino, in Quentin Tarantino, Robert Rodriguez, and Kurt Volk, *Grindhouse*, 155.
3. Carol Clover, "Her Body, Himself: Gender in the Slasher Film," 125.
4. Quentin Tarantino, in Quentin Tarantino, Robert Rodriguez, and Kurt Volk, *Grindhouse*, 155.
5. Carol Clover, "Her Body, Himself: Gender in the Slasher Film," 129–130.
6. Carol Clover, "Her Body, Himself: Gender in the Slasher Film," 135.
7. Tarantino, in Quentin Tarantino, Robert Rodriguez, and Kurt Volk, *Grindhouse*, 157.
8. Carol Clover, "Her Body, Himself: Gender in the Slasher Film," 143.
9. Carol Clover, "Her Body, Himself: Gender in the Slasher Film," 147.
10. Carol Clover, "Her Body, Himself: Gender in the Slasher Film," 152.
11. Carol Clover, "Her Body, Himself: Gender in the Slasher Film," 160.
12. Carol Clover, "Her Body, Himself: Gender in the Slasher Film," 160.
13. Carol Clover, "Her Body, Himself: Gender in the Slasher Film," 162.
14. Carol Clover, "Her Body, Himself: Gender in the Slasher Film," 155.
15. Stephen Prince, *Screening Violence*, 149.
16. Carol Clover, "Her Body, Himself: Gender in the Slasher Film," 149.
17. Tarantino, in Quentin Tarantino, Robert Rodriguez, and Kurt Volk, *Grindhouse*, 157.
18. Carol Clover, "Her Body, Himself: Gender in the Slasher Film,"165.
19. Sherrie Inness, *Tough Girls*, 17.
20. Carol Clover, "Her Body, Himself: Gender in the Slasher Film," 166.
21. Carol Clover, "Her Body, Himself: Gender in the Slasher Film," 166.
22. Sara Crosby, "Female Heroes Snapped into Sacrificial Heroines," 161.
23. Sherrie Inness, *Tough Girls*, 18.
24. Michel Chion, *Film, A Sound Art*, 159.
25. Tarantino, in Quentin Tarantino, Robert Rodriguez, and Kurt Volk, *Grindhouse*, 198.
26. André Bazin, *What Is Cinema?*, 45.
27. André Bazin, *What Is Cinema?*, 48.
28. Sergei Eisenstein, *Film Form*, 38.
29. Thomas Doherty, *Teenagers and Teenpics*, 189–198.
30. Thomas Doherty, *Teenagers and Teenpics*, 191–192.

CHAPTER 9

1. Reproduced in Rodriguez, Tarantino, and Volk, *Grindhouse*, 163.
2. Jeanine Basinger, *The World War II Combat Film*, 16.
3. Eli Roth, quoted in Naomi Pfefferman, "Eli Roth Fuels 'Basterds' Role With Holocaust Fury," *JewishJournal.com*, August 18, 2009, http://www .jewishjournal.com/cover_story/article/eli_roth_fuels_basterds_role_with _holocaust_fury_20090818/.
4. Quentin Tarantino, *Inglourious Basterds: A Screenplay*, 164.
5. Richard Slotkin, *Regeneration Through Violence*.
6. Richard Slotkin, *Regeneration Through Violence*, 8.
7. Richard Slotkin, *Regeneration Through Violence*, 21.
8. Richard Slotkin, *Regeneration Through Violence*, 55.
9. André Breton, *Manifestoes of Surrealism*, 9–10.
10. André Breton, *Manifestoes of Surrealism*, 26.
11. Jeanine Basinger, *The World War II Combat Movie*, 173–174.
12. Manohla Dargis, "Review: *Inglourious Basterds*," *The New York Times*, August 21, 2009, http://movies.nytimes.com/2009/08/21/movies/21inglourious .html?scp=2&sq=inglourious%20basterds&st=cse
13. Aaron Barlow, *The DVD Revolution*, 35–36.

CHAPTER 10

1. Thomas Hobbes, *Leviathan*, 84.
2. John McLeod, quoted in *Grindhouse*, 182.

Bibliography

Agee, James. 2000 [1958]. *Agee on Film: Criticism and Comment on the Movies*. New York: Modern Library.

Altman, Rick. 1996. "Cinema and Genre." In Geoffrey Nowell-Smith. 1996. 276–285.

Altman, Rick. 1999. *Film/genre*. London: BFI Publishing.

Aristotle. S. H. Butcher, trans. 1951. *Aristotle's Theory of Poetry and Fine Art, with a Critical Text and Translation of the Poetics*. New York: Dover.

Barlow, Aaron. 2005. *The DVD Revolution: Movies, Culture, and Technology*. Westport, CT: Praeger.

Barnes, Alan, and Marcus Hearn. 1999. *Tarantino A to Zed: the Films of Quentin Tarantino*. London: B.T. Batsford. 2nd edition.

Basinger, Jeanine. 1986. *The World War II Combat Film: Anatomy of a Genre*. New York: Columbia University Press.

Baudrillard, Jean. 1983. *Simulations*. Trans. Paul Foss, Paul Patton, and Philip Beitchman. Foreign agents series. New York: Semiotext(e).

Bazin, André. Hugh Gray, trans. 1967. *What is Cinema?* Berkeley: University of California Press.

Bernard, Jami. 1995. *Quentin Tarantino: The Man and His Movies*. New York: HarperPerennial.

Blakesley, David. 2003. *The Terministic Screen: Rhetorical Perspectives on Film*. Carbondale: Southern Illinois University Press.

Bloom, Harold. 1973. *The Anxiety of Influence: A Theory of Poetry*. New York: Oxford University Press.

Boggs, Carl, and Thomas Pollard. 2003. *A World in Chaos: Social Crisis and the Rise of Postmodern Cinema*. Lanham, MD: Rowman & Littlefield Publishers.

Bok, Sissela. 1998. *Mayhem: Violence as Public Entertainment*. Reading, Mass: Perseus Book.

Booker, M. Keith. 2007. *Postmodern Hollywood: What's New in Film and Why It Makes Us Feel So Strange*. Westport, CT: Praeger.

Bordwell, David. 2006. *The Way Hollywood Tells It: Story and Style in Modern Movies*. Berkeley: University of California Press.

Bordwell, David, Janet Staiger, and Kristin Thompson. 1985. *The Classical Hollywood Cinema: Film Style & Mode of Production to 1960*. New York: Columbia University Press.

Bouzereau, Laurent. 2000. *Ultraviolent Movies: From Sam Peckinpah to Quentin Tarantino*. New York: Citadel Press.

Breton, André. Trans. Richard Seaver and Helen Lane. 1969. *Manifestoes of Surrealism*. Ann Arbor: The University of Michigan Press.

Brooker, Will, and Deborah Jermyn, ed. 2003. *The Audience Studies Reader*. New York: Routledge.

Brooker, Peter, and Will Brooker. 1997. *Postmodern After-Images: A Reader in Film, Television, and Video*. London: Arnold.

Brown, Jeffrey. 2004. "Gender, Sexuality, and Toughness: The Bad Girls of Action Film and Comic Books." In Sherrie Inness, 2004. 47–74.

Carroll, Noël. 1996. *Theorizing the Moving Image*. Cambridge studies in film. Cambridge: Cambridge University Press.

Carroll, Noël. 1998. *A Philosophy of Mass Art*. Oxford, UK: Clarendon Press.

Charney, Leo. 2001. "The Violence of a Perfect Moment." In J. David Slocum, 2001. 47–62.

Charyn, Jerome. 2006. *Raised by Wolves: The Turbulent Art and Times of Quentin Tarantino*. New York: Thunder's Mouth Press.

Chion, Michel. Claudie Gorbman, trans. 1999 [1981]. *The Voice in Cinema*. New York: Columbia University Press.

Chion, Michel. Claudie Gorbman, trans. 2009 [2003]. *Film, A Sound Art*. New York: Columbia University Press.

Clarkson, Wensley. 1995. *Quentin Tarantino: Shooting from the Hip*. London: Piatkus.

Clarkson, Wensley. 2007. *Quentin Tarantino: The Man, the Myths and the Movies*. London: John Blake.

Clover, Carol. 2000 [1987]. "Her Body, Himself: Gender in the Slasher Film." In Stephen Prince, 2000. 125–174.

Connor, Steven, ed. 2004. *The Cambridge Companion to Postmodernism*. Cambridge companions to literature. Cambridge, UK: Cambridge University Press.

Constable, Catherine. 2004. "Postmodernism and film." In Steven Connor, 2004. 43–61.

Crosby, Sara. 2004. "Female Heroes Snapped into Sacrificial Heroines." In Sherrie Innes, 2004. 153–178.

Danto, Arthur Coleman. 1981. *The Transfiguration of the Commonplace: A Philosophy of Art*. Cambridge, MA: Harvard University Press.

Dargis, Manohla. 1998 [1994]. "Quentin Tarantino on *Pulp Fiction*." In Quentin Tarantino and Gerald Peary, 1998. 66–69.

Davis, Jessica Milner. 2003. *Farce*. Classics in communication and mass culture series. New Brunswick, NJ: Transaction.

Dawson, Jeff. 1995. *Quentin Tarantino: the Cinema of Cool*. New York: Applause.

Derrida, Jacques. Derek Attridge, trans. 1992. *Acts of Literature*. New York: Routledge.

Doherty, Thomas Patrick. 2002. *Teenagers and Teenpics: The Juvenilization of American Movies in the 1950s*. Philadelphia, PA: Temple University Press.

Donnelly, K. J., ed. 2001. *Film Music: Critical Approaches*. New York: Continuum.

Donnelly, K. J. 2001. "The Hidden Heritage of Film Music: History and Scholarship." In K. J. Donnelly, ed., *Film Music*, 1–15.

Donnelly, K. J. 2001. "*Performance* and the Composite Film Score." In K. J. Donnelly, ed., *Film Music,* 152–166.

Ebert, Roger, "One-Stop Mayhem Shop, 'Pulp Fiction' Hurtles Into Bizarre Universe," *Chicago Sun-Times,* October 14, 1994, Pg. 43.

Ebert, Roger, "Secrets of Pulp Fiction: Ebert Analyzes Film Shot by Shot—Now Try it at Home," *Chicago Sun-Times,* September 10, 1995, Show, Pg. 1.

Ebert, Roger, "Pulp Fiction: Great Movies," *Chicago Sun-Times,* June 10, 2001, Show, Pg. 5.

Eisenstein, Sergei Jay Leyda, trans. 1977. *Film form: Essays in Film Theory.* San Diego, CA: Harcourt, Brace, Jovanovich.

Everson, William K. 1978. *American Silent Film.* A History of the American film, 1. New York: Oxford University Press.

Fariña, Richard. 1966. *Been Down So Long It Looks Like Up to Me.* New York: Random House.

Foster, Hal. 1989. *Postmodern Culture.* London: Pluto Press.

Gallafent, Edward. 2006. *Quentin Tarantino.* On directors series. Harlow, UK: Pearson Longman.

Gans, Herbert. 1956. "The Creator-Audience Relationship in the Mass Media: An Analysis of Movie Making." In Bernard Rosenberg and David Manning White, 1957. 315–324.

Garner, Ken. 2001. 'Would You Like to Hear Some Music?': Music in-and-out-of-Control in the Films of Quentin Tarantino." In Garner, *Film Music,* 2001, 188–205.

Gladwell, Malcolm. 2008. *Outliers: the Story of Success.* New York: Little, Brown and Co.

Gledhill, Christine. 2000. "Rethinking genre." In Linda Williams and Christine Gledhill, 2000. 221–243.

Goodman, Peter S. 2009. *Past Due: The End of Easy Money and the Renewal of the American Economy.* New York: Times Books.

Gorbman, Claudia. 1987. *Unheard Melodies: Narrative Film Music.* London: BFI Pub.

Greenberg, Clement. 1957 [1939]. "Avant-Garde and Kitsch." In Bernard Rosenberg and David Manning White, 1957, 98–107.

Greene, Richard, and K. Silem Mohammad, ed. 2007. *Quentin Tarantino and Philosophy: How to Philosophize with a Pair of Pliers and a Blowtorch.* Popular culture and philosophy, v. 29. Chicago: Open Court.

Guerrero, Ed. 2001. "Black Violence As Cinema: From Cheap Thrills to Historical Agonies." In J David Slocum, 2001, 211–225.

Hirsch, Foster. 1999. *Detours and Lost Highways: A Map of Neo-Noir.* New York: Limelight Editions.

Hobbes, Thomas. 1904 [1651]. *Leviathan or the Matter, Forme & Power of a Commonwealth, Ecclesiasticall and Civill: Thomas Hobbes.* The text ed. by A. R. Waller. Cambridge: Univ. Press.

Holm, D. K. 2004. *Kill Bill: An Unofficial Casebook.* London: Glitter.

Holm, D. K. 2004. *Quentin Tarantino.* Harpenden: Pocket Essentials.

Horsley, Jake. 1999. *The Blood Poets: A Cinema of Savagery 1958–1999.* Lanham, MD: Scarecrow Press.

Inness, Sherrie A. 2004. *Action Chicks: New Images of Tough Women in Popular Culture*. New York: Palgrave Macmillan.

Inness, Sherrie A. 1999. *Tough Girls: Women Warriors and Wonder Women in Popular Culture*. Feminist Cultural Studies, the Media, and Political Culture. Philadelphia: University of Pennsylvania Press.

Jameson, Fredric. 1989 [1982]. "Postmodernism and the Consumer Society," in Hal Foster, 1989. 111–125.

Kael, Pauline. 1994. *For Keeps: 30 Years at the Movies*. London: Penguin.

Kael, Pauline. 1994. *I lost It at the Movies: Film Writings, 1954–1965*. New York: M. Boyars.

Kinder, Marsha. 2001. "Violence American Style: The Narrative Orchestration of Violent Attractions." In J. David Slocum, 2001, 63–100.

King, Geoff. 2002. *New Hollywood Cinema: An Introduction*. New York: Columbia University Press.

King, Geoff. 2004. "'Killingly funny': Mixing Modalities in New Hollywood's Comedy-with-Violence." In Steven Jay Schneider, 2004. 126–143.

Kracauer, Siegfried. 1997. *Theory of Film: The Redemption of Physical Reality*. Princeton paperbacks. Princeton, NJ: Princeton University Press.

Kramer, Peter. 2001. "'Clean, Dependable Slapstick': Comic Violence and the Emergence of Classical Hollywood Cinema." In J. David Slocum, 2001. 103–116.

Lawrence, Novotny. 2008. *Blaxploitation Films of the 1970s: Blackness and Genre*. Studies in African American history and culture. New York: Routledge.

Leitch, Thomas. 2004. "Aristotle v. the Action Film." In Steven Jay Schneider, 2004. 103–125.

Leonard, Elmore. 1990. *The Switch*. New York: Bantam Books.

Leonard, Elmore. 1992. *Rum Punch*. New York: HarperTorch.

Lyotard, Jean-Francois. 1984. *The Postmodern Condition: A Report on Knowledge*. Minneapolis: University of Minnesota Press.

LoBrutto, Vincent. 2008. *Martin Scorsese: A Biography*. Westport, CT: Praeger.

Macdonald, Dwight. 1957 [1953]. "A Theory of Mass Culture." In Bernard Rosenberg and David Manning White, 1957. 59–73.

McLuhan, Marshall. 1964. *Understanding Media: The Extensions of Man*. New York: McGraw-Hill.

Miklitsch, Robert. 2006. *Roll Over Adorno: Critical Theory, Popular Culture, Audiovisual Media*. The SUNY Series in Postmodern Culture. Albany: State University of New York Press.

Münsterberg, Hugo. 1916. *The Photoplay*. New York: Appleton.

Nabokov, Vladimir Vladimirovich. 1955. *Lolita*. New York: G. P. Putnam's Sons.

Neale, Stephen. 2000. *Genre and Hollywood*. London: Routledge.

Niall, Lucy, ed. 2000. *Postmodern Literary Theory: An Anthology*. Malden, MA: Blackwell Publishers.

Nowell-Smith, Geoffrey, ed. 1996. *The Oxford History of World Cinema: [The Definitive History of Cinema Worldwide]*. Oxford [u.a.]: Oxford Univ. Press.

Onderdonk, Todd. 2004. "Tarantino's Deadly Homosocial." In Steven Jay Schneider, 2004, 286–303.

Page, Edwin. 2005. *Quintessential Tarantino*. London: Marion Boyars Publishers.

Polan, Dana B. 2000. *Pulp Fiction*. BFI modern classics. London: BFI Pub.

Pomerance, Murray. 2004. "Hitchcock and the Dramaturgy of Screen Violence," in Steven Jay Schneider, 2004. 34–56.

Pound, Ezra. 1935. *Make It New: Essays.* New Haven, CT: Yale University Press.

Prince, Stephen, ed. 2000. *Screening Violence.* Rutgers Depth of Field Series. New Brunswick, N.J.: Rutgers University Press.

Prince, Stephen. 2003. *Classical Film Violence: Designing and Regulating Brutality in Hollywood Cinema, 1930–1968.* New Brunswick, NJ: Rutgers University Press.

Propp, Vladimir. 1968. *Morphology of the Folktale.* Publications of the American Folklore Society, v. 9. Austin: University of Texas Press.

Pynchon, Thomas. 1973. *Gravity's Rainbow.* New York: Viking Press.

Quart, Alissa. 2005. "Networked: Dysfunctional Families, Reproductive Acts, and Multitaking Minds Make for Happy Endings." *Film Comment;* Jul/Aug, Vol. 41 Issue 4, 48–51.

Quart, Leonard and Albert Auster. 2002. *American Film and Society since 1945.* 2nd Edition. Westport, CT: Praeger.

Read, Jacinda. 2004. "'Once Upon a Time There Were Three Little Girls . . . ': Girls, Violence, and *Charlie's Angels.*" In Steven Jay Schneider, 2004. 205–229.

Ritter, Kelly. 2003. "Postmodern Dialogics in *Pulp Fiction.*" In David Blakesley, 2003. 286–300.

Rodriguez, Robert, Quentin Tarantino, and Kurt Volk. 2007. *Grindhouse: "The Sleaze-Filled Saga of an Exploitation Double Feature."* New York: Weinstein Books.

Romanov, Peter A. 2006. *Soundtrack: the Significance of Music in the Films Written and Directed by Quentin Tarantino.* Thesis (M.A.), Wake Forest University. Dept. of Liberal Studies, 2006.

Rosenberg, Bernard, and David Manning White, ed. 1957. *Mass Culture: The Popular Arts in America.* Glencoe, IL: The Free Press, 1957.

Rothman, William. 2001. "Violence and film," In J. David Slocum, 2001. 37–46.

Schatz, Thomas. 1981. *Hollywood Genres: Formulas, Filmmaking, and the Studio System.* Boston, MA: McGraw-Hill.

Schneider, Steven Jay, ed. 2004. *New Hollywood Violence.* Inside popular film. Manchester, UK: Manchester University Press.

Shaw, Joseph T. 1946. *The Hard-Boiled Omnibus; Early Stories from Black Mask.* New York: Simon and Schuster.

Silver, Alain, and James Ursini, ed. 1996. *Film Noir Reader.* New York: Limelight Editions.

Sklar, Robert. 1994. *Movie-Made America: A Cultural History of American Movies.* New York: Vintage Books.

Slocum, J. David, ed. 2001. *Violence and American Cinema.* AFI film readers. New York: Routledge.

Slocum, J. David. 2004. "The 'Film Violence' Trope: New Hollywood, 'The Sixties,' and the Politics of History." In Steven Jay Schneider, 2004. 13–33.

Slotkin, Richard. 1973. *Regeneration through Violence; the Mythology of the American Frontier, 1600–1860.* Middletown, CT: Wesleyan University Press.

Smith, Jim. 2005. *Tarantino.* Virgin film. London: Virgin.

Stein, Atara. 2004. *The Byronic Hero in Film, Fiction, and Television.* Carbondale: Southern Illinois University Press.

Stone, Alan A. 2007. *Movies and the Moral Adventure of Life*. A Boston review book. Cambridge, MA: MIT Press.

Tarantino, Quentin. 2009. *Inglourious Basterds: A Screenplay*. New York: Little Brown & Co.

Tarantino, Quentin, and Gerald Peary. 1998. *Quentin Tarantino: Interviews*. Conversations with filmmakers series. Jackson: University Press of Mississippi.

Thompson, Kristin. 1988. *Breaking the Glass Armor: Neoformalist Film Analysis*. Princeton, NJ: Princeton University Press.

Todorov, Tzvetan, Richard Howard, and Robert Scholes. 1984. *The Fantastic: a Structural Approach to a Literary Genre*. Cornell paperbacks. Ithaca, NY: Cornell Univ. Press.

Wager, Jans B. 2005. *Dames in the Driver's Seat: Rereading Film Noir*. Austin: University of Texas Press.

Warshow, Robert. 1996 [1948]. "The Gangster as Tragic Hero." In Alain Silver and James Ursini, 1996. 11–16.

Webb, Theresa and Nick Browne. 2004. "The Big Impossible: Action-Adventure's Appeal to Adolescent Boys." In Steven Jay Schneider, 2004. 80–99.

Williams, Linda. 1997. *Viewing Positions: Ways of Seeing Film*. Rutgers depth of field series. New Brunswick, NJ: Rutgers Univ. Press.

Williams, Linda, and Christine Gledhill. 2000. *Reinventing Film Studies*. London: Arnold.

Willis, Sharon. 2000. "'Style,' Posture, and Idiom: Tarantino's Figures of Masculinity." In Linda Williams and Christine Gledhill, 2000, 279–295.

Wolfe, Tom. 1998. *A Man in Full: A Novel*. New York: Farrar, Straus and Giroux.

Woods, Paul A. 1998. *King Pulp: the Wild World of Quentin Tarantino*. London: Plexus.

Woods, Paul A. 2000. *Quentin Tarantino: The Film Geek Files*. London: Plexus.

Index

Note: Page numbers followed by an n indicate that the reference is to a note on the designated page.

The Matrix Revolutions (Wachowski and Wachowski, 2003), 108
Mayfield, Curtis, 98
McDonald, Dwight, 6–7
McGowan, Rose, 128
McLeod, Jon, 157
McLuhan, Marshall, 36
Mean Streets (Scorsese, 1973), 27
Medium Cool (Wexler, 1969), 38, 102
Menochet, Denis, 143
Metadiegetic, 91, 93
Mikels, Ted, 33
Miklitsch, Robert, 103
Mise-en-scène, 87, 89, 95, 135
Modern Times (Chaplin, 1936), 141–142
Monsieur Verdoux (Chaplin, 1947), 78–80, 83–87
Montage, 22, 64, 69, 87, 135–136
Monty Python's Life of Brian (Jones, 1979), 30
Moore, Michael, 39
Moss, Carrie-Ann, 108
Motion Picture Association of America (MPAA), 21, 46
Mr. Hobbs Takes a Vacation (Koster, 1962), 53
Münsterberg, Hugo, 68–69
Murphy, Audie, 149–150
My Fair Lady (Cukor, 1964), 20
Myers, Mike, 152

Nabokov, Vladimir, 35
Nashville (Altman, 1975), 30
National Lampoon's Animal House (Landis, 1978), 30
Natural Born Killers (Stone, 1994), 33, 78
Neale, Stephen, 16–18, 108
Network (Lumet, 1976), 30
New Hollywood, 13, 52, 140
New World Pictures, 27, 31
Nichols, Mike, 98, 101
Nicotero, Greg, 77
Nietzsche, Friedrich, 55, 58–60, 63, 67, 71–72
Nilsson, Harry, 133

Nouvelle vague, 21, 23, 34, 154
Novak, B. J., 144

The Old Dark House (Whale, 1932), 81
On Your Toes (Enright, 1939), 64
Once Upon a Time in the West (*C'era una volta il West*) (Leone, 1968), 35
Onderdonk, Todd, 82
One Flew Over the Cuckoo's Nest (Foreman, 1975), 30
Ophüls, Max, 67
Orwell, George, 140
Oscar (Academy Award), 33, 79

Pacino, Al, 80
Page, Edwin, 91
Palme d'Or (Cannes), 33
Parks, Michael, 113, 126
Pastiche, 7, 10, 12–16, 34–35, 95–96, 103
Peckinpah, Sam, 27, 47–48
Penn, Arthur, 21, 27
Penn, Chris, 62
Perkins, Anthony, 127
Phantom of the Paradise (De Palma, 1974), 15
Pink Flamingos (Waters, 1972), 26, 66
Pitt, Brad, 144
Planet of the Apes (Schaffner, 1967), 21
Plato, 16
Play It Again, Sam (Allen, 1972), 10
Plummer, Amanda, 51, 84
Poitier, Sydney, 124–125, 157
Porter, Edwin S., 69
Postmodern, 2–6, 8, 10–14, 16, 52, 90, 96, 103, 139, 154
Pound, Ezra, 58
Prince, Stephen, 21, 40–41, 44, 46
Production Code, 21, 46–47
Propp, Vladimir, 112–121
Psycho (Hitchcock, 1960), 127
Pynchon, Thomas, 1, 13, 36

Quart, Alissa, 10
Quart, Leonard, 21

ABOUT THE AUTHOR

Aaron Barlow teaches writing at New York City College of Technology of the City University of New York. Dr. Barlow has written three previous books, *The DVD Revolution*, *The Rise of the Blogosphere*, and *Blogging America*.